FLIRTING WITH
Pride & Prejudice

FLIRTING WITH

Pride & Prejudice

Fresh Perspectives
on the Original Chick-Lit Masterpiece

EDITED BY

Jennifer Crusie

WITH Glenn Yeffeth

BENBELLA BOOKS, INC.
Dallas, Texas

This publication has not been prepared, approved or licensed by any entity that created or produced the well-known book or films *Pride and Prejudice*.

BenBella Books, Inc.
6440 N. Central Expressway, Suite 617
Dallas, TX 75206
www.benbellabooks.com

Send feedback to feedback@benbellabooks.com

PUBLISHER: Glenn Yeffeth
SENIOR EDITOR: Shanna Caughey
ASSOCIATE EDITOR: Leah Wilson
DIRECTOR OF MARKETING/PR: Laura Watkins

Printed in the United States of America
10 9 8 7 6 5 4 3 2 1

Library of Congress Cataloging-in-Publication Data
Flirting with Pride and prejudice : fresh perspectives on the original chick-lit masterpiece / edited by Jennifer Crusie.
　　p. cm.
　　ISBN 1-932100-72-5
　　1. Austen, Jane, 1775–1817. Pride and prejudice. 2. Women and literature—England—History—19th century. 3. Women—Books and reading. 4. Women in literature. I. Crusie, Jennifer.

　　PR4034.P73F57 2005
　　823'.7—dc22

2005016568

Cover design by Mondolithic
Text design and composition by John Reinhardt Book Design
Original Artwork: *In Love* (1907), Marcus Stone; courtesy of The Bridgeman Art Library/Getty Images

Distributed by Independent Publishers Group
To order call (800) 888-4741
www.ipgbook.com

For special sales contact Laura Watkins at laura@benbellabooks.com

Contents

Contents

Jane and the Movies

Jane's Hero

Jane's Untold Stories

Jane in the Twenty-First Century

Introduction

Whᴇɴ ᴛʜᴇ ɢᴏᴏᴅ ᴘᴇᴏᴘʟᴇ at BenBella Books asked me to guest edit *Flirting with Pride and Prejudice*, I jumped at it. Then I thought, "Why did I do that?" It wasn't because the book's a classic; they could have offered me *Flirting with Bleak House*, and I would have claimed a previous deadline. It wasn't that it was my favorite book; I hadn't read it in fifteen years, not since I wrote that grad school paper defending Charlotte's choice of husband. It wasn't even that it was the mother of all romance novels; I love my genre, but I'm not a slave to it. So I thought about what it is that makes *Pride and Prejudice* such a prom queen of a topic, not only for me but for all the writers who signed on to write about it and all the readers who were going to pick this anthology up to read about it (that would be you).

To begin with, there's the author: Our Jane. People get passionate about Austen: the purity of her prose, the vividness of her characters, the reverberation of her underlying nineteenth-century snark. She wrote of a time, but also beyond it; her voice continues to enchant and enthrall; she's one of the Top Ten Dead People We'd Like to Have Dinner With. But if the BenBella people had offered me *Flirting with Emma*, I would still have had a pressing deadline.

So maybe it's the characters: poor but proud Elizabeth; rich and proud

1

Darcy; suffering Charlotte and insufferable Collins; Lydia the slut, Kitty the twit and Mary the prig; the Nightmare Mother and the Careless Father; Wickham the rake and Bingley the sweet; and Lady Catherine, the Character Most Likely to Crush a Tenant under the Wheels of Her Carriage. That's one heck of a cast Austen's got going there, and I admit that for the characters alone I might have signed on. Except I really did have a previous deadline.

But then there's that story: the wolf at the door, or at least at the gate, comic proposals and cutting asides, seduction and betrayal, disdain and heartbreak, the low raised high, the high brought low, and one in the eye for Lady Catherine. . . . Oh, there's a lot to love in this narrative. But it can't be just that; the story's been told and retold, adopted into other cultures and adapted into chick-lit, and I'm not standing in line for any of that. I'd have been too busy to do *Flirting with Bridget Jones,* too.

No, what makes *Pride and Prejudice* irresistible is the perfect combination of all those forces: the sly but ultimately sympathetic wit, the prose so clear you forget you're reading, the flailing, failing, enthralling cast and the richly over-plotted, understated story. It's like a great dessert that's good for you, a guilty pleasure you don't have to feel guilty about. The good are rewarded, the bad get burned and we close the book knowing they're still milling about in there, Wickham putting up with Lydia as his punishment for being a rat, Jane and Bingley in clueless contentment and Elizabeth teaching Darcy how to laugh while not inviting Lady Catherine to dinner.

And that, I think, is the key to this anthology. The novel is so alive in our hearts that we want to know what the characters were doing off the page while our attention was directed elsewhere, what happened to them after the book was done, how they'd fare today in modern London, modern Bombay, modern anywhere. We want to chat about what ten thousand pounds a year meant, why all those party boys were in uniform; we want to compare the plights of the characters to our plights, wonder what would happen if things had been different. . . .

Face it. We just like thinking about *Pride and Prejudice.*

What's wonderful about this anthology is that the writers are thinking about it in so many different ways, playing with the characters, messing with the plot, taking "what if?" to entertaining absurdity. We've got people who want to talk about history, people who want to talk about sociology, people who want to talk about literature, people who want to talk about Darcy. We've got essays and short stories and a quiz (one glaring omission: no crossword puzzle), we've got singing and dancing and cell phones, and it's all *Pride and Prejudice*.

Clearly, this is not an anthology of Studies on the Work (for that, see Norton, et al.). It's more of a series of Dates with Jane, where some writers were serious about her, some were looking for a good time and some, frankly, took advantage of her. But don't worry that any damage has been done. In one hundred and ninety-three years of wear, tear and academic assaults, not to mention countless adaptations, *Pride and Prejudice* has remained unchanged, except that Darcy now looks like Colin Firth. The affectionate attention these writers have paid can only enhance the experience of loving the novel. Really, all they did was, well, flirt a little.

How could I refuse to introduce a book like that?

So welcome to BenBella's party for *Pride and Prejudice*. It's informal, and we're easygoing, so get yourself a drink (negus, margarita or Diet Coke, your choice), kick back and read on. This is worth missing a deadline for.

—JENNIFER CRUSIE

Jane as Universal Social Commentator

"Jane Austen was born before those bonds which (we are told) protected women from the truth were burst by the Brontës or elaborately untied by George Eliot....Jane Austen may have been protected from truth: but it was precious little of truth that was protected from her."

G. K. CHESTERTON

"Does this petticoat make me look fat?"

Having It All in Jane Austen's Time and Today

BETH KENDRICK

One of the many things that make *Pride and Prejudice* a book to read again and again is that it's timeless; the longing, frustration, humiliation and betrayal that Elizabeth Bennet experiences are much the same longing, frustration, humiliation and betrayal that women are dealing with today. Beth Kendrick looks at the demands made on women in Austen's novel and argues that having it all is a myth, whether you're trying to get it in the nineteenth century or the twenty-first.

SATURDAY NIGHT AT THE NETHERFIELD estate and the claws are coming out: Elizabeth is chatting with Mr. Darcy and Miss Bingley about the qualifications of a truly "accomplished" woman. Mr. Darcy claims that through his entire life he has known only half a dozen women worthy of that title. You can practically see Elizabeth rolling her eyes as she replies he must have some pretty stringent requirements of womanhood. At this point, Miss Bingley jumps in and says no lady can be deemed accomplished unless she can: dance, sing, draw, converse fluently in the modern languages, net purses, cover screens and also possess a certain *je ne sais quoi* that announces to the world her inherent fabulousness. (So Beyoncé meets Martha Stewart, basically.) Darcy declares that on top of all that, an accomplished woman must also be well-learned and love to read. (Okay, Beyoncé meets Martha Stewart meets Marie Curie.)

Granted, Miss Bingley is only saying this because she wants Mr. Darcy to think she herself embodies the Beyoncé-Martha-Marie triad of perfection, but the point remains that women are harder on one another than men ever could be. When Mr. Wickham drops his flirtation with Elizabeth to pursue the more solvent Miss King, do the Bennets blame him for leading on one of their own? No. They excuse his behavior as the practical actions of a man with little fortune while denouncing Miss King as a "nasty little freckled thing." (Lydia says it, but Elizabeth agrees.) Bet she can't speak French worth a damn, either.

Yes, the women of *Pride and Prejudice* put a lot of pressure on themselves and on each other. Pressure to look fetching, master all the skills expected of a lady, climb the social ladder and generally comport themselves in a manner befitting a good girl from a good family. And who can blame them? Given their family's financial situation, it's either catch a rich husband or spend the rest of their lives mooching off relatives and living in the equivalent of a van down by the river (a hackney coach down by the Thames?).

But that was then. If the Bennets were transported to twenty-first-century suburbia, their character motivations would certainly be different. Or not. Why, after two hundred years and great strides toward achieving political and economic independence, do women still feel relentless pressure to live up to society's unattainable standards of feminine perfection? Can we blame the patriarch? Has "The Man" been plotting to keep us down, all the way from Bingley and Darcy to Clinton and Bush? Or are women the ones perpetuating the cycle, demanding the impossible from themselves and their peers?

Putting up a good front—that's what the Bennet girls are doing. Elizabeth pretends she's not humiliated by her mother's tackiness and her father's *laissez-faire* approach to parenting. Jane pretends first that she's only lukewarm toward her hunky dream man, then that she's not heartbroken when he blows town without so much as a forwarding address. Mrs. Bennet pretends that she can afford a staff of cooks and housekeepers when, in fact, she and her husband can barely scrape together a dowry for their daughters. And Mary, poor Mary, pretends to be too erudite to be bothered with preening and vanity when really she's mortified being the ugly duckling in a group of sisters so gorgeous they could have solved all their money problems with Estée Lauder endorsements had this option been available to well-bred ladies in the nineteenth century.

Compare this to the daily dilemma of the modern soccer mom. This is an age when women can have it all! And we'd better, or we're going to be branded the weak link in the carpool. Mothers today are expected to work, raise children, fit into those pre-pregnancy jeans *plus* have a beautiful home and a wonderfully fulfilling personal life…or else. The woman who dares to be a stay-at-home mom? Pathetic leech who sets feminism back fifty years! The woman who works full-time and drops the kids off at day care? Unavailable ice queen who'll suffer the consequences when little Brianna grows up to be a sociopath! And it's usually not the boyfriends and husbands who are saying this—it's the other moms at T-ball practice. If we can't figure out a way to do it all and be happy about it, we're not living up to our potential, or so the mantra goes.

The problem with all of us putting up the good front—in both the nineteenth and twenty-first centuries—is that none of us can appreciate that image where it most matters: in our own minds. We all *know* we're faking it, and we're terrified that the façade will crumble at any second, revealing us for the desperadoes we truly are. I will never forget the conversation I had with my labmates from grad school when we went out to celebrate the successful defense of my dissertation:

ME: Now I officially have a fancy-schmancy degree. I can stop obsessing about footnotes and snottily refuse to answer to my husband unless he calls me "Doctor." So why do I feel like I'm a complete fraud who doesn't know jack about jack?

POST-DOC RESEARCHER SITTING TO MY RIGHT: You know, I have that same feeling, like I'm going to be found out any day now and stripped of my credentials.

SECOND-YEAR STUDENT SITTING TO MY LEFT: Oh, God. You mean that never goes away?

TENURED PROFESSOR ACROSS THE TABLE: Never. Get used to it.

[*Huge gulps of wine all around*]

Moral of the story? External illusions count for more than internal truths in the game of having it all. In Jane Austen's day, females had a lot on their plates, at least as much as frazzled career women have now. Mrs. Bennet, for all her ditziness, works way harder than her husband. While he kicks back in the library all day with a few volumes of Samuel

Johnson and a glass of claret, she has to budget the household accounts, manage the servants, plan the meals, keep the family involved in neighborhood social events and, oh yeah, get all five daughters married off so they don't die penniless and alone. And while she's doing all this, she can't neglect her youthful appearance (because even though Mr. Bennet constantly mocks her for being so frivolous and superficial, the fact is he married her for her looks). Were Mrs. Bennet alive today, do you think she'd be caught dead going to the grocery store in sweats and a messy ponytail? As if. She'd be looking glamtastic just in case she ran into Mrs. Long or Lady Lucas. And she was considered a slacker mom.

Let the boys have their baseball. Competitive front-putting—along with competitive mothering, competitive dating and competitive consumption—has always been the national pastime for women. Reveal that you're thinking about getting a little work done because you just can't find time for the gym? Confess that your toddler isn't speaking in complete sentences way ahead of the developmental curve? Admit that you can barely make the payments on that shiny new SUV? Crazy talk! Mrs. Bennet would sooner have Mr. Collins think her girls actually *cook* instead of being served by a chef! (The family may not have any savings stashed away for the future, but hey, their guests can look forward to two full courses. Let's see them top *that* at Lucas Lodge!)

Where does this burning internal drive to be perfect originate? Why is it so important to hide the cracks and always make it look easy? I propose that today, just as in Austen's time, the burden of upholding the "family name" weighs heavier on women than men because women have a much narrower margin of error. So Darcy and Bingley went on a few benders at university, maybe caroused with a few actresses? No problem! What happens at Oxford, stays at Oxford! But when Kitty and Lydia get a little giggly at the ball and Mary delivers a less-than-virtuoso performance at the pianoforte? Elizabeth is covered with shame and begs her father to intervene. And then Lydia actually *runs away* with Wickham...well, Jane and Elizabeth might as well commit *hari kari* right then and there and get it over with. By the time Mr. Gardiner and Mr. Darcy track Wickham down like a dog in the street and force him to marry Lydia, it's too late to salvage the Bennet family's reputation. They have become the Hilton sisters of Longbourn. (Both Elizabeth and Jane end up marrying well in spite of their sister's indiscretions, but not without strong objections from the women in the grooms' families.)

At the end of the day women are the ones who make or break the family image. Public perception of powerful men, from King Louis XVI and Franklin D. Roosevelt to Ashton Kutcher and Brad Pitt, is indelibly colored by their choice of female companions. One of the prevalent themes in Jane Austen's novels is that selecting a spouse is the single most influential decision one makes in life, both on a public and personal level. This especially holds true for men (cough, cough—Prince Charles—cough, cough), so women must hold themselves to a higher standard if they want their families to get ahead. This self-imposed demand for perfection results in anxiety and plummeting self-esteem, which elicit burning resentment of "nasty little freckled things" everywhere. We know we don't have a hope in hell of meeting all the expectations, but we keep putting up that good front and pointing fingers at everyone else who falls short of the mark. Yes, okay, so secretly we're screwups who can't net a purse to save our lives, but at least we aren't:

A. pathetic old maids who settle for the first sniveling windbag who asks for our digits (Charlotte Lucas)
B. spoiled little rich girls who have money—but not enough money to buy class, ha ha (Miss Bingley)
C. panty-flashing party girls who boogie on the banquettes at night-clubs and get nailed in the gossip columns the next day (Lydia Bennet)

So there.

Do these vicious comparisons make us feel better about ourselves? No better than Elizabeth Bennet feels when her father assures her that her sister—"the most determined flirt that ever made herself and her family ridiculous"—won't diminish Jane's and Elizabeth's sterling reputations. Riiight. Tell it to Lady Catherine de Bourgh.

Then, as now, men like Mr. Bennet—who is, for all his lapses in paternal judgment, a good guy at the core—cannot begin to fathom the problems faced by the women who prop up his social order, probably because the girls are careful not to betray their image of effortless charm and grace. (It just wouldn't be ladylike.) In fact, Mr. Bennet considers the lot of his womenfolk very easy. All they have to do is sit around and trim bonnets and talk about the latest fashions from London, right?

When Elizabeth declares that no one woman can possibly attain all the feminine qualities society expects of her, Darcy scoffs, "Are you so severe upon your own sex, as to doubt the possibility of all this?"

Well...yeah. Because, even at the tender age of twenty, Elizabeth understands that "having it all" is a myth. And that's the truth, even if not universally acknowledged.

Beth Kendrick writes novels (*My Favorite Mistake*, *Exes and Ohs* and the upcoming *Fashionably Late*) when she's not procrastinating by shopping online or watching a Cubs game. She has a Ph.D. in psychology and reads *Pride and Prejudice* at least once a year. You can visit her Web site at www.bethkendrick.com.

A Little Friendly Advice

Is There Such a Thing When It Comes to Relationships?

Jennifer O'Connell

Do friends let friends marry losers? Jennifer O'Connell ponders the question as she compares Elizabeth's quandary in dealing with Charlotte's engagement to her own experiences with friends embarking on bad trips down the aisle.

WE'VE ALL SEEN THEM. The mismatched couple. Maybe he's an overbearing, egotistical bore who can spend hours talking about the merits of, well, himself. Maybe she's putting in sixty-hour weeks while he's at home breaking in the La-Z-Boy, demonstrating his ability to deftly juggle both the remote control and a cold bottle of Budweiser. Or maybe it's just a matter of chocolate versus vanilla. Ginger versus Mary Ann. Po-tay-to versus po-tah-to.

In any case, usually, way before the separation is announced and the words *irreconcilable differences* are typed in triplicate by some city hall clerk, there are signs.

When Elizabeth Bennet receives an offer of marriage from William Collins she recognizes him for the self-important kiss-up he is. And she's smart enough to gracefully refuse his kind offer, even if inside she's struggling not to laugh at the absurdity of his proposal. So, when her best friend Charlotte comes to Elizabeth with the news of her own engagement—an engagement to one self-important kiss-up who, not three days before, was requesting her own hand in marriage—Elizabeth has a choice to make. Option number one: She can accept Charlotte's explanation that she's not getting any younger, that this may be her last shot at marriage, and wish her luck. Or, option number two: Elizabeth can do what it takes to keep her friend from making a huge mistake. After all, isn't that what friends are for?

We've all heard the horror stories that sound like urban lore. Cautionary tales of brides and grooms and their friends who looked the other way even as signs flashing "WARNING: TROUBLE AHEAD" were practically fighting for attention with the six-tiered fondant-iced wedding cake and heart-shaped ice sculpture. Ask a few friends if they knew, just *knew*, that a marriage wasn't going to work out before the couple even declared, "I do," and the stories will start pouring in. I asked, and that's exactly what happened:

- The maid of honor who, while talking with guests at the rehearsal dinner, was told by a relieved best man, "Finally, Greg is getting married. After his third engagement we were beginning to doubt whether anyone would end up marrying him." Um, three failed engagements? That was news to the maid of honor—and the bride. Still, the wedding was on.
- The friend who knew it wasn't going to last when she discovered the bride cheated on her fiancé—during the wedding rehearsal. Yet they still tied the knot the next morning, before three hundred of their closest family and friends.
- The bridesmaid who, along with the bride, the bridal party and thirty family and friends, waited for over an hour for the groom to show up at his own rehearsal. He'd had a great golf round going and couldn't fathom walking off the course before finishing all eighteen holes. And the next day, the wedding went off as planned.

In hindsight, these women knew they should have spoken up. But did any of these friends express their concerns before the stretch limo pulled up to take the blushing bride to the ceremony? Not a chance. Are any of these couples still married today? No way.

So, if we really care about our friends, shouldn't we share our doubts with them before they put on that $4,000 Vera Wang gown and walk down the aisle toward certain disaster? If we see the signs that trouble is looming, aren't we obligated to tell our friends before they make one of the biggest mistakes of their lives? Sure, it's risky. Of course we could be wrong. But this isn't a matter of simply letting her choose the wrong entrée off the menu and holding her hair back the next day when her stomach is turning over and she's cursing those damn raw oysters. It's not just one day spent doubled over on the bathroom floor swearing off seafood forever—it's a lifetime of regret.

Why are we more likely to tell our friend that her bra is peeking out from beneath her strapless gown than we are to point out that we're worried about her relationship? We'd never let a friend enter the reception hall with her cathedral-length train tucked inside her pantyhose, so why do we balk at the idea of expressing our concern about her future? Obviously, the consequences of marrying the wrong man are far greater than those of exposing undergarments in the bridal party photo.

Why don't we say anything, and, if we did, would our friends even listen?

In all fairness, William Collins wasn't a philanderer, he had no ill intentions and he didn't ask for Charlotte's hand in marriage with an ulterior motive in mind (unless you count the fact that he'd already been shot down once on his trip and he still intended to return to Kent knowing he'd found a future Mrs. Collins). So why does Elizabeth shout "Impossible!" when Charlotte announces her engagement to Collins? Because she knows Charlotte deserves more. As her friend, Elizabeth wants Charlotte to be loved, not just provided for; to marry a man who cares for her emotionally, not just one who provides a comfortable home; and to spend her life with a man who sets her heart aflutter, not one who simply offers connections and a suitable situation in life.

Although she understands the societal expectations placed upon women of her age, Elizabeth has higher hopes for her own relationship. Although she concedes to the role society expects her to play, she's not willing to concede her idea of love. She doesn't believe that happiness is up to chance, as Charlotte does. Elizabeth believes that happiness is her right—is *every woman's right*. When Charlotte claims, "I am not a romantic," to explain her acceptance of Collins' proposal, Elizabeth's response could very rightly have been "Well, I am."

While some may say that Elizabeth is devoid of sympathy toward Charlotte's situation—after all, at the time it was the only honorable provision for well-educated young women of small fortune—I'd disagree. If anything, Elizabeth ultimately demonstrates extreme empathy and understanding toward Charlotte once she realizes that her friend's expectations aren't nearly as high as her own. But if Charlotte's "bride or bust" mentality is indicative of England in the early 1800s, why are women today still leery of expressing their relationship concerns to their friends? What's our excuse, when women no longer need a wedding ring to live a full life?

We've all seen the old movies in which the lone dissenter dramatically stands up at the wedding ceremony, her conscience called to action by the preacher's words and her refusal to keep her peace. But it seems as though the whole part about giving bystanders the opportunity to object to the marriage has been eliminated from modern ceremonies, as if our purchase of a Cuisinart off their Bloomingdale's registry provides our implicit acceptance and approval of the union.

Of course, no woman really needs her friends' acceptance and approval before slipping that dazzling cushion-cut solitaire on her finger and setting into motion a flurry of pre-wedding activity. Still, we have friends because we value their opinions, respect their points of view. We consult them when considering new career opportunities, take them with us to check out that new apartment before signing on the dotted line and put that pair of strappy sandals on hold until we can get them on their cell phones and consult about whether a gorgeous pair of purple snake-skinned stilettos really will go with everything in our closets like we've been telling ourselves. Although we might not always like what they have to tell us (nix the sandals), we assume that they want the best for us—that's why they're our friends.

But when it comes to romantic relationships, we stop asking, maybe for fear of the response. And, in turn, we don't offer our opinions, perhaps for fear of the repercussions.

For some reason, it was easier when we were younger. If our friend had a crush on the boy who put worms down our shirt on the playground, we'd tell her he was a jerk. If she was waiting for the moody boy in the white painter's pants and AC/DC t-shirt to ask her to the Valentine's dance, we'd point out that maybe a guy who drew barbed wire on his forearm in ballpoint ink wasn't the best candidate for a boyfriend.

But as we get older, things change. All of a sudden the guys our friends like have the potential to stick around a lot longer. After all, maybe the guy isn't just someone she enjoys having dinner with, maybe he'll end up being *the one*. Maybe if we told her how we felt we'd be doing more than just expressing our opinions—we'd be drawing a line in the sand. We'd be putting her in the middle of two people she cares about, forcing her to make a choice. Or worse yet, maybe she'd decide that if we can't peacefully coexist with the guy she loves, maybe we weren't meant to coexist as friends, either.

As friends, when relationships are past the point of no return, we tend to tiptoe around the subject for fear of creating problems. There's a sort of relationship "no fly zone" that exists between friends. Our friend is making a huge decision and we're supposed to support her, no matter what we think. We're not expected to be the voice of reason, to rain on her parade. Sometimes what it comes down to is this: we fear losing our friend more than we fear the outcome of her mistake.

By the time the caterer is selected and the band is told which song to play for their first dance, it's too late. We had our chance. Voicing our concern is a gamble that cuts both ways. If we express our doubt about the longevity of the relationship, even if time ultimately proves us right, we risk losing a friend. If she stays with him and lives happily ever after, it's possible we've still lost a friend.

Even if she could look at a board and see what odds her friends give her relationship, would she hesitate or think a little longer before committing to *forever*? Would it even make a difference?

My husband and I are convinced that half the friends at our wedding were betting on the endurance—or lack thereof—of our marriage. We were an unlikely pair with high highs and low lows. Eleven years later, we laugh about it. But if a friend had come to me beforehand and told me she thought I was making a mistake, I'd like to think I would have appreciated her thoughtful expression of caring, her genuine concern for my happiness, and have taken it into consideration. Truth be told, she probably wouldn't have been telling me anything I hadn't already told myself. But would it have changed my mind? I don't think so. Would I still remember our conversation years later and wonder if she had changed *her* mind? Would I watch her seemingly friendly conversations with my husband and question her sincerity? Would there have been long-term ramifications to our friendship that I couldn't imagine at the time? I really don't know.

There are friends I thought were perfectly matched, ideally suited to their partners, only to receive a phone call and hear my friend's sobbing on the other end as she describes her marriage's demise. There are people I thought wouldn't last long enough to wash the "Just Married" off their windshields or remove the tin cans dragging off their bumpers, only to find them happily celebrating yet another anniversary.

It would be nice to think that our intuition is keen enough to save our friends from making life-altering mistakes, to keep them from certain heartache. But in real life friends can't predict the certainty of relationships with the precision of Vegas odds makers. There is no Magic Eight Ball we can shake and find the answers. And, at best, any couple starts out even.

"I am convinced that my chance of happiness with him is fair, as most people can boast on entering the marriage state," Charlotte tells Elizabeth. Elizabeth considers this and decides to go along with her friend, to concede the fact that there are no sure things when it comes to marriage.

So Elizabeth doesn't press the issue with Charlotte. She doesn't point out that Charlotte truly deserves better or that Charlotte should hold out for more than marriage to a man who's merely suitable and up to the task. Instead, Elizabeth accepts her friend's decision and, like Charlotte, hopes for the best, knowing that if things don't work out she'll be there for Charlotte, to give her a shoulder to cry on and the encouragement she needs to move on. She'll be the friend Charlotte needs.

Because Elizabeth understands that we're all feeling lucky when we're staring down the aisle. We're all betting that we'll win. And that's why we let our friends roll the dice.

Bachelorette #1, Jennifer's bestselling debut novel, was called a "poolside page turner" by *Cosmopolitan* and declared "chick-lit at its most fun" by the *Denver Post*. *Dress Rehearsal*, Jennifer's second book, was selected as a "hot book pick" by *US Weekly*, hailed as a "sassy novel" by *LIFE Magazine* and dubbed "perfect" by *The Boston Herald*. Her third book, *Off the Record*, will be available September 2005, and *Plan B*, Jennifer's first teen chick-lit book, will be published by MTV Books in April 2006.

Jennifer received her B.A. from Smith College and her M.B.A. from the University of Chicago. She can be contacted via her Web site at www.jenniferoconnell.com.

High-Class Problems

Laura Caldwell

When I was teaching *Pride and Prejudice* in a high school English class, one of my students said, "This whole book is about getting married; it's just a Harlequin romance." After I'd smacked him upside the head for being snotty about romance, I pointed out that marriage in the nineteenth century was a life or death matter. It was *different* then, I said. Laura Caldwell has a much better answer: it wasn't that much different then. Relationship problems may be the problems of the privileged, but they're still very real problems. Attention should be paid.

Okay, I'm just going to admit it. When the publishers of this book asked me to write an essay on Jane Austen's *Pride and Prejudice*, I nodded and murmured, "Hmm, interesting." I pulled at an imaginary beard. I said I'd think about it. The tricky thing was, I'd never read *Pride and Prejudice*.

Sense and Sensibility, yes. And hey, I'd seen the *Sense* movie and *Emma* as well, but somehow *Pride and Prejudice* had escaped my Catholic high school curriculum and my Big Ten liberal arts education.

Nonetheless, I said yes to the project. A writer friend of mine recommended I read the CliffsNotes, claiming the book was too long. I did, and found them spare, to say the least. When I told my agent about the

19

anthology, she said, "Oh, just get the movie." So I rented the BBC version, which, at six hours long, didn't seem particularly economical in terms of time.

I still didn't know what in the hell I would write about, so I trotted off to the library and borrowed five treatises on *Pride and Prejudice*, two written before 1930. After slogging through over a thousand pages of theoretical musings on Elizabeth Bennet and her crew, I realized I could have read the damned book twice over by this time. And the fact was, I was intrigued.

So finally, at last, I went to my little neighborhood bookstore, and there it was, in a nice, trim paperback with a hot pink cover. Somehow I doubted the original cover had been so sassy.

I opened the book and dug in. By now, Elizabeth, along with the Bennet family and their friends, was as familiar to me as my own friends and family. And thanks to my research, I knew more about them than a suspect under FBI investigation. I knew what they were *really* about. I knew, for example, that Elizabeth and Darcy's marriage is the culmination of a journey toward social moderation. I knew that the wit embedded in the dialogue exposes their imperceptions and incongruities. I understood that Darcy represents heroism in his friendship with Bingley. And, of course, I realized that Elizabeth is an ironic and analytical spectator.

Yet within sixty pages my God-like perceptions of the characters floated away, and I moved on through the story as I would any other. As I did, I couldn't help but notice a similarity between *Pride and Prejudice* and many chick-lit novels published today. This similarity is that, instead of discussing the political situation of the time, Austen deals instead with what my friends and I call "high-class problems."

High-Class Problems, Defined

The term "high-class problems" was born for me one night while at a party with a friend who had spent the last year (and a hell of a lot of money) purchasing and rehabbing a house on Grand Cayman Island. She talked about the hurricane that had walloped the island only three days after she had moved in, and how she and her children had been evacuated and the house flooded.

A fellow partygoer, a man in his fifties wearing Buddy Holly glasses, listened to her story and then asked her if she still owned her house in Chicago. She replied that she did. "Well," he said, "sounds like you've got high-class problems."

Everyone laughed. He had a point, to be sure—my friend hadn't been killed or injured, nor, thankfully, had her children. But her spirit certainly was, along with her house, her furnishings, her clothes, her *shoes*, for Christ's sake.

Yet after that party, I started using the term "high-class problems," spreading it around amongst my friends. When I got a miserable massage by a woman with fingers the size of an infant's, I reminded myself that by definition a bad massage was a high-class problem. When the walls of my friend's big, brand-new kitchen began to shed random chunks of plaster, she called the architect to complain, and we decided this was also a high-class problem, since she was lucky to have a big, brand-new kitchen, not to mention an architect. When another friend of mine had a near meltdown on a plane after being robbed of her first-class upgrade by an evil gate agent (who then stuck her in a middle seat) we discussed anger management classes and then came to the same conclusion—high-class problem.

So the point of labeling something a high-class problem—or, as one friend called it, a "problem of privilege"—was to put things in perspective. It was the contemporary equivalent of saying, "There are children starving in Africa." But, over time, I noticed that I seemed in danger of belittling my experiences and those of my friends.

When I got my car stuck in a mud pit on the way to an anniversary dinner with my husband (a story too long and freakish to tell here), I finally wrestled my car from the oozing mass and, with shaking hands, called a friend on my cell phone to tell her about it. "But hey," I said, trying to breathe and smooth my hair. "High-class problem, right? I'm driving a Volvo, and I'm fine, and I'm about to go drink a bottle of expensive wine with my fabulous husband."

She snorted and said, "You and your *high-class problems*. You were trapped in a mud hole, for God's sake! You're entitled to be pissed off!"

This was a valid argument, I saw. Really, many of the problems my friends and I were calling "high-class" were more like "middle-class." These issues were not, after all, complaints about how one's $60 million trust fund wouldn't be available until next year, or how the Bentley was in the shop again. But, more importantly, I realized that the peril of labeling too many concerns high-class problems was in losing validation of the experience. By shrugging and telling myself or my friends that something they'd gone through, and that had just caused them great stress, was a high-class problem, I was in a sense saying, "Get over it, girlfriend."

Austen's Awareness of High-Class Problems

Either way, the conclusion I came to after reading *Pride and Prejudice* was that Jane Austen had mastered the art of high-class problems. She created characters like Mrs. Bennet, Elizabeth's indefatigable mother, whose demeanor approaches hysterical as she pines and plots for her daughters to find suitable husbands. She even denies her daughter Jane a carriage and sends her to a suitor's house on horseback, knowing it might rain, hoping it does rain, so that her daughter will be stuck at the suitor's house. When Mrs. Bennet learns that this same daughter, after traveling on horseback in a torrential downpour, is quite ill, she's delighted. Jane will have to stay at the suitor's house!

I chuckled as I read this. The characterization of Mrs. Bennet is certainly not black and white. She cares about her daughters, we know that much. But it's laughable how determined, how solely focused she is on the hope of her girls getting married. To be brief, she reminds the reader that getting married is a high-class problem. It's a problem faced by gentry who might lose their inheritance, girls like the Bennets who, while certainly not wealthy, have servants to deal with and balls to attend to.

And yet, as soon as Mrs. Bennet gets riled up, just when the reader feels almost distanced from this high-class problem of getting married, Austen introduces a new scene, like the ones between Elizabeth and her sister, Jane. We see that the girls love their mother, but that they know she is, to put it in contemporary terms, a head case. They know that her scheming is over-the-top and at times laughable. But through their touching discussions we see that not marrying properly could render them penniless; and to top it off they want to marry for love. We see that no matter how silly appearing it is at times, the issues that confront them are legitimate.

Put short, Jane Austen knew how to acknowledge a high-class problem and then address it and write about it in a sensible manner. She knew how to keep her characters in check and yet acknowledge that their problems, although not on the scale of starving children in Africa, are very real problems.

Similarities with Chick-Lit

Chick-lit is often dismissed for dealing with trivial women's issues (for example, which Prada shoe to buy definitely falls into the category of high-class problems) much the same way in which Austen was once criticized for not dealing with her political landscape. Austen, however, with Elizabeth Bennet and the surrounding *Pride and Prejudice* characters, manages a tongue-in-cheek nod to high-class problems while dealing with them at the same time. She puts a sympathetic face on the issues. She wrote with a confidence that insists that although some might call Elizabeth's concerns (and those of her sisters and family) trivial or high-class, they are still legitimate concerns; they are still very real issues.

And that's precisely why *Pride and Prejudice* is so popular today, in the same way chick-lit is popular. Readers want something that touches on their world in some small way—yes, I, too, have spilt coffee on a white blouse so that it looked like I was lactating; yes, I have also felt like a fool after being scolded at work by a boss so young I could have babysat him; and yes, I have also wanted to register for a handgun and meet my ex-boyfriend in the alley where he throws away his garbage.

Most chick-lit, like *Pride and Prejudice*, has characters who remind us about our high-class problems. There's the kooky friend with the shopping addiction or the friend who will stop at nothing to get engaged by her self-imposed deadline of New Year's Eve. There's the mother who hits the gym like a boxer training for the ring, and as a result has the body of a fifteen-year-old. There's the boss who's rumored to live under her desk at the office. Each of these characters in turn, like Mrs. Bennet in *Pride and Prejudice*, reminds the main character, as well as the reader, that the issues of buying the right dress, finding the right man, getting into the right workout groove and climbing the right corporate ladder are indeed high-class problems. No one is starving, and many people have it oh-so-worse. But the main character does care about these things, and so we do, too.

Chick-lit, much like *Pride and Prejudice*, gives us a view of someone struggling with *our* issues. It's not big business, it's not a murder at the Louvre, it's not a hunt to uncover a terrorist plot. Instead, it's women looking for fulfillment, whether that fulfillment takes the form of a husband, a new job or a pair of strappy sandals. It's girls occasionally behaving badly. It's friendships and fashion and fun, and it's growing up, at least just a little.

After reading thousands of pages of, or about, *Pride and Prejudice*, after seeing the movie and studying the CliffsNotes, I consider myself an expert on the novel, and therefore, on Jane Austen's handling of the problems of the Bennet girls—their high-class problems. And after all this studying and pondering and research, I've decided not to abandon the term "high-class problems" myself. I'll use it when I'm enraged by a cab driver who takes Clark Street instead of Lake Shore Drive, and I'll toss out the term to my friend when she moans about how the cleaning lady forgot to wash the dish towels. But I'll remember, just as Austen did, that whether they are high-class problems or not, these are problems just the same. They're my problems.

Laura Caldwell, who lives in Chicago with her husband, left a successful career as a trial attorney to become a novelist. She is the author of *Burning the Map*, *A Clean Slate*, *The Year of Living Famously*, *The Night I Got Lucky* and a novel of suspense, *Look Closely*. She is a contributing editor at *Lake Magazine* and an adjunct professor of law at Loyola University Chicago School of Law.

Jane and History

"[Austen was] rather a heartless little cynic...
penning satires about her neighbors whilst the
Dynasts were tearing the world to pieces and
consigning millions to their graves....Not a breath
from the whirlwind around her ever touched her
Chippendale chiffonier or escritoire."

FREDERIC HARRISON

A World at War

LAWRENCE WATT-EVANS

Jane Austen wrote of drawing room battles, not, as Lawrence Watt-Evans points out, of the real wars that drained England during her lifetime. Was it because Austen felt that pointed tongues were more lethally interesting than bayonets? Or is the answer inherent in Austen herself?

ONE OF THE ODDEST FEATURES of *Pride and Prejudice* for some modern readers has nothing to do with the class structure, sexual morality, mercenary marriages or other oft-cited differences between Austen's time and our own, but rather, the realization of just when the story is taking place and what was happening in the world at that time.

According to detailed analyses by Frank MacKinnon and R. W. Chapman, *Pride and Prejudice* opens in September of 1811 and reaches its happy conclusion late in 1812. This may be incorrect—they need to fudge at least one date, claiming Mr. Gardiner mis-dated a letter—but it does fit well with what we know of the story.

P. B. S. Andrews argues that the calendar better fits dates from 1799 through 1803.

In either case, however, England was in the midst of the French/Napoleonic Wars at the time. Thousands of men were fighting and dying on the Continent, yet Austen never once mentions France; the word "war" appears exactly once, in a reference to Elizabeth's hope that the War Office will not send another regiment of militia to Meryton after the first is removed to Brighton.

Yes, England is raising militia at Meryton and then sending them to Brighton, presumably to defend against the possibility of a French invasion, but this does not appear to be a matter of any great concern to the Bennets or Darcys. When Wickham is given a commission in the regulars, the possibility that this might get him shot on a battlefield in Spain or Belgium is never mentioned.

In England, the militia was only summoned when the bulk of the regular army was abroad—as of course it was, from that earliest suggested date of 1799 through the novel's publication in 1813, fighting the French Wars. This is never mentioned.

If Messrs. MacKinnon and Chapman are correct in their chronology, then the militia's move to Brighton is in direct response to Napoleon marching east from Paris with 750,000 men, bound for Russia. The United States declared war on Britain around the time of Lydia's sixteenth birthday.

And what's more, much of the English militia of the time was employed in putting down unrest in the industrializing counties to the north; the Luddites were active from 1811 to 1816, sabotaging machinery in Yorkshire, Nottinghamshire, Leicestershire and Mr. Darcy's own Derbyshire, and being hanged for it.

There is no hint of this in Ms. Austen's narrative.

But there is one truly curious item in the final chapter, Chapter 61, when Austen describes the fate of Wickham and Lydia: "Their manner of living, even when the restoration of peace dismissed them to a home, was unsettled in the extreme."

"Restoration of peace"? Except for the brief interruption of the Peace of Amiens from March 25, 1802, through May 18, 1803, England was at war for all of Jane Austen's adult life prior to the publication of *Pride and Prejudice*. (She was sixteen when England entered the French Wars.) Was this wishful thinking on Austen's part?

Or it might be that Andrews is correct about the dates, and the peace referred to is indeed the Peace of Amiens. In that case, however, it was careless of Austen to leave that line there in 1813 when she knew very well how brief that peace had been. She seems to be referring to a lasting peace, one that would keep Wickham safely on England's shores, but no such peace had been brought about prior to the book's publication. It did not even look terribly certain—Napoleon had suffered tremendous losses in the Russian campaign, but assuming MacKinnon and Chapman are correct, his retreat from Moscow had not yet begun when Elizabeth Bennet became Mrs. Fitzwilliam Darcy, and *Pride and Prejudice* had been in print for months before Napoleon's first abdication.

Yet nothing else makes sense but to assume that Austen was predicting an early end to hostilities and a solid peace thereafter.

As it turns out, she was correct, as after the false start of 1814 and Napoleon's subsequent escape from Elba, a real peace did settle upon Europe in 1815, and Britain managed to remain free of major wars for the next few decades—but how could Austen have anticipated that, after living through more than twenty years of almost constant conflict?

It's not as if no war could last longer than twenty years—the Thirty Years' War and the Hundred Years' War easily put the lie to that notion.

And it's not as if such optimism is universal in wartime—quite the contrary. During World War I the futile trench warfare had many people convinced the fighting could drag on for a decade or more.

In 1933 H. G. Wells, in *The Shape of Things to Come*, accurately predicted that World War II would begin with a Japanese invasion of China and that Europe would join in as a result of a staged border incident between Germany and Poland. He missed the exact start date of the European war by a little over three months, setting it in January 1940 rather than September 1939, but he assumed the war would drag on until at least 1950 and last until both sides were too exhausted to fight by conventional means anymore, whereupon biological weapons would be deployed.

No optimism there; Wells assumed that civilization would have to be utterly destroyed—by war, plague, famine and total economic collapse—before matters could improve and a new and better civilization be built.

And when the war actually began—well, I've read a great many science fiction stories written during World War II, and most that gave a date for the end of the war set it in 1947, 1948, 1951—very few, if any, thought it would be over as soon as 1945.

And the soldiers fighting in it certainly weren't expecting it to end as soon as it did; remember that they were still finding isolated Japanese soldiers holding out in the 1970s.

I grew up during the Vietnam War, and I remember very well that everyone in my cohort assumed the war would drag on for decades. The possibility that it might end before we were all draft age never even *occurred* to any of us—it just wasn't going to happen; we all knew this, despite Richard Nixon's claims during the 1968 election. When the draft ended in 1973 we were astonished and disbelieving—and I was twenty-six days too young to be drafted—an outcome I had never imagined

Nor was it just my own age group. In the original off-Broadway version of the musical *Hair* (the show was cut considerably for its Broadway run) one of the characters has a vision of the end of the war described in the song "One-Thousand-Year-Old Man"—and that's apparently in a far distant future. If the title is to be taken literally, *centuries* in the future.

In the 1980s science fiction authors such as William Gibson and Lucius Shepard wrote stories that assumed the guerrilla wars in El Salvador and Colombia would continue into the middle of the twenty-first century.

And of course, any number of authors and pundits assumed that the Cold War would continue indefinitely.

In general, it's been my own experience that people tend to be pessimistic about how long any given war will last. Why, then, did Jane Austen, who had seen the wars last twenty years already, take it for granted that they would soon be over? After ignoring the outside world for sixty chapters she could easily have avoided the issue for one more, yet she did not.

It seems unlikely that she didn't think it was *possible* for the wars to continue; the England she describes in *Pride and Prejudice* hardly seems to be straining to support itself. In fact, the England she describes seems utterly untroubled by the war, or by the disturbances in the industrial north.

Read any story set during one of the World Wars, or during Vietnam, and even if the story is set far away from the theater of battle, the war is a constant presence hanging over everything. Any young man may be called upon to fight, any soldier may die at any time. Yet in *Pride and Prejudice* even the soldiers don't worry about these gruesome possibilities, and the young men not already in service—Bingley, Darcy and other potential husbands—are obviously in no danger.

Technically, although the army and militia were manned by volunteers, England *did* have conscription after a fashion at the time, in the form of naval press gangs that shanghaied able-bodied young men to serve below decks. Of course, this only affected the lower classes, and only in ports; Bingley and Darcy were quite right to be unconcerned. This was a time and place when an unfortunate young man might, under the right circumstances, be snatched away and bound to hard labor aboard a man o' war, but that had nothing to do with the landed gentlemen among whom the Bennet sisters hoped to find spouses.

This, I believe, is one of the greatest differences between Austen's world and our own—she was able to ignore the war because it simply didn't affect her directly. Despite occasional propaganda to the contrary, there was no real chance that Napoleon would invade Britain; the Royal Navy dominated the seas, and the French had no way to transport troops across the Channel. England was making a serious effort, sending ships and troops into the fray, but it did not even begin to resemble the sort of total war effort that became the norm in the twentieth century.

In fact, very little that happened on a larger scale intruded upon the inhabitants of England's country homes. Wars abroad, press gangs in the ports, riots in the industrial north and the decisions of kings and parliaments simply didn't have any real effect on these people. There was no mass communication—even newspapers did not reach rural communities, let alone anything like radio or television. News traveled by word of mouth—and that wasn't especially fast, since there were no highways, no railroads, nothing faster than a good horse.

Austen could ignore the wars and other events outside her own sphere without any real consequences and without anyone thinking the less of her for it. Her world was one compartmentalized by class, location and gender in a way difficult for us to imagine. About 130 years later cinema audiences would hear Humphrey Bogart tell Ingrid Bergman, "The problems of two little people don't amount to a hill of beans in this crazy world," and it would resonate with them, because everyone everywhere was caught up in the war then going on—but Jane Austen wrote about the problems of two little people as if they very much *did* amount to rather more than a hill of beans, even though a comparable war was going on around them.

Any novel set in 1944 that ignored World War II as completely as Austen ignored the Napoleonic Wars would be seen as eccentric, at the very least.

And any story *written* in 1944 that talked blithely about the housing problems of a ne'er-do-well lieutenant after the war would probably have been seen as in rather poor taste.

So why *did* Austen assume that the wars would end soon and set Wickham at liberty?

We'll never really know, but perhaps it was merely that she could not imagine anything as disorderly and unpleasant as a war continuing for much longer. Twenty years was quite long enough for such foolishness.

After all, although she is sometimes accused of cynicism and a mercenary view of things, Austen seemed to have maintained an optimistic outlook in most regards. She knew perfectly well that bad things could happen and not be undone—misfortunes do befall her characters—but in the end, most things do work out well enough. Compromises are accepted, adjustments made, the irreparable endured, but all in all, Providence is generous enough. Lydia's ruination is mitigated rather than avoided, Charlotte's marriage to Mr. Collins is tolerable but hardly ecstatic, Mary and Kitty are left unwed, but Jane has Mr. Bingley and Elizabeth has Mr. Darcy, which is more good fortune than they might have reasonably expected. Predicting an end to the war may well have seemed no more outrageous than establishing Elizabeth as mistress of Pemberley; after all, she never did specify exactly *when* peace would be restored, merely that it would come while Lydia was still young.

Surely, it is a sign of her inherent optimism that she took it for granted that the French Wars would end soon.

But before we start thinking of her as *too* light-hearted, it may be worthy of note that she speaks of peace being restored, but never mentions who *won* the war....

Lawrence Watt-Evans is the author of some three dozen novels and over a hundred short stories, mostly in the fields of fantasy, science fiction and horror. He won the Hugo Award for Short Story in 1988 for "Why I Left Harry's All-Night Hamburgers," served as president of the Horror Writers Association from 1994 to 1996 and treasurer of SFWA from 2003 to 2004 and lives in Maryland. He has two kids in college and shares his home with Chanel, the obligatory writer's cat.

Gold Diggers of 1813

JO BEVERLEY

Mrs. Bennet has alienated many a modern reader by her avaricious evaluation of her daughters' suitors, but Jo Beverley points out that she was less greedy than needy. How choppy were the financial straits the Bennet girls were sailing into? Read on.

"A Gift from Heaven," to the tune of "Hey, Big Spender"

Mrs. Bennet:
The minute I heard about our neighbor,
I knew at once he was a gift from heaven
A rich, single man, dear.
Five thousand
And Netherfield!
He has to meet our dear daughters
Ahead of the field.

We need you to call right away.
A chance like this just doesn't hang on every tree!
My dear Mr. Bennet,
Please call—for your daughters and me!

Chorus of daughters:
We're so glad you've moved near.
(There's two, girls! Two!)
Please attend our assembly.
We'll make sure you enjoy it!

Being new to the area . . .
(Bingley! Darcy!)
. . . you must want to see the country.
We can show you our . . . beauty spots.

Mrs. Bennet:
Now that we've met our charming neighbor.
I'm convinced he is a man of perfection,
Ideal for sweet Jane.
Only think, dear,
What comes with a ring.
He can provide for her sisters when you haven't done a thing.

And then there's Elizabeth and Darcy.
I fear the man's too proud to ever bend the knee.
But, oh, Mr. Bennet,
Oh, Mr. Bennet,
Ten thousand and Pemberley!

Elizabeth Bennet linked with the good-time girls of the show *Sweet Charity*? Horrors! And, of course, she does stand against the guiding principle of her world by twice refusing offers of marriage from eligible men of property. However, *Pride and Prejudice*'s theme is stated in the famous first sentence and continues throughout. A rich, single man was like a fox to the Quorn hunt, or the cigar-smoking big spender in the nightclub—a natural quarry. Mrs. Bennet gets a harsh rap from modern readers because we now prefer to think that money weighs lightly in decisions of love, but in Jane Austen's age, genteel poverty was a dreadful fate, and it is what the Bennet ladies face, entirely because of the improvidence of Mr. Bennet.

For a Regency gentlewoman, money was key to a bearable life. It was almost always necessary in order to marry, and marriage brought children, quite possibly a child every couple of years for twenty years. Raising them without adequate finances would be drudgery, though poverty could ease matters by killing a number of them. Educating them would be extremely difficult, and thus their prospects would be dismal, leading to yet more misery. Who would support Mother in her old age?

Remaining single was no improvement. Marriage was the Regency gentlewoman's only path to social dignity. Agnes Porter (*A Governess in the Age of Jane Austen: The journals and letters of Agnes Porter*. Ed. Joanna Martin, The Hambledon Press, 1998) had what in Regency times was an excellent career. She was governess to the children of Lord Ilchester and very well-treated, in many ways like one of the family. Even so, she longed for a husband. She bought a lottery ticket thinking of a fortunate young woman who won £1,200 and was then courted by a rich man, "... and now she rides in her own coach and proves a woman of good sense and merit." At another time she writes: "I could not forbear...reflecting on the ills that single women are exposed to...from being the property of no one." (Property here is clearly used in the warmer meaning of our "belonging.")

In 1799, the Marquess of Bute put it bluntly: "Ladies of quality without fortunes are perhaps worse off than any other class." Though Jane Austen was not of aristocratic rank, she suffered the predicament. She probably lost her true love, Tom Lefroy, because she lacked the money he needed to establish himself in life. He married an heiress and did very well.

As Lefroy and the lottery winner illustrate, gentlemen were gold diggers, too, and were not despised for it. If they had no money they married it, and a promising future in a profession or the military was considered fair exchange. If they were rich, they would think it folly not to bring yet more wealth into the family. Great wealth gives Darcy the freedom to be a fool for love, but Wickham can only be brought to marry Lydia by bribes of considerable amounts.

Wickham secures the promise of Lydia's meager dowry of £1,000 and the addition of £100 a year from her father, a considerable sum when a modest house could be rented for £20 a year. Mr. Bennet says that Lydia's £1,000 would bring only £50 a year, so he's assuming a 5% return on investment. Using that figure, the fortunate lottery winner above did not bring as much as Lydia; her £1,200 invested would be unlikely to produce more than £60 a year. £100 per annum would, therefore, equal an additional dowry of £2,000 or more invested.

In addition, Darcy pays Wickham's debts and buys him a commission in the regular army, which would cost between £500 and £1,500, depending on regiment and other details. Contrast that, however, with what Wickham lost with Darcy's sister—a very handsome £30,000, which could translate to £1,500 a year and comfort.

It's very difficult to relate these figures to modern values. Labor was cheap, so a maid-of-all-work could be hired for £10 a year plus room and board. Contrast that with the mere tax on keeping a four-wheeled carriage and two horses to pull it—£30. Add in a coachman and a groom for about £40, and keeping a modest carriage would cost seven times the price of one overworked housekeeper.

If the employers took that carriage on a journey and stayed at an inn, their bill for room and meals, without considering the care of their carriage, horses, coachman and groom, would probably exceed £2. No one today could hire a live-in housekeeper for five times the cost of a night in a good hotel. On the other hand, most people run a car (note, the above figures are only for maintaining the horses and carriage, not purchase) without thinking they can afford a servant, except possibly an occasional cleaning service. But then, appliances and premade goods are our cheap servants today.

We have to remember, too, that in Regency times people at different levels of society had vastly different requirements for a "decent life." But then, perhaps it's not so different than today, when some need the food bank at the end of the month while others pay $1,000 for a handbag; or when some will pay for a meal at a restaurant an amount that could keep a family for a year in a third-world country ($300 in Burkina Faso).

This way of looking at things might clarify why money was so important to the gentry in Regency England. A lower income did not merely mean a little economy. It brought danger of sliding to an entirely different level of life.

Jane Austen is unusually specific about money in *Pride and Prejudice*, proving that it is indeed the theme of the novel. I can find no period slang for the concept of the gold digger, almost certainly because it was considered a normal state of affairs to want to marry wealth.

To understand why snagging a rich spouse was so important, we have to understand the financial realities of Jane Austen's time.

Entail was a common way of preserving the integrity of estates. The property inheritor had only a life interest in it. He had free use of the income, but could not sell or mortgage the property, and it passed on according to the terms of the entail, almost always to the next male in line. Because the Bennets have no son, Longbourn is entailed on Mr. Collins. As soon as Mr. Bennet dies, Mrs. Bennet and her daughters will lose both access to the estate income and to their home. Like the Dashwoods in *Sense and Sensibility* they face a penny-pinching life in a cottage, or employment that will never offer them the dignity that in their circles comes only from marriage.

Jane Austen comments on the unfairness of this through Lady Catherine de Bourgh: "I see no occasion for entailing estates from the female line." I don't think either Lady Catherine or Austen would have questioned the right of sons to inherit before daughters, but for a property to bypass a man's children entirely is another matter.

Given the legal settlement governing Longbourn, however, the Bennet women's situation could have been improved if Mr. Bennet hadn't been a foolish, selfish, improvident man. Instead of gold-digging, he chose to marry a pretty girl with no money. His plan to cover this was to have a son. When his son came of age they could together break the entail and any daughters would be provided for by depleting the estate. If the daughters didn't marry, they would still have their home and their brother's support. When that son didn't appear, he should have cut current spending to put aside money for his widow and daughters, but that would have affected his comfort.

When Mr. Bennet made his foolish marriage, however, he couldn't have foreseen demographic and economic changes. In earlier times a bevy of well-bred gentlewomen would have had a reasonable chance of making satisfactory marriages with well-bred gentlemen neighbors of modest but adequate means, but by the early nineteenth century, things had changed.

The supply of young gentlemen available for marriage was reduced by an ongoing war. When it didn't kill or maim the men it kept a lot of them out of England. It has been estimated that in 1812–14 the male population of Britain between the ages of fifteen and sixty was 2,700,000. More than 10 percent, around 330,000, were under arms, not counting the navy (*The Armies of Wellington*, Philip J. Haythornthwaite, Brockhampton Press 1998). The percentage in prime eligibility years—twenty-five to forty—must have been much higher. Moreover, in an age where officers led their men into battle, casualties among officers were much higher than among the ranks.

At the same time, many gentlemen at home were reluctant to marry, especially women who brought little income. Why? Because life expectancy was generally increasing. This period saw a decrease in infant mortality and an increase in longevity, especially among women. This might seem like a blessing, but it put many upper class families in a predicament.

A system had been devised for property stability. The key element was male primogeniture, by which the oldest son inherited the whole estate, usually under the strict controls of an entail. The other children were taken care of through a marriage settlement. The settlement specified income for the wife, known as pin money, and for her widowhood, called jointure. Once the settlement was signed, these were her legal rights, not subject to the whim of her husband. The settlement also usually included an amount put in trust for the younger children of the marriage, to be divided into equal portions—dowries for the girls, starter money for the boys.

However, preservation of the estate was still the intent, so while a husband was expected to support his wife and children from his income during his life, the demands upon the estate after his death—the jointure and portions—were based on what the bride brought into it. Mrs. Bennet and Mrs. Dashwood (*Sense and Sensibility*) brought little as dowry and thus they and their children could take little out.

Mrs. Bennet and her daughters are expected to live on the interest of £5,000 (about £250 a year). If any of the girls married, her portion must come out of the capital, leaving less income for the rest. If a woman did not marry, she was expected to live on the interest generated by her portion. If Elizabeth Bennet was left a spinster trying to survive alone on the interest of her £1,000, £50 a year would provide only the bare necessities.

Because the amount set aside for the children was usually a fixed sum, large families meant inadequate portions. In this situation, wiser fathers than Mr. Bennet put money aside to increase the portions, and sons often gave over their share to their sisters. One route for these sons was the navy, which required little outlay and provided opportunity for advancement and wealth. This was the course taken by two of Jane Austen's brothers.

Longevity created another problem. Many estates were carrying the burden of long-lived widows, and maybe more than one. Consider the fix of the young man who inherited an estate with multiple jointure obligations. His fifty-five-year-old mother is entitled to five hundred a year for life and could easily live for another thirty years. Eighty-year-old granny is still alive and due another five hundred a year. If this were rich Mr. Bingley, a fifth of his £5,000 per annum must go to the widows, and it could be that way for most of his life.

Many upper-class men were land rich (entailed, remember) but had incomes of only a few thousand. It is hardly surprising if some seem to have decided not to risk adding another widow for a generation, especially as their "Regency buck" lifestyle, especially fox hunting, made the bachelor life appealing.

Fox hunting? Horses were the Regency man's passion, and fox hunting, with its long, dangerous runs, the favorite activity of many. Various factors led to the expansion of fox hunting in the Shires in the late eighteenth century, but by the Regency era, many young men took up residence around Melton Mowbray from November to March, turning the place into the best men's club around. Marriage generally meant an end to it, however, as a wife and family couldn't be abandoned for that length of time and weren't welcome there.

This didn't, of course, mean doing without sex. "Cyprians" were acceptable in Melton, and some even rode to the hunt. In all places, the Regency buck had easy access to sex, and if he preferred a type of monogamy, he could set up house with a mistress without any of the legal and financial complexities of marriage.

Jane Austen lived and wrote in a time when eligible husbands were in short supply, spinster gentlewomen had little status and spinster gentlewomen with small portions had only faint hope of marriage. It's hardly surprising if that predicament permeates her work. Perhaps only her contemporaries could truly appreciate the breathless hopes of the ladies of Longbourn when two single, wealthy men appeared among them, but if she didn't describe the Bennet ladies as gold diggers, it's only because hunting down that "gift from heaven, a rich, single man, dear" was a natural part of her world.

Jo Beverley is the bestselling author of twenty-seven historical romance novels, most set in and around the Regency period. She is a five-time winner of the RITA award, the top award in romance fiction, and a member of the RWA Hall of Fame for Regency romance. She is also on the RWA Honor Roll. Her latest publication is *A Most Unsuitable Man*, NAL February 2005. www.jobev.com

Jane and Academe

"The key to Jane Austen's fortune with posterity has been in part the extraordinary grace of her facility, in fact of her unconsciousness: as if, at the most, for difficulty, for embarrassment, she sometimes over her work basket...fell...into woolgathering, and her dropped stitches...were afterwards picked up as...little master-strokes of imagination."

HENRY JAMES

Any Way You Slice It

Elisabeth Fairchild

What is it that keeps Austen's story so fresh that it can be reinvented again and again? Elisabeth Fairchild sorts through her literary vegetable bin and gets the answer from her onions.

A SHELTERED TWENTY-YEAR-OLD romance writer from the early 1800s helped launch two popular fiction genres from beyond the grave. I'm talking Regency romance and a hot, sassy new fiction genre known as chick-lit. I'm talking about the movies *Pride and Prejudice, Emma, Sense and Sensibility* and *Persuasion*.

How does Jane Austen do it? How do her witty, romantic, quill pen scribblings continue to impress readers after almost two hundred years? What magic convinces the big screen to tell and retell her tales, even morphing them into more contemporary knock-offs like *You've Got Mail, Clueless* and *Bridget Jones's Diary*?

The answer is simple: love and onions.

We relish Jane's work because she wrote romance with biting humor and delving insight. Humankind adores a wonderful love story. Always has. Hopefully, always will. There is undeniable potential for our species as long as love enchants us.

Jane, a kid-gloved feminist, would savor the idea that fresh crops of women's fiction writers are employed today because of her writing, and in two very different romance genres.

Regency period historical romances owe their roots to Jane Austen. Think *Pride and Prejudice* and you've a good idea of the witty tone, Regency period settings and comedy-of-manners romantic leanings of virtually every book within the genre.

More recently, a fresh crop of authors have sprung into bloom courtesy of Jane cultivating the sassy seeds of new fiction known as chick-lit. Think *Bridget Jones's Diary*. Think spicy dialogue, hip attitudes and romantic shenanigans.

Regency romance and chick-lit tell, in essence, the same story. Jane's story.

Hey, wait a minute. How can that be?

That's right. Bridget Jones is a modernized Elizabeth Bennet—a brilliant and captivating knock-off. *Bridget's* screenwriter made no secret of Jane Austen's influence. After all, Mr. Darcy retains his name in both works. But there is more to the connection than that.

Which brings me to onions. You see, three different vegetables offer the keys to driving fiction: broccoli, Mr. Potato Head and onions.

The most popular choice is broccoli.

Plot-driven fiction is "events driven" and built like broccoli, with a strong storyline or turning point event that branches out. Something happens, which makes something else happen, which triggers something else to happen.

A classic literary example: Alexander Dumas wrote lively, swashbuckling broccoli in *The Man with the Iron Mask*.

Here's how it works:

CENTRAL PLOT LINE: A young man is locked away in an iron mask. No one knows why except an evil Prince and his most trusted advisor, a Musketeer.

PLOT BRANCH #1: The Musketeer asks fellow Musketeers to free the man in the mask,

PLOT BRANCH #2: who is discovered to be the spitting image of the evil Prince,

PLOT BRANCH #3: which gives the Musketeers the idea to put a new and less evil prince on the throne.

What about Jane Austen's plotting skill? Certainly interesting, tension-laced events unfold in every one of her stories, but plot is not her primary driving force, which is why the plot lines of *Pride and Prejudice*, *You've Got Mail*, *Bridget Jones's Diary* and the Bollywood musical hit *Bride and Prejudice* vary, but still echo one another.

The second most popular choice in driving story is to put Mr. Potato Head behind the wheel. Many readers are under the mistaken impression that Jane Austen writes character-driven work in which memorable characters color every element, every forward thrust of the story. Like the plastic nose, eyes and hat all connect to a Mr. Potato Head, all story elements in a character-driven work connect to character.

A classic literary example: Sir Arthur Conan Doyle's *Sherlock Holmes* is Mr. Potato Head armed with a Meerschaum pipe, a deerstalker hat and a magnifying glass. Without Holmes, there is no story. Same holds true for James Bond, or the television series *Monk*, or Bernard Cornwall's *Sharpe's Rifles* series. These are exemplary character-driven pieces. Take away the key spud and the story fabric falls apart.

Characters are not really what drive Jane Austen's work. That's why even though *Pride and Prejudice*, *You've Got Mail*, *Bridget Jones's Diary* and *Bride and Prejudice* are peopled with entirely different characters, the *Pride and Prejudice* story structure remains intrinsically the same in all of them. Don't get me wrong. Jane Austen wrote wonderfully memorable and intriguing characters: noble, comic, quirky and original, but her stories are not character-driven.

Which brings us to the lynchpin of Jane's longevity—onion story structure. Compare *Pride and Prejudice* and the screenplay for *Bridget Jones's Diary*. Both are theme-driven works.

Theme. It is a truth universally acknowledged that the very word strikes a breathless "Oh, no, I'm not ready for a pop quiz" mentality into the hearts and minds of many. Perhaps due to all-nighter memories of the dreaded college theme paper?

Well, Jane loved theme. Reveled in theme. Wrote thematic masterpieces. Okay, I'll stop. I can see some of you giving me that glassy-eyed "Let's keep this a little kickier" look.

Back to the onion. Any way you slice into Jane Austen's work, it comes up theme. Layer upon layer, nuance upon nuance of a single idea is built around a central truism. Jane's themes are not always initially seen or understood until the repetitive pattern of that core truth is recognized, but like an onion's pungent flavor, theme permeates whatever it touches. Its essence affects plot, character—virtually everything in a story. Try to remove theme from Jane Austen's work and the story fabric falls apart.

Jane is not just clever with her onions; she is a master. She trusts in the intelligence of her reader. Peel back the layers of *Pride and Prejudice* (or any of its knock-off permutations) and discover one savory truth from beginning to end.

Pride and Prejudice (originally titled *First Impressions*) is an onion all about impressions: first impressions, mistaken impressions, false impressions, impressing and being impressed.

Have a go! Search out the onion layers in *Pride and Prejudice.* It's great fun—like a *Where's Waldo?* word game for adults.

Start with the opening line: "It is a truth universally acknowledged, that a single man in possession of a good fortune must be in want of a wife."

This line offers a snarky, tongue-in-cheek statement of potential theme, but beware: it offers a *flawed first impression* of what the story is all about.

Then look at how Jane introduces characters; each personifies the theme of *impressions* in some way. The reader's first impression of the heroine, Elizabeth Bennet, given by Mrs. Bennet: "Lizzy is not a bit better than the others; and I am sure she is not so handsome as Jane, nor half so good-humored as Lydia." But Mrs. Bennet is an unreliable witness and offers a *flawed first impression.*

The reader's first impression of the hero, Mr. Darcy, given by the narrator: "Mr. Darcy soon drew the attention of the room by his fine, tall person, handsome features, noble mien, and the report...of his having ten thousand a year." Another *flawed first impression.*

By the end of the evening Mr. Darcy has rudely insulted Elizabeth with his pride, which also turns out to be a *flawed impression.*

The first impression of the heroine, Elizabeth Bennet, given by Darcy: "She is tolerable; but not handsome enough to tempt me...." Another *flawed first impression.*

The first impression of the villain, Mr. Wickham, given by Elizabeth: "... Mr. Wickham was beyond them all in person, countenance, air and walk...." Another *flawed first impression.*

Keep searching and you will find that all of Jane's characters are touched by theme.

How does theme affect plot development in *Pride and Prejudice*?

Beginning: Mrs. Bennet wishes Mr. Bennet to make a good *first impression* by calling upon a new neighbor, whom everyone in the neighborhood is trying to *impress*. She is under the hopeful *impression* Mr. Bingley might marry one of their many daughters.

The Bennets go to a local Assembly (to *impress* and be *impressed*), where the local community receives its first shallow, *social impression* of Darcy and Bingley, and Elizabeth is wounded by a distinctly poor *first impression* of Darcy's pride. Bingley gives the *impression* he is interested in Jane, and Jane gives the *false impression* her heart is not truly engaged.

Middle: Wickham misleads Elizabeth with an ironic *mistaken impression*. "The church ought to have been my profession," Wickham claims. "I was brought up for the church...."

The shoe is on quite the other foot. Wickham fails to mention his reputation as a dissipated, debt-ridden idler who ruined his future by seducing Darcy's underage sister. Wickham further misleads Elizabeth with the *mistaken impression* he is interested in her, while repeating his wicked pattern by seducing Elizabeth's younger sister Lydia.

Climax: Darcy resolves to ride to Lydia's rescue to disprove Elizabeth's *mistaken impression* of him as "ungentlemanly." Elizabeth is left with the *mistaken impression* Darcy's horrible *impression* of her family drives him away.

Turning Point: The imposing Lady de Bourgh's dour and condescending *mistaken impression* that her nephew intends to marry Elizabeth Bennet offers fresh hope to Darcy and Elizabeth, who have both been suffering under the *mistaken impression* that their relationship is at an insurmountable impasse.

Impressions. Impressions. Impressions. Onion. Onion. Onion. When theme is analyzed and pointed out it may feel as though Jane repeatedly bangs the reader over the head with her Vidalia. Not true. Her onion-layering technique is exquisitely subtle. Many readers never realize they are biting into a big mouthful of theme; they just sense resonance and connections without being able to immediately identify the ingredient.

Theme explains why Jane Austen's works are considered classics. Any way you slice into her carefully crafted words, you find continuity of purpose. Randomly thumb through the pages of *Pride and Prejudice*. Over and over again you touch upon essence of onion. Every possible mutation and permutation of impressions and false impressions is explored, such as:

- The annoying Mr. Collins, a man of the cloth who should be least *impressed* by worldly goods and status, is in fact the biggest fawning toady of a woman of worldly goods and status.
- Mr. Darcy's negative *impression* of Elizabeth Bennet undergoes change when she is not trying to *impress* anyone at all and walks three miles to stay with Jane, who is ill, despite bad weather and a muddied petticoat.
- Elizabeth's horrid *impression* of Darcy is forever changed when she visits his *impressive* estate. His servants speak well of him, clarifying her mistaken *impression* of Wickham and Darcy.

In *Pride and Prejudice*, Mr. Wickham prejudices Elizabeth Bennet against Darcy by misleading her with a *false impression* of the past. In two of the recent rewrites of *Pride and Prejudice*—*You've Got Mail* and *Bridget Jones's Diary*—mistaken first *impressions* involving the human failings of pride and prejudice figure into the updated versions of the story.

- In *You've Got Mail*, Meg Ryan's e-mail savvy Shopgirl's online hopes for love are threatened by her prejudiced impression of the megastore bookstore magnate, Fox of Fox Books. Tom Hanks plays a dual (hero/villain) role by misleading Ryan's character as to his online identity. *You've Got Mail* even gives a big-screen nod to Jane Austen's inspiration. Meg Ryan and Tom Hanks discuss the book *Pride and Prejudice* several times as the two rebuild their relationship.
- In *Bridget Jones's Diary*, an office assistant bent on improving herself is prejudiced against Mr. Darcy, a divorced lawyer, by the mistaken impression offered up by her handsome, womanizing flirt of a boss (*Bridget's* version of Wickham).

But how does Jane's choice of theme as the driving force behind her works impact how we view *Pride and Prejudice* today?

Dig deep into well-written themes and you find truth.

Humankind recognizes and honors universal truths. Discerning readers, screenwriters, producers and directors revere truth well-told. Universal expressions of truth resound year after year, in print, on screen, in our hearts and souls. More than telling a story, or building a vivid world, or captivating readers with wonderful characters, Jane Austen captures the truths of a flawed humanity. As a result, her works are treasured and emulated as literary classics.

Just how long did it take Jane (working with quill, inkwell, blotter and pounce box) to create a fresh, witty thematic onion like *Pride and Prejudice*? She initially penned *First Impressions* at age twenty, from October 1796 to August 1797, immediately following a spurned love interest in a young Irishman convinced by family he must marry better than a mere Jane Austen. Jane poured wounded feeling onto the page. A first draft was completed in eleven months. Not bad, even by today's standards. Two years later Austen rewrote and renamed the book.

Austen scribbled fast, completing *Elinor and Marianne* (retitled *Sense and Sensibility*) and *Susan* (retitled *Northanger Abbey*). She sent *Pride and Prejudice* to an editor and suffered (horrors!) a rejection. In 1802, Jane, twenty-six and in danger of becoming a pitiable spinster, received a respectable marriage proposal. She accepted the offer, but that night suffered second thoughts. The following day she scandalized friends and family by gently refusing her suitor.

Once again Jane Austen turned to *Pride and Prejudice* as a catharsis of romantic emotion and rewrote the book.

In 1812 *Sense and Sensibility* had been published and was earning favor. Emboldened, Austen gave *Pride and Prejudice* one last rewrite. In a letter to her sister she says that much of the prose had been removed, a quarter of the book "lopt and cropt." Indeed, the opening passages of the book are crisp, fresh onion, witty and spare, almost the beginning of a play. Every word reflects Austen's theme: first impressions. After seventeen years of perfecting, in January of 1813, *Pride and Prejudice* was released in its first printing, the work destined to become the most popular and widely published of Jane Austen's writing career.

Austen admitted, "I am quite vain enough, and well-satisfied with *Pride and Prejudice*." She should be. True to its theme, the book made quite an impression. It is a truly delicious onion—words worth savoring.

Biographies of Jane Austen wholeheartedly endorse her as "one of the greatest writers ever known." High praise. I have to agree. I personally owe a lot to Jane, and to *Pride and Prejudice*. It shaped my life more than any other literary work. I love word play, puns and double entendres because of Jane. I trust in the intelligence of the reader and write theme-driven Regency romances because of Jane. I live a life personally influenced by themes of love, persistence, accountability, awareness and openness to learning—because of Jane.

My heartfelt thanks go to a lovely young woman who quietly revolutionized the way I look at the world, words, love and onions.

Awarded the romance industry's top trade magazine Career Achievement Award for Regency-period romance, Elisabeth Fairchild's work is described as "theme-driven, lushly set and lyrically layered wit—Jane Austen style." Half English (her mother still maintains UK citizenship) with a keen ear for British voice, a sharp eye for accurate and evocative setting and a wry tongue-in-cheek wit, the award-winning author is also published in Germany, Italy, Bulgaria and the Netherlands.

Her last three releases, *Sugarplum Surprises*, *A Game of Patience* and *Valentine's Change of Heart* have been chosen as "Top Pick" releases. She is currently working on a new book and dabbling with a Regency period screenplay. For a sneak peek at sample chapters, visit www.gimarc.com/fairchild.html. Write Elisabeth at fairchild@gimarc.com.

Jane Austen and the Masturbating Critic

ADAM ROBERTS

Readers and critics make strange bedfellows, especially romance readers and literary critics. Adam Roberts imagines a dialogue between the two and discovers there's common ground.

CONSTANCE READER: And let me begin by saying that I do not merely *like* Jane Austen's books. No, I *love* Jane Austen. I know all of her novels, and I reread them regularly. Indeed, reading is one of my chief pastimes. I have many favorite authors, but Jane occupies a special place in my affections.

PROFESSOR ACADEMICUS: I am pleased to hear it, madam. As a salaried university professor of English Literature, I have built my reputation as a scholar of the early years of the nineteenth century, with a number of articles and monographs on Austen's novels. I share your approbation of her writing.

CONSTANCE READER: And there, sir, is precisely my problem. I do not believe that you, and your kind—

PROFESSOR ACADEMICUS: My *kind*? Madam! What do you mean?

CONSTANCE READER: I mean the type or species of academic critic   I cannot believe that any of *you* truly understand what it is about Austen that makes her worthy of her readers' love. I know what *I* love about her writing.

PROFESSOR ACADEMICUS: And what is that?

CONSTANCE READER: I love her portrayal of love. All of her novels tell the same story, all follow the same broad narrative arc, and this is a plot that speaks to one of the deep human narrative needs: girl meets boy, an obstacle is placed in the way of the love between girl and boy, the obstacle is overcome, girl marries boy and everybody lives happily ever after. Ten thousand such love stories ("romances") are produced every year, but people have not grown tired of reading them. They make us feel good; they reassure us of the value and importance of love—perhaps they remind us of our own stories that led to our own romantic partnerships; or perhaps they give us an ideal to which to aspire. The template they provide, in which love is a profoundly satisfying, free emotional exchange between partners, is neither trivial nor escapist. On the contrary, working out *how* to love one another is one of the most challenging tasks facing humanity.

What differentiates Austen's classics from the vast body of mundane romantic fiction is its sheer *quality*. She is so completely in command of her materials; her fluency and tone are so witty, so sparkling, so entertaining; her characterization is so deftly yet penetratingly done; her pacing and form so perfect. Nobody has told this core human story better than her.

PROFESSOR ACADEMICUS: I do not disagree with you, madam. This is, indeed, a crucial part of the satisfactions that Austen offers her readers.

CONSTANCE READER: Then why, sir, does your profession not *say* so?

PROFESSOR ACADEMICUS: But we do!

CONSTANCE READER: I beg to differ, sir, you do nothing of the sort. Thinking that reading critical studies of Austen might deepen my appreciation of her novels, I recently spent a few hours in the university library.

PROFESSOR ACADEMICUS: Are you, might I ask, a student?

CONSTANCE READER: No, I am an ordinary working adult, a member of my local community. I am what is known as "a general reader." Yet I have been told that universities exist in part to serve the community, to help disseminate knowledge and understanding. I asked the university librarian if I was free to browse, and he said I was. Moreover, I asked him to recommend to me some criticism on Jane

Austen, and he put before me, as I sat at one of the library's broad pinewood desks, two articles. These, he told me, were two of the most influential critical readings of Jane Austen of the 1990s, by two of the most highly regarded critics in the field of English Literature. They were required reading for the Literature students studying at the university. And so I read them. And this is the kernel of my complaint to you, sir. For in neither of them did I even *recognize* Jane Austen—the Austen that I so often read and reread. It seems to me that something has gone very wrong somewhere...that academic criticism has become an idiom so obscure and oblique, so counter-intuitive and complex, so far removed from the ordinary apprehensions of most book lovers, that it is now merely irrelevant.

PROFESSOR ACADEMICUS: I see. Before I attempt to refute your charges on behalf of my profession—

CONSTANCE READER: Refute! There you have it, sir! That, in a nutshell, is what is wrong with academic criticism: its pride. Its arrogance. Its certainty that it knows better than ordinary readers and that it can condescend and dismiss ordinary reactions to books.

PROFESSOR ACADEMICUS: [*Bridling a little*] And *your* problem, madam, is a prejudice against the academy so embedded that it will not even allow you to hear the contrary case. [*Calming*] But I do not mean to lose my temper. Before I *address* your *concerns* and attempt to defend my profession, might I ask what the two articles in question were?

CONSTANCE READER: One was by a man named Edward Said, and was entitled "Jane Austen and Imperialism." It took for granted that Austen's novels were not about men and women falling in love and marrying, but were instead oblique and complex critiques of imperialism, slavery and patriarchy. At least I *think* that's what he was arguing; it wasn't clear.

PROFESSOR ACADEMICUS: The librarian did not lie: Said is (or was, for sadly he died not long ago) one of the most highly regarded critics in the world, and his account of Austen—you are referring, I think, to a famous chapter from his book *Culture and Imperialism*—has indeed had an enormous impact on Jane Austen studies over the last decade.[1] What was the second?

---

[1] Edward Said, *Culture and Imperialism* (Knopf: 1993).

CONSTANCE READER: An article in a certain scholarly journal by a professor called Eve Kosofsky Sedgwick entitled "Jane Austen and the Masturbating Girl."[2]

PROFESSOR ACADEMICUS: Yes, I know it, of course. Another very famous critical intervention in the field of Austen studies. Did you find the article unilluminating?

CONSTANCE READER: On the contrary, I found it *most* illuminating. But what it illuminated was not Austen. It was whilst reading that article that the truth dawned on me: the thousands upon thousands of articles, the scores of critical monographs published on the subject of Austen—the deconstructions of Austen's novels, the positioning of Austen in Cultural Materialist, Formalist, Feminist, Marxist, New Historicist or other theoretical-philosophical contexts—all this has *nothing to do with Austen*. It is all about tribes of academics declaring their ideological affiliations: "I'm a Marxist, therefore every book I read seems to me about Marxism!" "I'm interested in sexuality, therefore I find explicit sexuality in every novel whether it's there or not!" "I consider imperialism a weightier and more important topic than the triviality of men and women falling in love; therefore when I read a Jane Austen novel it magically becomes all about the evil of empires and has nothing at all to do with romance." Is it not the case that you academics must publish—that your career advancement, promotion and reputation all depend on adding myriad scholarly publications to your CVs?

PROFESSOR ACADEMICUS: Well, yes, I concede that.

CONSTANCE READER: There you are! *That's* what these articles are about—not Jane Austen, but rather about *the critics themselves*; critics shoehorning Austen into whichever conceptual pigeonhole happens to be *á la mode* at the moment. Critical responses that owe everything to political correctness and intellectual vanity and faddishness, and nothing to close attention to what Austen is actually saying! Is it any surprise that ordinary readers never buy books of academic criticism? Most of it is written in a gibberishical university-ese that is ungainly and ugly when it isn't flat incomprehensible; and when we make the effort we discover that the books we love, passed through the weird prism of academic conscious-

[2] Eve Kosofsky Sedgwick, "Jane Austen and the Masturbating Girl." *Critical Inquiry* 17 (1990–91) 818–37.

ness, have become unrecognizable. So you academics are writing all these books and articles for—whom, exactly? For one another, at cliquey little conferences, or published in obscure little journals that only academics read. Which is to say: for yourself. Criticism is no longer about communicating your love for an author; it's about impressing yourself with your own cleverness. You're alone in your bedroom giving yourself obscure and unsocial pleasures. Jane Austen and the Masturbating Girl? Jane Austen and the Masturbating *Critic* more like!

PROFESSOR ACADEMICUS: Well! You've certainly made your case with great, ah, *emphasis*.

CONSTANCE READER: Are you going to tell me that general readers of Austen can expand their appreciation, enhance their knowledge or really learn anything *about Jane Austen* from an article called "Jane Austen and the Masturbating Girl"? It's ridiculous! Because the plain fact of the matter is that *there are no masturbating girls in Austen at all*. Austen makes no reference of any kind to masturbation, or any explicit reference to sex, in any of her books. This is not to say that her books are unsexy, of course. On the contrary, I have always felt that her well-bred reticence on the sexual life only enhances the pervasive sensuality and erotic charge of her books. Darcy, fully clothed and reserved, is *far* sexier than Colin Farrell dancing about stark naked on screen. But to suggest that "Jane Austen and the Masturbating Girl" is a valid topic for criticism? It's absurd.

PROFESSOR ACADEMICUS: The story behind Sedgwick's famous article is quite interesting, actually, and relevant to what you are saying. An American conservative called Roger Kimball, horrified (rather like you, Ms. Reader) at what he saw as the degeneracy of contemporary criticism, published an attack on academia in 1990 under the title *Tenured Radicals: How Politics Has Corrupted Our Higher Education*. In it he mocked the sorts of academic papers presented at the convention of the Modern Language Association of America, or MLA (one of the professional organizations of academics and critics in the field of literature), quoting that title, "Jane Austen and the Masturbating Girl," as the *ne plus ultra* of academic idiocy and corruption. Professor Sedwick published her article, deliberately taking that title, the following year: it is an article that explores not only the connections between three sorts of solitary pleasure ("literary pleasure, critical self-scrutiny and autoeroticism"), but also surveys the ways in which the prejudice against masturbation itself (an activity, many believe, not only harmless but positively beneficial to good health, and yet one that has suffered for centuries under active prohibition, or censorious dismissal) is part of a larger hidden cultural desire to *control* sexuality, particularly female sexuality. And these issues of control (both self-control and the metaphorical harness placed upon women by society and the expectations of others) are exactly what Jane Austen is about.

CONSTANCE READER: Pah!

PROFESSOR ACADEMICUS: But might I *suggest*—without wishing arrogantly to *insist*—that you rein in your prejudice for a moment, and allow me to continue?

Sedgwick (a brilliant critic, I might add) challenged Roger Kimball's unspoken assumptions. Why, she wondered, was "Jane Austen and the Masturbating Girl" so absurd a topic for the critic of literature to explore? Of course, Austen does not represent any of her female characters *actually* masturbating, unlike (say) James Joyce in *Ulysses*. But that refusal to show, that reticence, that sense of things going on *beneath* the surface of things, is precisely one of the most significant of Austen's genius. Sometimes it is called irony. So, for example, on one level the sentence, "It is a truth universally acknowledged, that a single man in possession of a good fortune must be in want of a wife" (forgive me for choosing so obvious an example), means just what it says. The story of *Pride and Prejudice* will eventually prove that several such men do eventually fulfill their want and find wives. Within the universe of Austen's novel the sentence holds true. But, of course, it is also ironic: wittily amusing in its subtle revelation of the obsessive insistence of Mrs. Bennet on finding husbands for her daughters. It is ironic because when we read it we bring to it our knowledge of the way the world actually is, a world in which it does not hold true.

CONSTANCE READER: I will concede that Austen's greatness lies as much in what she does *not* say as what she says.

PROFESSOR ACADEMICUS: Quite—and this is something she has in common with the greatest literature. Just to take one example from the same period as Austen—what is Coleridge's *Rime of the Ancient*

Mariner but a rather silly story about a sailor who shoots a seabird, which action somehow kills his crew and leaves him with a compulsion to tell his story to everybody? But to say so is of course to misrepresent the effect of this great poem: for it does not seem to those who read it to be silly, but instead profound, powerful, haunting. It is what the poem *implies*, the fuses of association its images and scenes set alight in our minds, that makes it great: not some story about a sailor and a bird. I put this in a deliberately extreme way, of course, but the general point holds true. In the greatest literature it is not what is actually said, but what is implied, what is below the surface, those secret and hidden nexuses of textual pleasure, that are truly important.

One of the tensions of a novel such as *Pride and Prejudice* is precisely that between public duty and private desire. In all of Austen's novels, society, in the form of family, acquaintances, the polite world of middle- and upper-class England, acts as a restraint upon the indulgence of merely selfish pleasure. The characters who flaunt that social restraint, like Lydia eloping with Wickham, inevitably find themselves excluded from social acceptability. In all Austen's novels the heroines negotiate a path between what is expected of them as civilized and refined ladies on the one hand, and what their hearts yearn for, and perhaps require, on the other. It is one of the things that make Austen so *civilizing* to read, that she places so high an emphasis on the civilized virtues: courtesy, consideration, attentiveness, perception, kindness.

CONSTANCE READER: These are not trivial virtues.

PROFESSOR ACADEMICUS: Indeed they are not! And there is, Austen believes, an appropriate public forum for the expression of physical love (you said yourself that Austen's books are very aware of sexual attraction, however reticent they are about that subject on the surface) and that is marriage. All her novels move toward marriage precisely as that consummation, the balance between the private sexual desire of the heroine and the duties of public propriety. But there is always a moment in Austen's novels in which her heroines—who are usually highly aware of and sensitive to what is publicly required of them—put their feet down, as it were, and insist upon their right to *wholly private* pleasures. It is a function of their growth as human beings, their assertion of their own rights. In *Pride and Prejudice*, for instance, there is the scene in which Lady Catherine attempts to browbeat Elizabeth into giving up Darcy by reminding her of the public prejudices against their marriage. Describing Elizabeth as an "upstart," a "woman without family, connections, or fortune," she insists that she give up her desire to marry Darcy. But Elizabeth refuses, in effect declaring that there are private pleasures to which, since they harm nobody else, she is entitled: "I am only resolved to act in that manner, which will, in my own opinion, constitute my happiness, without reference to *you*, or to any person so wholly unconnected to me."

CONSTANCE READER: But that's hardly the same thing as masturbation. . . .

PROFESSOR ACADEMICUS: Of course not; but in saying so you're reading the novel in only a shallow, literal sense. Yes, *speaking literally* there is no masturbation in the novel; but in the broader sense, in the sense of a life going on behind and beneath the glittering surfaces Austen presents to us—the sense of the broader symbolic signifying structures of her novels—guilty, self-oriented pleasures are very present in her work. I wonder: do you object to the notion of studying "masturbation" as a metaphorical trope within Austen because you are prejudiced against masturbation itself? Perhaps you believe it turns people blind, or insane? Perhaps you believe God punishes those who partake of it? Yet everybody has *done* it, no? Will we all go blind and face God's wrath?

CONSTANCE READER: [*In a low voice*] You are baiting me, sir.

PROFESSOR ACADEMICUS: [*Sincerely*] I apologize. But my point is that the ways society and "authority" talk about masturbation have always been enormously disproportionate: that it will lead to physical incapacity, madness, death or even the wrath of the Deity! In *Pride and Prejudice* society reacts with similar disproportionate anguish to Lydia's elopement with Wickham, or Darcy and Elizabeth's decision to marry: yet Austen makes plain that it is the intimate, personal, individual aspects that are the truly important ones in such matters.

CONSTANCE READER: Perhaps I see your point. But I remain unconvinced. I am not a prude; it is not that I object on principle to the very idea of masturbation in literature. But I *do* object to critics importing their own shibboleths and hobby-horses into books. This

Mr. Said, whom you described as a world-famous critic—how can he claim that Austen is about *slavery*? Empire? Oppression? And, for all I know, the dictatorship of the proletariat and any and all sacred cows of political correctness!

Don't misunderstand me: slavery was of course a terrible thing. If I read a novel such as Toni Morrison's *Beloved*, I come to a deeper understanding of just how terrible, how dehumanizing and how profoundly violent and distorting slavery is. *Beloved* is a very great book, a masterpiece and the sort of reading Mr. Said proposes is quite proper to it. But Jane Austen's novels are simply not about slavery. The word is not so much as *mentioned* in her books!

PROFESSOR ACADEMICUS: You're quite correct. It's also true to say that Austen does not mention so much as one contemporary political figure, one current issue, one famous battle or treaty. Her books have a timeless quality precisely because of their focus on the private lives of a small group of families. Consider *War and Peace*, another novel set (as is *Pride and Prejudice*) at the time of the Napoleonic Wars. In Tolstoy's famous novel history is ever-present, with a wealth of references to the sorts of things history books are full of: battles, treaties, sieges, political machinations. There is no history in Jane Austen. She never, in any of her novels, so much as mentions Napoleon's name.

CONSTANCE READER: Exactly.

PROFESSOR ACADEMICUS: Except that we've already agreed that one of the most distinctive things about Austen's genius is the way she weaves deeper truths into the apparently simple, sunny textures of her writing. This is her irony; the gap that she deliberately opens up between what she seems to be saying on the surface, and what she is actually saying when you think about it a little, when you look a little harder. Are the Napoleonic wars really absent from *Pride and Prejudice*?

CONSTANCE READER: I suppose there do seem to be a lot of soldiers in the neighborhood....

PROFESSOR ACADEMICUS: Yes. And why are there so many soldiers? Because the nation is at war; practically a world war, in which most Britons feared French invasion as a real threat, in which people feared for the stability of England, the English family and way of life. This anxiety is part of *Pride and Prejudice* too. Or to dwell for a moment on Edward Said's actual example: he was particularly interested in *Mansfield Park*. Yes, on the surface that novel seems, like *Pride and Prejudice*, to be merely a witty and charming love story in which Fanny Price and Edmund Bertram overcome the obstacles and find happiness together. But that's just the surface. What happens, Said wondered, if you ask more penetrating questions? Like, for instance, where does Sir Thomas Bertram's wealth come from? We might assume that characters like Bertram, or Darcy, are wealthy because they just are: but that's a childish view of things. Wealth must come from somewhere. And in the case of *Mansfield Park* Austen tells us where the wealth does come from: it comes from his extensive West Indian plantations. Sir Thomas even leaves his stately home to visit those plantations during the first half of the novel. In the early nineteenth century, those plantations would have depended upon slave labor. So even though Austen does not explicitly say so, we can infer (if we are used to reading Austen for her hidden depths as well as her sparkling surfaces) that Bertram is wealthy because he exploits slaves. This in turn connects with a ubiquitous fascination in the novel about authority, the proper and improper manifestations of it, the responsibilities as well as the privileges that authority carries with it. Said simply points out that the privileged lifestyles of Austen's aristocrats are deeply complicit with the misery and exploitation of slavery. Of course she doesn't say so explicitly: exploitation never does admit to itself explicitly that its privileges are obtained at the cost of other people's misery.

CONSTANCE READER: Still—*slavery*? Really?

PROFESSOR ACADEMICUS: Slavery is simply the most extreme, and most unpleasant, manifestation of a lamentable feature of human history: the tendency of one human being to assert absolute authority over another. Slavery is the turning of a human being into a possession, a thing. Austen's novels are all of them deeply fascinated with the logic of authority, of the way one set of people assumes authority over another set: men over women, aristocrats over the middle classes, beautiful stupid girls over plainer, more thoughtful girls, and so on. These are the examples she takes, because this is the world with which she was familiar. But the principle is what is important and the principle is that these seemingly embedded hierarchies are not necessarily valid. That you should not simply accept something because it is conventional; that you should look more deeply into it.

CONSTANCE READER: Perhaps I have judged a little hastily...there may be more in these critical approaches than I first admitted.

PROFESSOR ACADEMICUS: And perhaps I, and my profession, do not make enough allowance for the common readers of the world. It is true that you would not expect to open the professional journal of a mathematician, or a physicist, or an engineer, and expect to be able to understand everything written inside. In those cases you accept that professions have their own professional idioms, their own technical jargon, which enables them to talk about their business precisely and without ambiguity; and that to master that professional idiom requires time and training. Yet you are impatient when you discover a similar idiom in the professional journals of literary critics....

CONSTANCE READER: Because it is not *necessary*! Physicists may need technical terminology to describe the inner workings of the atom...but no literary critic needs technical terminology more arcane than "character," "plot," "style" and "metaphor" to talk about literature. Literary criticism used to be accessible to the general reader; it could be again.

PROFESSOR ACADEMICUS: Perhaps you are right. I have been, sometimes, unregarding of the needs of the broader reading public...perhaps even arrogant in my self-absorption....

CONSTANCE READER: And I have been, perhaps, too quick to judge, too hasty in my prejudice.

PROFESSOR ACADEMICUS: Ms. Reader...

CONSTANCE READER: Yes?

PROFESSOR ACADEMICUS: I love you! You are what I have been looking for all my life. For too long have I sojourned with specialists and dry-as-dust professors. I need you in my life!

CONSTANCE READER: Professor Critic—this is most unexpected....

PROFESSOR ACADEMICUS: Could you ever agree to make me the happiest Professor alive?

CONSTANCE READER: Oh, my darling, yes! Yes!

PROFESSOR ACADEMICUS: My love! For too long my pleasures—my reading of Austen, my writing about Austen, my dreaming of Austen's worlds—have been solitary pleasures, secretively and even furtively undertaken. But now, with you, I have someone with whom I care share my pleasure!

CONSTANCE READER: And I too, my love! For too long Jane's novels have been, in my life, merely a lonely substitute for the love-connection they describe. I have wallowed in this solitary emotional pleasure instead of making that outward connection with another human being...but no longer!

[*They embrace.*]

Adam Roberts is a professor of nineteenth-century literature at the University of London (Royal Holloway College). There seems to him no contradiction between teaching and publishing academic criticism on the classics of Romantic and Victorian English literature on the one hand and writing science fiction novels on the other.

The Original Chick-Lit Masterpiece

SHANNA SWENDSON

Jane Austen is generally acknowledged to be the mother of the romance novel. Shanna Swendson takes that one better and argues that Austen wrote the first chick-lit novel, complete with a smart, beleaguered heroine who relies on her friends for support as she searches the social jungle to find her Mr. Right.

SAY YOU'VE GOT A BOOK about a smart, sassy young woman with one sane sister and an otherwise impossible family. She approves of her sister's new boyfriend but can't stand his arrogant best friend. The last man in the universe she'd ever want anything to do with (even if he does have friends in high places) decides she's his ideal wife, and when she finally gets it through his thick skull that she is so very much not interested, really—and she's not just saying that to make him even more interested—her best friend marries him because it beats being single.

Our heroine bonds with the charming, handsome new guy in town over their mutual dislike of the arrogant guy, but before she manages to truly fall in love with him, he ditches her for someone better able to help him climb the social ladder. Much to her surprise, the arrogant guy confesses that he's fallen in love with her, though he has a funny way of letting her know, making it sound more like an insult than a compliment. She puts him in his place with all the dirt she'd heard about him, only to find out she'd heard only one side of the story. He starts to look more appealing to her as she gets to know him better—and when she finds out just how rich he really is. When he comes to the rescue after her crazy family gets into yet another crisis, she realizes that it might be true love. Then she just has to explain to her friends and family why she changed her mind about a guy she'd sworn she had good reason to hate.

It sounds like something you'd find on the "new in paperback" table at the front of your neighborhood Barnes & Noble or Borders, probably with a cartoon cover with either shoes or a martini glass on it. The color pink would most likely be involved. But this isn't the latest chick-lit novel. It's perhaps the first, written nearly two hundred years ago.

Those who write off chick-lit as a passing fad should probably take another look at Jane Austen's *Pride and Prejudice*, which has a lot in common with those cartoon-covered confections about the lives and times of young women. The term "chick" wasn't in use—at least, not with today's connotations—but Austen honed in on the elements that make chick-lit popular today.

A Smart, Self-Aware Heroine Who Is a Keen Observer of the World around Her

ELIZABETH: I hope I never ridicule what is wise or good. Follies and nonsense, whims and inconsistencies *do* divert me, I own, and I laugh at them whenever I can. —But these, I suppose, are precisely what you are without.

A strong, sympathetic and believable heroine—what the publishing industry often calls "relatable"—is key to a chick-lit novel. That's what puts the "chick" in "chick-lit," after all. Elizabeth Bennet, the heroine of *Pride and Prejudice*, is the prototype for this kind of heroine.

Lizzy is keenly perceptive, finding wry amusement in the follies of those around her. She's an observer of human nature and of the quirks of her society. She's equally critical of herself and quite willing to own up to her own perceived flaws. She's a devoted daughter (even if her mother does drive her insane), a loyal sister and a true friend.

But she's no paragon of feminine virtues, and she'd be the first to tell you so. She's no raving beauty and doesn't expect the admiration of men. She's most often described as "pretty." At first glance, Mr. Darcy isn't at all impressed, and it's only on subsequent meetings that he begins to appreciate her fine eyes. Instead of inspiring love at first sight, she's someone who grows on men gradually. At nearly twenty-one, she's fairly old to remain unmarried for her time and culture, but she isn't desperate to be married. She's what her literary descendent Bridget Jones would call a "singleton."

She reads more than the average woman of her time, but admits to being no great reader. She plays the pianoforte passably, but knows she doesn't practice nearly enough to show any real skill. When she meets someone new, she makes a nearly instant judgment, then clings to that opinion until the evidence is too overwhelming for her to deny it. This blend of good qualities, quirks and flaws adds up to a heroine readers of any century can relate to, someone you'd want to be and someone you could imagine yourself being.

Pride and Prejudice is Lizzy's story. Although the other characters have their own stories and subplots, their prime importance is in how they affect Lizzy and her growth as a person. Through the course of the book, Lizzy has to come to terms with her family complications, her friend's choices and her own misguided prejudices as she finally discovers what (and who) she wants out of life. Even her romance with Mr. Darcy is part of this story arc, showcasing how she has changed as a person. Lizzy herself admits that the change was not in Mr. Darcy himself, but rather in the way she learned to see him.

This sets the pattern for the chick-lit heroine, whose story is about how she interacts with her world and the people who inhabit it. She may have a romance, but the story is more about how she has to grow and change in order to open to that romance when it comes along than it is about the relationship itself.

Female Friendships: Sharing, Secrets and Shopping

ELIZABETH: Compliments always take you by surprise and me never. What could be more natural than his asking you again? He could not help seeing that you were about five times as pretty as every other woman in the room. No thanks to his gallantry for that. Well, he certainly is very agreeable, and I give you leave to like him. You have liked many a stupider person.

You may find a chick-lit novel without a romance in it, but you'll seldom find one without female friendships in it. *Pride and Prejudice* devotes more pages to interactions between Lizzy and her sister Jane, her friend Charlotte and her Aunt Gardiner than it does to her interactions with Mr. Darcy, the romantic hero of the piece. Their conversations are very much like what you'd see in a chick-lit novel written a couple of centuries later, only taking place in carriages, bedrooms and drawing rooms rather than at Starbucks over lattes or at a bar over martinis.

The women of *Pride and Prejudice* talk at length about men. They analyze their every word or action during lengthy post-mortems of every social event. They warn each other about the bad ones, agonize when the good ones fall off the face of the earth and vent when they believe a man's actions have been inexcusable. Adjust the language a bit, change "write" to "call," and Jane's agonies about Mr. Bingley's disappearance from her life could fit easily into any modern chick-lit novel.

Austen also deals with a dilemma women of any century can relate to: what happens when your friends get married while you're still single, especially when you don't approve of their choice of husband? Lizzy's friend Charlotte marries the obnoxiously obsequious Mr. Collins—whom Lizzy has just rejected for herself—with the reasoning that it's the best she can hope for. Lizzy recognizes that her relationship with her friend will be forever altered and has to find a way to overcome her personal feelings in order to support her friend.

And Manolo Blahnik may not have started designing shoes yet in the early 1800s, but that doesn't mean the women of *Pride and Prejudice* don't go shopping. A visit to the milliner is a convenient excuse for a walk into town to check out the guys. Lizzy's sister Lydia even shops like a modern woman, buying a bonnet she's not crazy about just because she wants to buy something, and she hopes she can later alter it to make it better.

The Men in Her Life: Jerks, Cads and Mr. Good-on-Paper—But Which One Is Mr. Right?

ELIZABETH: I am going tomorrow where I shall find a man who has not one agreeable quality, who has neither manner nor sense to recommend him. Stupid men are the only ones worth knowing, after all.

One key differentiator between a romance novel and a chick-lit novel with romantic elements is that in a chick-lit novel the identity of the romantic hero isn't always immediately apparent. In a romance novel, if the heroine meets a handsome man in the first chapter, it's a good bet that he's the hero. If a chick-lit heroine meets a handsome man in the first chapter, he could be the hero. He could also turn out to be a jerk who breaks her heart, or he could become her gay best friend. On the other hand, Mr. Wrong can look like a viable option, at least for a time.

Mr. Darcy is the romantic hero of *Pride and Prejudice*, and he does make his appearance early in the book, but Austen stacks the deck against him. If you hadn't heard enough about the classic story to know how it comes out, or you hadn't known that Colin Firth played Mr. Darcy in the television miniseries (and you didn't have fond memories of him emerging dripping from the lake in that white shirt), you might not be sure you wanted him to end up with Lizzy.

Quite frankly, he's a bit of a jerk. He makes a terrible first impression. He's rude. He insults Lizzy behind her back, but within earshot. We get Mr. Wickham's stories about Darcy's misbehavior long before we learn Darcy's side of the story. The only reasons we don't hate Darcy entirely (if we're not picturing Colin Firth) are his stated appreciation for Lizzy's pretty eyes and his snarky way of putting down Caroline Bingley when she cattily attacks Lizzy.

On the other hand, Wickham appears to be the perfect romantic hero. He's handsome and charming. He knows how to flatter a woman. He's even a put-upon underdog struggling to make it in the world. Too bad he's also a pathological liar, a cad and a scoundrel; but Austen makes us sympathize with him before she reveals his true colors.

Then there's Mr. Good-on-Paper, the man who would appear to be ideal by logical standards, but who is so very, very wrong. Mr. Collins stands to inherit the Bennets' estate, so Lizzy marrying him would secure a future for her mother and sisters. He's a clergyman with connections. But he's also an idiot and the worst kind of brownnoser, and we never seriously consider that Lizzy should marry him, even if it makes all kinds of sense. Mr. Collins is the nineteenth-century equivalent of the ambitious junior executive who sounds like he should be a good match and who would give you a comfortable life, if only you could stand to be in the same room with him. He's the man of last resort, and Lizzy isn't yet that desperate, but Charlotte is.

Sifting through these men, all of whom have their drawbacks, is a large part of Lizzy's task throughout the book, a task many modern chick-lit heroines share.

A Not-Necessarily Hearts-and-Flowers View of Love (Even with a Happy Ending)

ELIZABETH: I wonder who first discovered the efficacy of poetry in driving away love?

DARCY: I have been used to consider poetry as the *food* of love.

ELIZABETH: Of a fine, stout, healthy love it may. Everything nourishes what is strong already. But if it be only a slight, thin sort of inclination, I am convinced that one good sonnet will starve it entirely away.

Although it's often used as an example of romance, *Pride and Prejudice* isn't actually a romance novel, for reasons I've already touched upon. In its treatment of love, the book has far more in common with modern chick-lit novels than with modern romance novels.

For one thing, the book is more about Lizzy's growth as a person than it is about her relationship with Darcy. Darcy remains offstage for much of the book, only coming into Lizzy's life at a few key moments. We can see how she's changed by the different ways she reacts to him in each of these encounters. There's her initial prejudice in the first period of togetherness in the country, her obstinate dislike when she encounters him again in Kent, her seeing him in a new light when she runs into him in Derbyshire and, finally, her awareness of love when he and Bingley return to Netherfield.

But even as Lizzy becomes aware of her love and finds herself defending Darcy to her family, she can't help but acknowledge a little cynicism about her reversal of opinion. She points to the moment she saw his estate—and realized just how rich he was—as the start of her love for him. She may love him enough to stand up to both his family and her family, but she has to admit that it's a very beneficial arrangement for her. That kind of honesty about the practicality of a match is rare for a traditional romance heroine but key to the irony in chick lit.

Helen Fielding may get the credit for launching a genre with *Bridget Jones's Diary*, but the foundation was laid centuries earlier with *Pride and Prejudice*—which was the basis for Fielding's novel. A smart publisher would put a cartoon cover on *Pride and Prejudice* and reissue it in a trade paperback edition, where it would fit in perfectly with all those other chick-lit novels on the "new in paperback" table at the bookstore. All that's really changed since then are the fashions, a few social mores and the technology that facilitates communication (and miscommunication) between men and women.

Shanna Swendson sold her first book at the age of twenty-four and went on to sell four more short contemporary romances before the age of thirty. She didn't know it at the time, but she was always writing what we now call chick-lit, just published in romance novel form. Now that the publishing niche actually exists, she's building a real chick-lit career. Her latest book, *Enchanted, Inc.*, was a June 2005 release from Ballantine Books. A sequel to this book is scheduled for 2006.

Plenty of Pride and Prejudice to Go Around

LAUREN BARATZ-LOGSTED

Lauren Baratz-Logsted agrees with Shanna Swendson: Austen wrote the first chick-lit. But then they differ: Baratz-Logsted thinks that modern would-be Austens have "devolved" Elizabeth into ditzes and worse. And then there are the modern critics....

"It is a publishing truth, universally acknowledged, that anyone professionally involved in the pursuit of 'Lit-e-ra-ture,' must, by definition, despise chick-lit.

"I first met Frank D'Arcangelo, Editor-in-Chief of the *New York Times Book Review*, at the annual National Book Awards ceremony and while it was definitely not the best of times for me, it was a close runner-up for the worst.

"Of course, being the kind of person I am and writing the kinds of books I do, I didn't actually receive anything so mundane as a printed invitation to the ceremony. Rather, my agent, perennially dateless, said I could be her guest."

Thus begins *Chick-Lit: A Love Story*, my upcoming novel that pits the much-maligned subgenre against the conventional literary press. Here's one more quote: "I hated the *Times* with their uppity tone of voice.... They were Pride, as far as I was concerned, and I was Prejudiced."

71

And therein lies the rub. It's ironic that writers of chick-lit, proud inheritors of the mantle of the now much-honored Jane Austen, get so little respect, experience so much prejudice. Is our pride deserved? Is the prejudice warranted? I'll come back to this, but first let's take a closer look at those deceptively simple words: pride and prejudice.

Let's start with Elizabeth and Darcy. Which one is Pride? Really, can someone tell me which one is which? Apparently I wasn't paying sufficient attention in the graduate course I took on Austen and Brontë, because I've never been able to tell them apart. And, no, I don't mean Austen and Brontë. I mean, even *I* can tell them apart; the former wrote about societal conventions, the latter wrote about moors. And I don't mean Elizabeth and Darcy themselves, because I can readily tell that she's the girl with the intelligent eyes while he's the boy with the rather large, er, estate. But what I cannot for the life of me figure out is if Elizabeth is Pride and Darcy is Prejudice. Or is it the other way around? Or could it possibly be, perhaps, they each are—gasp!—both?

Time to pull out *Merriam Webster's Collegiate Dictionary, Tenth Edition.* True, the copyright is 1996, so I should probably invest in a new one, but, really, the words are mostly the same, right?

Okay, here we go, then. Ignoring the definitions that use the actual word itself or some version of it as part of the definition—which always seems lame to me—we have:

> **pride** *n* (bef. 12c)* **1 a:** inordinate self-esteem : CONCEIT **b:** a reasonable or justifiable self-respect **c:** delight or elation arising from some act, possession, or relationship **2:** proud or disdainful behavior : DISDAIN **3 a:** ostentatious display **b:** highest pitch : PRIME **4:** the best in a group or class **5:** a company of lions **6:** a showy or impressive group.[1]

I'm not even going to comment about the lions, but I think we can all agree that both Elizabeth and Darcy exhibit everything listed under

---

[1] It was something of a relief when, having done a double take concerning the creation of the word pride, I saw that it was created before the twelfth century. This was a relief because, on the first take, I confused it with the entry above it, prickly poppy, which had a date of 1724, so close to Jane's own dates, she could have invented it. Of course, then I became upset all over again when, flipping to the biographical portion at the back of the dictionary to confirm Austen's dates, I realized that she was born in 1775, which would have been too long after even prickly poppy for her to have coined it, and that—here's the depressing part, for me—she died in 1817, meaning she was exactly as old when she died as I am at the writing of this essay, 42…and I haven't done anything yet!

1 and 2, and that Austen intends them to be and they are in fact 4. For myself, I'm not sure exactly what 3 means, but I can state categorically that 6 does not apply since, Elizabeth and Darcy each being very much individuals, they cannot then each also constitute a group.

Now for the other pesky word (and it really is pesky, since I don't think you can define it without using elements of its construction as part of the definition; or, at least, *Merriam Webster* is having trouble doing so):

> **prejudice** *n* (13c) **1**: injury or damage resulting from some judgment or action of another in disregard of one's rights; *esp*: detriment to one's legal rights or claims **2 a** (1): preconceived judgment or opinion (2) an adverse opinion or leaning formed without just grounds or before sufficient knowledge **b**: an instance of such judgment or opinion **c**: an irrational attitude of hostility directed against an individual, a group, a race, or their supposed characteristics.

I would say the 2s have it here.

And I would further say that, having reviewed *Webster*'s definitions of **pride** and **prejudice**, Elizabeth and Darcy are definitely each both.

IT IS A TRUTH UNIVERSALLY ACKNOWLEDGED—here we go again!—that many authors writing in the subgenre of chick-lit today take as their model Austen's most talked-about book. One need look no further than the woman most often cited as the modern originator of chick-lit, Helen Fielding, to see how true this statement can seem. After all, Ms. Fielding, writing in *Bridget Jones's Diary*, even goes so far as to name the romantic object of her eponymous heroine's attentions Mark Darcy. Could her intentions *be* any clearer?

And yet...and yet....

Considering that the books I've written so far have been labeled chick-lit; considering that I actually have a book in the hopper called *Chick-Lit: A Love Story*, I do not spend an inordinate amount of time reading in the subgenre. Since the age of ten, thirty-two years ago as of this writing, I've averaged between 100 and 250 books a year (this year I'm trying for a book a day, but that's my own personal insanity and final proof of the fact that—yes!—I'm a geek). So while I read some chick-lit each year, it by no means makes up a large percentage of what I read. But in preparing to write *Chick-Lit: A Love Story*, as part of my research I felt it only wise to reread *Pride and Prejudice* as well as *Bridget Jones's Diary*. I wanted to see what Austen had done with the original; I wanted to see what Fielding had done with the modernization. Then, as further research, I read some more chick-lit, and a curious trend began to emerge: a wide difference between the mistress and her handmaidens.

(Parenthetically, I'd like to point out here that I have nothing against modern writers modeling their work on a classic, giving it some new spin. Indeed the greatest writer of all time, Shakespeare, was the supreme master at this.)

We, as women, like to think that we have progressed as time has gone on: we can work at nearly anything we want to, provided we're willing to work hard enough; we can choose to have families or not, and if we do choose to, we can even arrange those families in any one of a myriad of configurations. Why, then, decades after the ostensible Women's Revolution, rather than evolving the prototype of Elizabeth Bennet, have we chosen to *devolve* her into characters who, however lofty their careers, however many modern choices arrayed before them, are charming ditzes at best, babbling and insecure bumblers at worst? A quick survey of many modern offerings reveals that many of the descendents of Elizabeth are just that. On the other hand, Darcy has survived intact. No matter which book you encounter him in, he is still handsome, still scowlingly intelligent if sometimes pompous, if given to the sin of pride, if always prejudiced, and, as such, is portrayed as the most perfect of imperfect men. But Elizabeth? She is not only given to pride, not only prejudiced, but she is a klutz. She wears a vulgar costume to a party that is meant to be anything but, she trips over her own Manolo Blahniks at the feet of the hero, she accidentally sets fire to something, causing Darcy-as-Fireman to come to her aid. Not only does she not know her own heart, as is the case of Elizabeth Bennet, but sometimes it appears that she knows almost nothing at all!

Elizabeth Bennet is not a ditz. Elizabeth Bennet is not a babbling bumbler, nor is she noticeably insecure, despite taking offence to Darcy's snubbing of her at the dance. After all, wouldn't *you* be offended? Elizabeth Bennet is not concerned with fashion, indeed cares little enough about it that she worries not a whit about her own appearance when she dashes off to take care of her sister Jane, who has fallen ill away from home. Surely, she wouldn't have attempted *that* journey in a pair of Manolo Blahniks! Elizabeth Bennet is *smart*. She is smart enough to be her intelligent father's favorite daughter; she is smart enough to know most of her sisters are silly, but that Jane is good; she is smart enough not to marry the odious Mr. Collins. So what if, based on first impressions, she is foolish enough for a time to think the nefarious Wickham all things good while thinking the hiding-his-goodness-under-a-bushel Darcy all things bad? She has pride! She's prejudiced!

It's. The. Name. Of. The. Book.

So perhaps we've earned a little of the prejudice that seems to surround chick-lit; perhaps some of our pride is misplaced. Sometimes. Occasionally. But chick-lit is also filled with smart, competent women; fair matches to Elizabeth Bennet and worthy successors.

I have no doubt that if Jane Austen were writing today, she would get labeled as a writer of chick-lit. There is no denying the fact that no matter how far we have come, no matter how far we *think* we have come, there is still the tendency on the part of the conventional literary press to deem works written by, about and primarily for women as being automatically less than. After all, when academics talk about the classic literary greats, they talk about Dickens, they talk about James; they only talk about Austen and Brontë as a pretty pink sop to pacify the Women's Lit classes. And when they talk about the modern literary greats, they talk about Updike, they talk about Roth, they talk about DeLillo, Wolfe and Mailer, but only as an afterthought and with great prodding, do they toss in Ozick.

But I also like to think—and perhaps this is just my own fancy here—that Jane Austen, being Jane Austen, would not much care. She'd just go on writing the books she wants to write, telling the stories she wants to tell.

Of course, I suppose it's always possible that I'm just plain *wrong* about the conventional literary press. Maybe I'm just proud. Maybe I'm just prejudiced.

> Lauren Baratz-Logsted is the author of three published novels, *The Thin Pink Line*, *Crossing the Line* and *A Little Change of Face*. In July 2006 her fourth novel, *How Nancy Drew Saved My Life*, will be released. Lauren is a former independent bookseller, book reviewer, freelance editor, sort-of-librarian, window washer and doughnut salesperson. She lives in Danbury, Connecticut, with her husband and daughter.

Jane and the Movies

"To paraphrase Jane Austen: it is a truth universally acknowledged that Hollywood in possession of good fortune must be in want of a good love story."

ELIZABETH FARNSWORTH

Elizabeth . . . On the Roof

JENNIFER COBURN

Tolstoy said all happy families are alike (both of them). Jennifer Coburn says families with five daughters have a lot in common, too—in particular, rebellion, disgrace and redemption. Mr. Bennet may never have sung "If I were a rich man," but he must have thought it often enough.

THE FIRST TIME I READ *Pride and Prejudice* was during my freshman year of high school, right around the same time my friends and I were auditioning for the school production of *Fiddler on the Roof*. I tried out for the musical because that's what I was into at the time. We were the musical-chick clique that performed in the school shows, the Madrigal group and the "beauty shop" octet. In our spare time, we taught ourselves the lyrics of every Broadway musical and took acting and dance lessons on the weekends.

I would have auditioned for any show the school was doing, but I felt a particular affinity for this production. Though the story took place in turn-of-the-century Russia, it was about my people—Jews. It was about an issue I could understand—grappling with one's identity during a time of change. Not only were our teen lives changing, but the world around us was, too. I was the fourteen-year-old daughter of a divorced, new age secretary and hippie musician who came of age in Manhattan in a decade when greed was good and preppies aspired to become yuppies.

I was less than thrilled to read *Pride and Prejudice*, but did because it was assigned. I wondered how I would relate to the story of nineteenth-century Brits in a "comedy of manners." Manners weren't the sort of thing that interested any teen, much less me, whose father said they were "bullshit rules prescribed by an oppressive establishment." My mother felt that as long as everyone's chi was flowing, the idea of manners was just a silly mainstream notion. Neither of their ideals resonated with me. The reality is that manners sounded like work I didn't want to be bothered with—much like the assignment of reading *Pride and Prejudice*.

I expected to be dreadfully bored by *Pride and Prejudice*. I even bought the CliffsNotes just in case. But, like many teens who know it all, I was mistaken. I found myself drawn into the plight of the Bennet family, wondering how Jane and Elizabeth would fare, what was up with those bitchy Bingley sisters and whether or not Darcy would come through in the end. It reminded me a lot of what was going on in ninth grade, where mean girls plotted to break up couples through gossip, rumors and schemes. Typical of most American schoolkids, we had a well-guarded class system defined not by economics or religion, but popularity. I had fallen prey to a modern-day Caroline Bingley, and loath as I am to admit it now, I wove a web or two in my day.

Unexpectedly, I started seeing overlaps between *Pride and Prejudice* and *Fiddler on the Roof* and realized that the families had far more in common than I'd ever imagined. Not only did they share similar experiences with each other, but with families and daughters and young women everywhere.

Despite the difference in their religion, geography and era, both Tevye's brood and the Bennet clan are poor families with daughters whose actions usher in a new era of familial and individual identity. Their ideas about love, in particular, serve as a catalyst for the patriarchs to confront and adjust their notions about propriety, tradition and tolerance.

Tevye and Mr. Bennet have five daughters, the eldest two of whom are of marrying age—and a younger one who surprises them by eloping. They each have spirited wives who freely air their grievances with their spouses in a time when female submissiveness was the expectation in a marriage.

The two families also live on a similar fault line. They share the threat of loss of their home. The Bennets face entailment by their rogue cousin, Mr. Collins. Tevye's family, along with the other Jewish villagers, is always painfully aware that they could lose their home and community at any moment to the Cossack army. Pogroms plagued Russian Jewish communities and Anatevka was vulnerable.

Perhaps most importantly, the two families are dealing with intensely personal issues during times of great cultural shift. The roles of the individual, women and families transform before them.

As an adult, I wonder if teachers assign *Pride and Prejudice* to their English students because they know that teens will identify on some level with the story about their lives and roles in the family changing before them. I know I quickly tossed out my CliffsNotes and began talking back to the pages the same way my grandmother would interact with the characters on *The Young and the Restless*. I was drawn in at a level I never expected. The story wasn't just about the deftly crafted characters Jane Austen developed. It was about all of us.

The Eldest Daughters, Jane and Tzeitel

If their paths crossed, the eldest daughters of the families from Hertfordshire and Anatevka might well be friends. They share an idealism and sweetness that sets them apart from their peers. They both share a fairly modern desire to marry for love. While Jane's trip to the altar is undoubtedly longer than Tzeitel's to the chuppa, both are severely challenged by issues of social class and family status.

Didn't we all have a boyfriend our mothers thought were beneath us? While dating is certainly a lower-stakes game than marriage, I now feel for my mother, who claimed that the total cutie Paul had "a bad aura."

In one of the opening scenes in *Fiddler on the Roof*, Tevye negotiates the marriage of Tzeitel to the widowed butcher, Lazar Wolf. He is far older than Tzeitel, but is still considered a good match because of his affluence. Tevye and his wife Golde are ecstatic about the marriage because their social and economic status had limited Tzeitel's prospects. But Tzeitel has her heart set on marrying the poor tailor, Motel. Tzeitel convinces her father to let her marry her true love. This is the first time Tevye considers the modern notion of romantic love and questions whether he and his wife share such feelings. Sadly, Mr. and Mrs. Bennet never have the opportunity to discuss their feelings for each other. Some might argue that they are comfortable enough to tease and cajole each other, while others say their relationship ranges from tolerable to antagonistic. Nonetheless, each family has the opportunity to examine its values, weighing enduring tradition against individual desire.

Jane falls in love with Mr. Bingley fairly early in *Pride and Prejudice*, but is separated from her love by a plot of snobbery. Neither Mr. Darcy nor the Bingley sisters feel that country-bred Jane is worthy of the wealthy gentleman and convince him to leave for London, where he will be far away from Jane. When Jane travels to the city, the Bingley sisters fail to inform their brother that she is in town, while Darcy actively interferes to keep his friend apart from Jane. Like Tzeitel, Jane has an opportunity to marry an older, undesirable man—her cousin, Mr. Collins. Of course, Collins is also interested in marrying her sister Elizabeth and their friend Charlotte Lucas. Clearly, he is, like Lazar Wolf, a lonely old guy looking for a wife—any wife.

Jane and Tzeitel ultimately marry their soulmates. Though Bingley and Motel are men of different economic means, they are both happy-go-lucky, somewhat goofy young men. Can't you just see Bingley running through Meryton singing "Wonder of Wonders" after he is reunited with Jane?

The Second Daughters, Elizabeth and Hodel

These are the spunky, independent girls of both *Pride and Prejudice* and *Fiddler on the Roof*. While Elizabeth is the lead sister in the tale of the Bennets, Hodel is the star of Tevye's girls. Okay, maybe not. (Perhaps this would be the time to disclose that Hodel is the role I played in *Fiddler*.) But she is the rebel of the five sisters, leaving home to marry the liberal student Perchik after he is arrested and sent to Siberia for political activism.

While Elizabeth and Hodel enjoy different social and economic status as married women, their journey into wedlock is similar. Elizabeth is disinterested in Darcy when she meets him at the ball in Hertfordshire. Considered proud and boorish, Darcy does little to endear himself to the locals. Though he is also an outsider, when Perchik came to town, he immediately joined Tevye and his family at Sabbath dinner and began tutoring his youngest daughters. Overhearing Perchik's lesson, Hodel chimes in to challenge him. He is charmed—as is Darcy when Elizabeth reveals her intellect and wit.

Both Elizabeth and Hodel choose outsiders who are a little rough around the edges. While Perchik is certainly more endearing than Darcy, he ruffles more than a few local feathers when he encourages dancing with a partner of the opposite sex at Tzeitel and Motel's wedding. Only free-thinking, feisty daughters would find themselves attracted to men like Darcy and Perchik. Sure, it doesn't hurt that they're cute guys (at least in the movies), but it's their fire that lights that of the second daughters.

The Younger Daughters, Lydia and Chava

Though Lydia and Chava do not share the same birth order, they have two key elements in common. First, they both elope with military men, much to the dismay of their parents. Second, their relationships are key to each story, in terms of defining the changing role of family in culture. That is, their controversial marriages force characters to confront the issue of individual choice and family status.

Lydia and Chava have two entirely different temperaments. Lydia is the wild child of the Bennet girls, while bookish Chava is described as "sweet little Chavala." Their passion leads them to men who are considered undesirable by their families, forcing them to choose between the two.

True to character, Lydia gives little thought to how her actions will affect others, including her family; but, to some extent, she must know that her unseemly elopement with Mr. Wickham will shame the Bennets. (If Meryton had a marriage and family counselor, he might ask if that was half of the attraction.) After all, Lydia is a mere sixteen years old and runs off in the middle of the night, leaving only a smug note for the colonel's wife to find in the morning.

Lydia poses a striking contrast to the genuinely in-love Chava, who is deeply pained by her tough choice. She falls in love with Fyedka, a Russian soldier who belongs to the army that ultimately forces the villagers to leave Anatevka. When Tevye learns that his favorite daughter has eloped and was married by a priest, he immediately pronounces her dead.

Mr. Collins suggests the same course of action for Mr. Bennet. He suggests that the only way for the family to recover from the disgrace of Lydia's actions is to proclaim her dead and cut all ties from her and Wickham. Ultimately, neither family can go through with it and ultimately find a way to accept their daughters' choices.

Individual versus Family Identity

In both *Pride and Prejudice* and *Fiddler on the Roof,* the daughters force their families to examine the issue of individual identity versus family status. Is Jane Bennet first seen as a quiet, good-natured young woman? Or do people first think of her as the eldest of the Bennet daughters?

The families' social and economic standing affect virtually everything at the beginning of each story. Elizabeth is snubbed by Darcy because he feels the Bennet family is "beneath" him. The Bingley sisters conspire to keep Jane and Mr. Bingley apart for the same reason. Tevye believes his daughter is lucky to receive a marriage offer from Lazar Wolf because his family is of modest means. As both stories progress, we see that individual character eclipses family status in terms of outside perception.

The defining moment in each story, in terms of personal versus familial identity, is when the young daughters elope. In fact, the severity of the perceived betrayal is worthy of disownment. In the days between Lydia's disappearance with Wickham and their marriage, Collins suggests that the Bennets consider their youngest daughter dead. Elizabeth is furious that her sister's indiscretions will undermine the family's social standing, the sisters' ability to marry well in particular. Of course, she is still feeling the sting from Darcy's blundering marriage proposal during which he articulates the differences between his aristocracy and her commonness. In the end, Wickham is forced to make an honest woman of Lydia, saving the family from disgrace; however, we clearly understand how high the stakes are. Having a sister who lived in sin would devastate the entire Bennet family. We never have the opportunity to see how the people of Hertfordshire would react to Lydia had she returned unmarried, but one has the feeling that Darcy's adoration for Elizabeth and Bingley's love for Jane would remain strong. Though it is Darcy who is the key instigator of the marriage between Wickham and Lydia, he is primarily motivated by his feelings for Elizabeth (and his antipathy for Wickham), not his contempt for Lydia's promiscuity.

Chava's plight is a more wrenching one because she is initially disowned by a father who loves her dearly, and whom she adores. Her marriage is not the act of a capricious teen, but a young woman deeply in love. Tevye's first concern is not about what the neighbors will think about his daughter marrying outside the Jewish faith, but rather what God will think. Still, in the end, he finds room in his heart to begin to see Fyedka as an individual, rather than one of the "Cossacks." Sadly, this revelation occurs only moments before Tevye and his family are forced to leave Anatevka.

Each story forces us to question how much of a role our family plays in our own identity. Of course, any therapist would say that we are defined by our childhood experiences and interactions with family. I believe this to be true. As a Jewish New Yorker raised as an only child, I can see the many differences between myself and my friend who grew up as the youngest of nine kids in a Puerto Rican family in Grand Rapids, Michigan. Coming to the table with an entirely different cultural and familial background is another friend who was raised as one of two daughters in a WASPy family in Orange County, California. But this explains who we are internally and how we react to the world around us. How the world sees us is an entirely different story. While I typically don't know about a friend's family background until a few weeks into the relationship, the Bennet sisters were known—and to some extent characterized—by their families before Darcy and Bingley ever set eyes on them.

Pride and Prejudice and *Fiddler on the Roof* share more than a few fun similarities in plot and character. Really, they are both universal stories about shifts in perception that cause people to examine the importance of family identity versus individual character, and allow young women to understand who they are in life's ever-changing social contexts.

Jennifer Coburn is a chick-lit author of *The Wife of Reilly*, *Reinventing Mona* and the soon-to-be released *Tales from the Crib*. *The Second Wife of Reilly*, a novella, will be included in Jane Green's holiday anthology, *This Christmas*, which will be released in November. She is currently working on her fourth novel, a sequel to *Tales from the Crib*. Her first novel has been optioned for film. Coburn lives in San Diego with her husband William and their eight-year-old daughter Katie, who is a delightful blend of both Jane and Elizabeth Bennet. When she's not writing, Coburn enjoys playing soccer, reading and worrying.

Bride and Prejudice

LAURA RESNICK

Jane Austen goes out in the noonday sun, and Laura Resnick approves with reservations as she analyzes the Bollywood version of the Meryton Follies. What did India keep and what did it change? Well, for starters, the Assembly still dances, but now it also sings.

"All mothers think that any single guy with big bucks must be shopping for a wife."

This line of dialogue, spoken with good-natured exasperation in the opening scene of the 2004 film *Bride and Prejudice: The Bollywood Musical*, closely echoes, of course, the famous opening line of Jane Austen's *Pride and Prejudice*: "It is a truth universally acknowledged, that a single man in possession of a good fortune must be in want of a wife."

Bride and Prejudice is an Indian film directed, cowritten and coproduced by Gurinder Chadha, who previously directed the delightful British film *Bend It Like Beckham*, about an Anglo-Indian girl in London who defies the traditional values of her immigrant family by playing soccer. Adapted from Jane Austen's still-compelling two-hundred-year-old novel, *Bride and Prejudice* transports the story across time and space to set it in twenty-first-century India, England and the United States.

A rather unusual feature of *Bride and Prejudice* is that, although it is in many ways a traditional Bollywood movie, it's filmed entirely in English. This is an attempt to make this Austen-based tale even more accessible to Western audiences—and particularly to American audiences. The Bombay movie industry makes no secret of its desire to develop a larger audience in the United States. *Bride and Prejudice* is not the first recent Bollywood film to be set partly in the U.S. (indeed, the immensely successful 2003 film *Kal Ho Naa Ho* was set entirely in New York City), but it is rare (perhaps unprecedented) for a film from this industry to be presented in English.

In *Bride and Prejudice*, the English Bennet family of Jane Austen's novel is now an Indian family named Bakshi. Instead of Longbourn near Meryton in Hertfordshire, they inhabit a falling-apart villa in Amritsar, a provincial city in India. The family's quantity of daughters is reduced from five to four, of which Lalita (played by reigning Bombay cinema queen and former Miss World, the luminous Aishwarya Rai) takes the place of Elizabeth as the smart, vivacious second daughter of the family. It is she who utters the line in the early moments of the movie about all mothers assuming that wealthy single men want to get married. Of course, she means *her* mother; like Austen's Mrs. Bennet, Mrs. Bakshi is extremely eager to make good marriages for her daughters.

In this story, the amiable Mr. Balraj Bingley (played by Naveen Andrews, whom you may remember as the Sikh anti-landmine lieutenant in *The English Patient*) comes to India for a few weeks to attend the engagement ceremony and wedding of a friend. The friend has come to Amritsar to marry a traditional Indian girl, the result of his having asked his parents to find a bride for him. Balraj Bingley is a wealthy NRI (nonresident Indian); although familiar with and comfortable in India, his home and his life are in England. He is accompanied by his fashionable sister, Miss Kiran Bingley, as well as by an American friend, Mr. Will Darcy.

Will Darcy is a workaholic from an extravagantly wealthy, California-based family of hoteliers. He takes an instant dislike to India, despite his equally instant attraction to Lalita, who is a friend of the bride in these ceremonies. Balraj Bingley meanwhile becomes attracted to Jaya Bakshi, Lalita's sweet-natured elder sister. After the wedding, Bingley invites Jaya to accompany his party on a trip to Goa, where Darcy is thinking of buying a hotel. Since the girls' father, Mr. Bakshi, feels it would not be appropriate for Jaya to go unchaperoned, Lalita accompanies her, despite her intense dislike of Darcy.

While Will Darcy keeps trying to make a better impression on Lalita and, due to his arrogance, just keeps making a worse one instead, Lalita becomes attracted to Johnny Wickham, a young man backpacking around India. By remarkable coincidence, Johnny's mother was Darcy's nanny, and he tells Lalita that Darcy treated him cruelly and unfairly after old Mr. Darcy died.

As if her love life weren't already complicated enough, with Johnny Wickham and Will Darcy both pursuing her, Lalita is soon also being courted by the nerdy Mr. Kholi (the novel's Mr. Collins), an NRI living in Los Angeles who has returned to India in search of a traditional Indian bride. By still further remarkable coincidence, he, too, knows Will; Kholi is an accountant whose firm does business with Mrs. Catherine Darcy (a.k.a. Lady Catherine de Bourgh).

With the wedding over and the trip to Goa completed, it's soon time for Darcy and the Bingleys to return to their respective homes overseas. Johnny Wickham, too, heads off to London. While Lalita pines for Johnny, Jaya pines for Balraj Bingley—who, despite his affectionate "I'll call you soon" farewell to her, never contacts her again.

Meanwhile, to Mrs. Bakshi's horror, Lalita rejects Mr. Kholi's marriage proposal. He rebounds quickly and is soon engaged to her good friend, Chandra. Like Miss Charlotte Lucas in Austen's novel, Chandra explains to Lalita that she herself is not romantic; she's just pleased to marry a kind man who makes a good living, treats her well and is taking her to America. Before long, the Bakshis are invited to Los Angeles to attend the wedding of Chandra and Kholi...which will take place at a lavish hotel owned by his business acquaintances, the Darcy family. While touring the hotel, the Bakshis meet Mrs. Darcy, a domineering mother and a generally snide, tactless person.

During Lalita's visit to California, Will courts her more successfully this time around, and she develops fond feelings for him. However, only moments before he proposes marriage (in a stumbling, pompous fashion), she learns that his negative influence is the reason Bingley has abandoned Jaya, and she leaves Los Angeles, heartbroken and determined to forget all about him.

While the Bakshis are staying in London on their way home to India, the family's youngest sister, Lakhi, disappears with Johnny Wickham. Darcy pops up in time to explain that his enmity with Wickham is due to Wickham having gotten his sixteen-year-old sister pregnant and then abandoning her, and he fears the same thing will happen to Lakhi. Luckily, though, Will and Lalita find the missing couple before anything serious happens, and they bring Lakhi safely back to her family.

Having realized the error of his ways, Will convinces Bingley to resume contact with Jaya, and the two soon become engaged. Lalita realizes she loves Will despite his arrogance, and they, too, get married.

So, despite substantial changes (such as turning it into a story about an Indian family and setting it on three continents), the plot of the movie is very faithful to Austen's novel, using much the same story structure and events, albeit adapted to a contemporary setting. For example, it is absurd to suppose that a woman in modern Amritsar would stay for days (and soon be joined by her sister) at the house of people she hardly knew just because she'd caught a cold upon leaving home for lunch at their house. Upon falling ill, she'd get a lift home, of course. So, instead of the cold Jane catches in the novel, which creates enforced isolation and intimacy with Bingley's group early in the story, Jaya and Lalita are now Bingley's guests on a trip to a popular resort town.

Characters and their circumstances also change to suit the contemporary setting. Johnny Wickham simply running off with a willing young woman in this day and age wouldn't create the kind of sheer horror (at least not with American audiences) that it does in the Regency-era novel; so now he's someone who impregnated and abandoned an underage girl and seems likely to do so again. Landed gentry isn't a cultural concept in modern America, so now the Darcys possess—and work hard at—a successful business empire. The sense of distance and new surroundings created in Austen's novel when characters relocate to London or to another county is created in our era of air travel by moving the characters halfway around the world. Rather than awaiting letters, the pining Bakshi women keep checking their e-mail accounts.

And, of course, instead of all being members of different subsets of the English gentry, the characters now come from different cultures and countries. Mr. Darcy is a wealthy American; Lalita is a "poor" Indian, by comparison; Mr. Kholi is Indian-born but emphatically identifies himself, above all, as the holder of an American green card; Mr. Bingley is an NRI who speaks with a British accent. The conflicts of class and situation in Austen's book are reshaped in this Indian film as conflicts of values between Indians "at home" and NRIs, as well as between Indians and non-Indians.

According to Mr. Kholi, "India is decades behind" America in all things; and yet the hypocrisy of his attitudes is exposed by his desire to marry a "traditional Indian girl" rather than an NRI or an American woman. The Bingleys enjoy India and, indeed, prefer their British household to be staffed by servants brought over from India; yet their speech, attitudes and lifestyle are European, and even their fond comments about India are rather condescending. They are diasporic Indians who want India to remain colorful and traditional without wanting the burden of living their *own* lives on those unpaved streets or according to those traditions.

Meanwhile, Will Darcy's attitude toward India is a less-comedic mirror of Kholi's. He finds the country backward in all things. He's awkwardly uncomfortable in Indian clothes at the wedding he attends, and he's afraid Indian food will make him ill. He's shocked at the notion of arranged marriages, he's critical of the failings of Indian plumbing and electricity and he seems insensitive to (or perhaps just ignorant of) the problems of poverty in India. Yet, as the child of a chilly American marriage, he's envious of the way families regularly get together and share their lives in Amritsar; and his hypocrisy is exposed when Lalita learns his mother is trying to arrange *his* marriage to Anne, a wealthy young American woman whose family's business empire Mrs. Darcy would like to merge with her own.

Lalita, highly vocal in her representation of corresponding Indian prejudices about the West, assumes that no one in America reads books, values culture at all, honors marriage vows or cares about anything but money. Will and Kholi seem to confirm some of these beliefs, since they are both money-obsessed workaholics. Kholi's rhapsodies about the house he has bought in L.A. for his prospective bride are based on what the house cost and how much it has appreciated in value since purchase. Will is always either working or trying to get back to work throughout his trip to India, because time is money. And back in California, his mother states that since we've got yoga, curry and Deepak Chopra here in the U.S., there's no need to go to India at all.

However, while Austen's novel shrewdly conveys many perpetual truths about human nature, the core of the story is difficult to adapt directly to a modern setting. Bollywood is a milieu more suited to this endeavor than American cinema; yet, despite this, and despite the film's energy and charm, *Bride and Prejudice* nonetheless inevitably falters in portraying certain aspects of Austen's story two centuries after it was written.

Bombay cinema is also known—indeed, probably *better* known—as "Bollywood." Since this is a derivative of the name "Hollywood," of course, a number of Bombay filmmakers object to the term, considering it demeaning, as if Bombay's film industry were a shabby would-be Hollywood. In fact, although it has yet to become popular with mainstream American audiences, Bombay cinema is an even bigger industry than the Hollywood dream factory, releasing more films per year and playing to an even bigger audience, both domestically and internationally. However, despite objections to the term "Bollywood," it is nonetheless the common term for Bombay cinema at this time. It's used in this essay because it's used by distributors advertising Bombay-made films and DVDs; it's used in the titles of books, articles, interviews and even scholarly writings about Bombay cinema; and, indeed, the word is in the official international title of Gurinder Chadha's film: *Bride and Prejudice: The Bollywood Musical.*

Which brings up another point. Bollywood films are *always* musical films. The vast audience for this industry's films expects—and gets—about half a dozen musical numbers per movie, many of them quite lavish. This can be disconcerting to Americans who see a Bollywood film for the first time, particularly if the film's subject matter (war, assassination or terrorism, for example) strikes us as an unlikely backdrop for inspiring the characters to burst into song and dance every so often. (Equally confusing to American audiences is the standard and unconcealed Bollywood custom of the actors all lip-synching to songs recorded by someone else for these musical numbers.)

As it happens, though, *Bride and Prejudice* is a romantic comedy in which the musical numbers slide easily into the tale. The first of these numbers is an elaborate full-cast performance in formal Indian dress to celebrate an engagement. This is a particularly standard staple of Bollywood movies, in which engagements and weddings are a very common cinematic event (and, indeed, often a central feature of the plot). This and a similar musical number later in the film seamlessly fill in for the balls and assemblies where the characters of Austen's novel exchange news, develop their relationships and further the plot. Such gatherings being a very common feature of Bollywood portrayals of contemporary

India is one example of why Bombay cinema is an ideal vehicle for a modern-day version of *Pride and Prejudice*.

Other examples of standard Bollywood musical numbers in the film include a love-song duet, a song of one lover pining for the other and a number where the entire local population breaks into synchronized song-and-dance in the streets of the city. Probably the most charming musical number in the film is the lively, humorous one in which Lalita's three sisters tease her about the nerdy Mr. Kholi's plans to woo and marry her.

Another standard feature of this film, one which is in perfect harmony with Austen's story, is the sexual discretion of Bollywood cinema. Censorship is so strict in Indian cinema that Bollywood films rarely even portray a kiss on-screen; and the explicit French kisses, nudity, graphic sexual conversation and simulated sex scenes that are by now a predictable feature of most American movies are virtually unknown in Bollywood films. Bombay cinema is frequently sensual, often even erotic. Indeed, the hip-grinding, blatantly suggestive, "soaking wet sari" dance routine, whether performed solo or as a passionate *pas de deux*, is yet another common feature of Bollywood cinema. Nonetheless, Bollywood typically portrays conservative sexual values.

So it isn't at all surprising that Mr. Bakshi says it would be inappropriate for Jaya, a woman in her twenties, to accompany the Bingley group to Goa without a chaperone, thereby creating the need for a reluctant Lalita to go with her. This kind of restriction on a grown woman's social life would be absurd beyond even Hollywood's ability to play it with a straight face if the heroine were American. But in Bollywood cinema, respectable young women live by a set of standards and restrictions that we in America think of as belonging to a long-ago era. Therefore, Lalita's courtship with Will doesn't involve sex any more than Elizabeth Bennet's courtship with Fitzwilliam Darcy does.

Another typical aspect of Bollywood is the portrayal of a large family inhabiting the same dwelling. In America, the elder girls would most likely have moved out of the house already, and the younger girls would be preparing to go off to college. In this Bollywood film, though, they all still live at home, as did all the Bennet women. Their lives are not just their own, but also their family's; and they don't have any more privacy from Mrs. Bakshi's prying eyes than Lizzy and Jane have from Mrs. Bennet's interference.

Additionally, Mrs. Bakshi's obsession with marrying off her daughters, as well as her conviction that marriage comes first and *then* you learn to love your spouse, is a very credible rendering of Austen's Mrs. Bennet—and one that would translate badly in a modern American mother. Yes, even most American mothers want their daughters to marry well; but in our culture, Mrs. Bakshi's obsession with this ambition would come across as the neurosis of a woman who desperately needs to get a life of her own.

However, despite marriage and the involvement of elders in arranging marriages being a common staple of Bollywood, this is also an example of how difficult it is to translate Austen's novel into modern culture even in Bombay cinema.

Mrs. Bennet's obsessive desire to marry off her daughters in *Pride and Prejudice* has a sensible, realistic basis. The subject is fraught with dramatic tension due to the inevitable, inescapable poverty the Bennet girls face if they are still unmarried when their father dies and the corresponding difficulty of finding suitable husbands for them because they lack dowries. All of this is due to the entailment of the estate, which will go to Mr. Collins when Mr. Bennet dies, rather than to any of the Bennet women. And, as Austen points out, in the Bennets' world, matrimony is "the only honorable provision for well-educated young women of small fortune." The Bennet girls *must* marry. There are few other paths in life open to them at *all*, and the others are all quite unpleasant.

The Bakshi women, however, have opportunities and choices available to them that don't exist for the Bennet girls, who cannot possibly go out and get jobs, become professionals and support themselves as career women. When Kholi proposes to Lalita, he lists the advantages she would encounter by marrying him, just as Mr. Collins does when he proposes to Elizabeth. However, when Kholi points out that she'd never have to work again, Lalita responds reasonably, "But I *like* working."

Additionally, when Elizabeth rejects Mr. Collins' proposal, she's not just rejecting matrimony, she's also throwing away the income on which she, her mother and her sisters could continue to survive after Mr. Bennet's death. Therefore, however repellant Mr. Collins may be, Mrs. Bennet's fury and hysteria when Lizzy rejects him are understandable, whereas Mrs. Bakshi's fury and hysteria when Lalita rejects Kholi just seem self-indulgent and irrational. There's nothing at stake, beyond the fact that Mrs. Bakshi wants the prestige of married daughters and the pleasure of grandchildren. Even if we count these things as important, they're not reason enough for her to have hysterics because her attractive, still-young, socially outgoing daughter doesn't want to marry a man whom the rest of the family, including Mr. Bakshi, all despise.

The credible, imminent threat of a truly dire future if the Bennet girls don't marry is the tension running through this novel about young women who want to marry for love. That dramatic tension is wholly absent from *Bride and Prejudice*. Its absence makes the movie a weaker story than the book. Yet it's difficult to imagine a modern version of this tale wherein the need to marry for financial survival could ever be as urgent among educated, intelligent people as it is in Austen's novel.

Another aspect of the novel that doesn't translate well in *Bride and Prejudice* is Mr. Darcy. The class-based arrogance of Austen's hero makes him difficult even for the people of that long-ago era to like. And it's not as if Lizzy's dislike of Darcy is due to her having egalitarian views. On the contrary, when Mr. Collins wants to introduce himself to Mr. Darcy at the Bingleys' ball at Netherfield, Elizabeth tries to dissuade him, pointing out that "it must belong to Mr. Darcy, the superior in consequence, to begin the acquaintance," and that it should be wholly up to Darcy whether or not there will even *be* an acquaintance. Elizabeth takes pride in being a gentleman's daughter, and this does not refer to her father as a man of good manners, but rather as a man who doesn't work for a living. And yet even in a world where such values are held by the heroine, Darcy comes across as pompous, stiff and conceited.

There may not *be* a way to make this character translate well to a modern tale, however much we may excuse his behavior in Austen's novel because we all know that Regency-era aristocrats just didn't know any better. The principle of social equality is so deeply embedded in our twenty-first-century ideology that the off-putting but ultimately forgivable behavior of a nineteenth-century English gentleman like Mr. Darcy seems repellant when assigned to a modern American character. And if there is a way to make such arrogance about one's own position in the world acceptable in a contemporary story, it definitely doesn't consist of portraying him as a stereotypical, money-obsessed, ugly-American tourist who makes insensitive comments to his hosts about their "backward" country The romantic hero of the movie, alas, becomes the character we keep trying to *overlook* as Lalita's story progresses.

Nonetheless, despite core aspects of *Pride and Prejudice* that do not adapt well to the twenty-first century, the charm, wit and human heart of Austen's beloved two-hundred-year-old novel *do* translate well to our own era in this colorful, energetic Bollywood adaptation.

One of the reasons for this is that we like and respect Elizabeth Bennet even from the perspective of our twenty-first-century social values. So this intelligent, vivacious, loyal and strong-willed heroine translates wonderfully into a modern, educated Indian woman who, like Elizabeth, has to deal with a matchmaking mother, a lovelorn elder sister and a rather bewildering array of suitors.

Moreover, the balance that Jaya, Bingley, Lalita and even Darcy are trying to find between being part of their families (including meeting their families' marital expectations for them) and being individuals in search of their bliss is the same personal struggle that Jane, Elizabeth and their English beaux experience throughout *Pride and Prejudice*—and the same one that each of *us* is inherently familiar with in our own lives. The older generation talks about security and sense, the younger generation dreams of love and takes some missteps in the search for it. That's true in Elizabeth Bennet's Regency-era England, and it's true in Lalita Bakshi's musical India; and we feel that truth in their stories because it's also so true in *our* lives, though we, Elizabeth and Lalita are separated by time, space and culture.

Bollywood fan Laura Resnick has watched dozens of movies made by the Bombay film industry, and she's also read *Pride and Prejudice* twice. Her fantasy novels include *Disappearing Nightly*, *The White Dragon* and *The Destroyer Goddess*. The author of numerous short stories, essays and articles, she has also written fourteen romance novels under the pseudonym Laura Leone.

Times and Tenors

Or, What the Movies Have Done, and Failed to Do, to Pride and Prejudice

SARAH ZETTEL

Jane Austen didn't write for the movies—if she had, *Pride and Prejudice* would have had at least one lip lock and probably an explosion in the haha—so the movies have had to adapt her. Sarah Zettel argues that what they kept and what they changed says a lot more about the moviemakers than it does about Austen.

*H*i.
My name's Sarah...
And I'm a PBS Janeite.
(Hi, Sarah!)
I fell in love with the works of Jane Austen through the movies and the television specials, and for the longest time I stayed away from the actual novels. I thought I could get along with the lovely old BBC presentations, and when I saw the 1995 miniseries starring Colin Firth as Mr. Darcy, I was sure I could be set for life. But...there was an empty feeling within. Somewhere deep down, I knew there was a problem....

Okay. Maybe it wasn't all that Marianne Dashwood-level dramatic. But, it is true, I watched *Pride and Prejudice* long before I actually sat down and read it. Then, my husband bought me a lovely, old edition of Austen's collected works for Christmas. That was when I discovered, as do all who read Austen, that these books were much more than what their media interpretations portray. I also came to realize that what those interpretations pull out of the story says far more about the time and place the filmmaker lives in than it does about Austen's time.

All filmmakers who work with literature make choices. Unfortunately, it really is impossible just to film the book, whatever book it might be. Decisions have to be made about what to leave in, what to take out and what to make up. All this is done according to a complicated combination of what the filmmaker thinks the audience will like, what the money-bags will accept and what their vision of the original story is. As a result, a story, especially an old story, will inevitably be updated and changed, sometimes blatantly, sometimes subtly, to suit the new times into which it is being brought.

There've been a lot of *Pride and Prejudice* adaptations done over the years. The BBC has done the book as a miniseries at least three times. A number of new films have come out in the past five years that take the plot and redo it for modern times, including *Bridget Jones's Diary* (which is a film adaptation of a book adaptation of Austen's novel...good, but dizzying), and one subtitled "A Latter-Day Comedy" that moves the action to a college in Salt Lake City. Since I don't have the word-space for all of them, I'm going to make my own choice and concentrate on three: *Pride and Prejudice*, 1940, starring Greer Garson as Elizabeth Bennet and Laurence Olivier as Mr. Darcy; *Pride and Prejudice*, 1995, starring Jennifer Ehle as Elizabeth Bennet and Colin Firth as Mr. Darcy; and *Bride and Prejudice*, 2004, starring Aishwarya Rai as Lalita Bakshi and Martin Henderson as Will Darcy.

Each of these sticks very close to the basic plot of *Pride and Prejudice*: There is a family with a whole lot of daughters. The mother is a clueless and incorrigible matchmaker. Two rich men come to the area and fall in love, willingly and not, with two of the daughters. Events are complicated by an unbelievably stupid male relative who wants to marry one daughter, and a charming rogue who runs off with another.

What's interesting about each of these is that despite the different times, cultures and way different visions, there are some remarkable similarities in all of them, beyond the basic plot elements lifted from Austen's novel.

All of them make the understated sexual themes in Austen overt, one way or another. In the 1940 movie both Mr. Collins and Mr. Darcy chase Elizabeth around the study and kiss her, in the best Hollywood drawing room fashion of the time, but in a way that never would have occurred to Austen. Okay, maybe it would have *occurred* to her. But it would have radically changed the nature of the book, taking it from satire to farce. In the 1995 miniseries, we have the delightful but completely made-up scene with Mr. Darcy standing up in the bathtub and giving those so inclined to admire such things an excellent view of his person. We also have him diving partially clothed into the estate pond so he meets Elizabeth essentially in his dripping wet underwear. In the 2004 version…it's Bollywood, friends. There are lots and lots of extremely pretty people around and some are wearing not much at all, not to mention the sisters speculating on whether Mr. Kholi (Collins) might be any good in bed. Added to this is the change that Will Darcy's sister, Georgie, is not just emotionally seduced by Wickham, but gotten pregnant.

The "sexing up" of *Pride and Prejudice* is an easy change to make and to understand. Not only has sex been a part of movies since the get-go, but as our communities have expanded and effective birth control has become widely available, even in the 1940s, sex has become a more frequent and common subject of discussion. Also, even as we obsess more and more about it, sex is actually less serious a life event for a woman. It is made light of in modern storytelling because it *can* be made light of. It is interesting to me that in the newest of the versions, the Bollywood production, while Wickham does sleep with Georgie, he *doesn't* get a chance to actually sleep with "Lucky" Bakshi. Lalita and Will stop him before he gets her into bed. In India, a young girl getting deflowered, if I may use the term, is still a far more serious matter than it has been in mainstream America for a long time. The beauty of the human form is on display in *Bride and Prejudice*, but the act of sex is not taken lightly.

There is another feature all these productions have in common that surprised me, and that is how well Mr. Bennet comes off. In her book, Austen is scathing toward Mr. Bennett. She speaks of his indolent neglect of his daughters' characters and education in the strongest terms. She several times criticizes his lackadaisical manner and shows up his failure to take charge when his wife proves incompetent as a major factor in Lydia's downfall. In the 1995 miniseries, which strives to be faithful to the book, Mr. Bennet is winked at. He remains a charming, slightly absent old man, who is really fond of his daughters and is content with their rescue, but not really to blame for them being in need of rescue. In the 1940 version, Mr. Bennet is a charming, slightly rascally man who is mildly approving if not actually supportive of his wife's matchmaking efforts. In the Bollywood version, he's almost not there, except for a few scenes where our Balraj Bingley shows his good manners by addressing him for permission to take his daughter out, and, of course, for the necessary confrontation scene when Our Heroine refuses to marry her cousin, Mr. Kholi.

This is a factor of the kabuki quality that pervades the movies. In film, women are responsible for the health and life of the family (unless they are dead). If there is neglect in the family sphere, it's primarily the woman's fault, no matter what the man has done. Alternate on-screen interpretations of the family dynamic are rare in the extreme, and they've never been applied to *Pride and Prejudice*. Mr. Bennet firmly remains the good parent and is off the hook.

The other person who comes off lightly in every version is Charlotte Lucas. In Austen, she is a mercenary. Not on Wickham's grand scale, but she marries for security and security only as soon as the opportunity presents itself, and arranges her life to be as comfortable as possible within the security she bargains for. She has no regrets in Austen's book. She does what she does for sound reasons and is content with the results. In both the 1940 and 1995 productions, we are made to feel her wistfulness and to understand that her regret will grow over time. In 2004 the situation is softened with a tearful scene in which she begs Lalita to understand that her new husband is really very kind, and he does adore her.

The woman who could be content with security is as much a forgotten figure in the mythology of our modern times as the woman who cannot be married for lack of a dowry was in the 1940s. We know women still do such things, but a contented ending for them has no place in a current-day romantic fiction. Which is what is left of *Pride and Prejudice* by the time most of the filmmakers are done with it: romantic fiction conforming to the romantic notions of the present day.

Not all those romantic notions are about human love, either. What's most notable about the 1940 production, aside from the usual Hollywood historical inaccuracies of costume and behavior and the violence done to the characters, is the reversal in importance of two dominant factors in the Bennets' lives: class and money.

In the novel, both of these are obstacles to the eventual marriages of the Bennet girls, but the lack of money is decidedly more important. Class is an issue, in that one can be sneered at for having been a shopkeeper before being knighted. Such transgressions, however, can be conveniently forgotten within a generation. But money (or, rather, the lack thereof) is a major stumbling block, and it is not so easily dismissed. Without the expectation of a dowry, many young men even within the Bennets' social circle cannot be enticed to marry into the family. A woman without money who wants to marry a man with money must be a fortune hunter, or be from a fortune-hunting family, which, you must admit, the Bennet girls can claim.

But in the 1940s presentation, the great stumbling block is shown to be an issue of class. Mr. Darcy slights Elizabeth at the initial assembly ball, not because she has been slighted by other men, as in the book, but because he is not interested in amusing the "middle classes." By the forties in the U.S., dowry is an almost forgotten custom, and money, according to the romantic myth of the time, is something anyone of sufficient intestinal fortitude can acquire. So, money cannot be portrayed as any kind of obstacle to people of character. No, it's got to be the English caste system that gets in the lovers' way. Those stuffy English with their stuffy, inflexible ways cannot see the inherent goodness of the solid middle class, which was expanding rapidly in 1940s America, had just dug its way out of the Depression, and, oh, yeah, was just about to go to war.

What makes this an even more radical, shall we say, reinterpretation of the original is that Austen's way of dealing with the class issue was to reveal it as an issue only from Lady Catherine's point of view. Lizzy points out, "He is a gentleman, I am a gentleman's daughter. Thus far we are equal." But that would apparently not do for an America looking to laugh at a light romantic comedy. We as Americans still carry the belief that we are free of the class hang-ups that bother much of the rest of the world, most particularly England. In some ways we are. In some ways we are not, and certainly were not back then. Here's a thought experiment: how would this self-congratulatory American reinterpretation have been received if the Bingleys had been white and the middle-class Bennets black? That's our most stubborn American class issue, but one that could not even begin to be addressed at the time, and certainly not as Austen addressed the issues of class and money in her time.

But the 1940s movie was not made to be serious social commentary, and that was the greatest change of all. Austen writes lightly about things that are of utter seriousness to the lives of women at the time. Money, lack of property and the ability to marry could be life and death issues and reputation was all-important. She writes about all of these with a sharp wit, but she repeatedly shows the importance of these matters. In the 1940s movie, all of these things are treated as complete frippery. Nothing is regarded seriously by any of the characters, not even Lydia's elopement, which surprised me. Jane and Lizzy breeze through the day, attending their mother's nerves, and agreeing to move out of the house to get away from the problem (one of the worst anachronisms in the whole film). The only serious thing in the film is love itself. It is the only situation permitted to be important—again, almost in direct opposition to Austen's original. The money was dead serious. If the girls could not get married, they really would end up destitute.

What none of the productions have retained is the bite of Austen's novel. To my surprise, *Bride and Prejudice*, for all the musical numbers and delightful Bollywood absurdity, comes the closest, but it still pulls the knife back via character moderation (such as of Mr. Kholi and Mr. Bakshi) and also by lightening the seriousness with which the core of the story is treated. Austen carved out her stories with sharp and exacting strokes. She is unsparing of her criticism of her characters, and her works are as much social satire and commentary as they are romances. While showing the importance of the situations her heroines find themselves in, she points out the absurdity, not of the system always, but of the people within that system—the forgetful women, neglectful men, malicious neighbors and clueless relatives—from whom there is no escape.

Which may be the most difficult point about trying to translate *Pride and Prejudice* into modern times, and why neither the comparatively modern sensibility (I know, that's another book, but bear with me) of the 1940s production or the modern setting of Bollywood can quite match the tone of the book. In the novel, the Bennet girls are literally trapped in their home. They have no money, they have no mobility, and they are all underage. They could not work, and they could not leave. This is where the 1995 miniseries is best. Because it stays with the original setting, it can provide that feeling of imprisonment the others cannot. Even in India, in the modern age there are options for a young

おはい

woman. As for the U.S., we have from the beginning been a land where one could flee a bad past or a bad family. The rigid fixity of life that was such a binding factor of the women of Austen's time is simply not something that has come down to us, but it is what makes the brushes with tragedy in the book so intense.

So, am I now a complete convert to the original text, eschewing film remakes and staying stubbornly at home with my books? Heck no! Or perhaps I should say, oh, my dear, of course not! I admit, I'm not going to be rewatching the 1940s silliness any time soon. However, while the seriousness and the satire of the original have not been retained by filmmakers, when the delightful characters, the continually entertaining story and the setting which lends itself to lavishness fall into the hands of a director with a little sensitivity to the underlying tensions, they make for wonderful viewing.

Forget the meeting. Pass the popcorn. And the hanky.

Enjoy.

Sarah Zettel was born in Sacramento, California. Since then she has lived in ten cities, four states, two countries and become an author of a dozen science fiction and fantasy books, a host of short stories and novellas as well as a handful of essays about the pop culture she finds herself immersed in. She lives in Michigan with her husband Tim, son Alexander and cat Buffy the Vermin Slayer. When not writing, she drinks tea, gardens, practices tai chi and plays the fiddle, but not all at once.

Jane's Hero

"There are those who are deluded by the decorousness of her manner, by the fact that her virgins are so virginal that they are unaware of their virginity, into thinking that she is ignorant of passion. But look through the lattice-work of her neat sentences, joined together with the bright nails of craftsmanship, painted with the gay varnish of wit, and you will see women haggard with desire or triumphant with love, whose delicate reactions to men make the heroines of all our later novelists seem merely to turn signs, 'Stop' or 'Go' toward the advancing male."

REBECCA WEST

My Darling Mr. Darcy

Why Is the Unattainable So Irresistible?

TERESA MEDEIROS

What is it about Darcy that makes him such a sigh-inspiring hero? He's arrogant, he's monosyllabic and, when he's not monosyllabic, he's rude. It has to be more than just Pemberley, although, as Elizabeth points out, Pemberley is not chump change. No, Teresa Medeiros says, what makes Darcy the granddaddy of Difficult Men We Love is all the things he is beneath that upper-crusty exterior.

EVERYONE KNOWS WHAT AMERICAN women want—thinner thighs, darker chocolate and a dashing Englishman who looks more like Hugh Grant or Colin Firth than Prince Charles or Dame Edna. George Clooney might charm us with his bedroom eyes and easygoing manner, but deep in our hearts we yearn for a quintessential English gent who will declare both his scorn and his love for us in clipped, upper-crust tones. He will mock, infuriate and adore us—preferably from afar so we won't be able to tell when his teeth start going bad as English teeth invariably do. (In a recent interview, Hugh Grant confessed that his were already starting to go.) To achieve the true pinnacle of desirability, this paragon of manhood must be always in our hearts, yet forever out of our reach.

It's precisely these qualities that make Jane Austen's Mr. Fitzwilliam Darcy in *Pride and Prejudice* the great-great-grandpappy of all the dark and brooding anti-heroes who would come after him. Whether embodied by Sir Laurence Olivier in 1940 or Colin Firth in the 1995 BBC production or Colin Firth again as attorney Mark Darcy in *Bridget Jones's Diary*, Mr. Darcy is one of the most compelling romantic characters ever to grace the page, stage or the screen.

Darcy is first introduced to us as the Simon Cowell of the Meryton assembly. There's not even a sympathetic Paula Abdul to soften the blow or a 1-800-number to call in protest when he passes ruthless judgment on Elizabeth Bennet, dismissing her as "tolerable, but not handsome enough to tempt me." His collar is as stiff as his demeanor and his aristocratic nose is fixed firmly in the air, no doubt breathing deeply of the rarified stratosphere that can only be coveted by lesser mortals like Miss Bennet and her sisters.

He is proud, arrogant, insufferable...and utterly irresistible. It's no accident of Ms. Austen's clever prose that we fall in love with him long before Elizabeth does. After all, who could resist a man who leaves this first impression?: "He was the proudest, most disagreeable man in the world and everybody hoped that he would never come there again." He might drive a coach-and-four instead of straddling a Harley, but that doesn't make him any less of a bad boy. His behavior is impeccable, but his temperament is deliciously deplorable.

Darcy becomes even more intriguing when compared to his devoted friend, Mr. Bingley: "Bingley was sure of being liked wherever he appeared, Darcy was continually giving offence." How is it that the amiable Bingley makes us yawn into our tea while Mr. Darcy, the most unlikely of heroes, still possesses the power to make us swoon nearly two hundred years after Jane Austen first created him? Are all women closet masochists, or do we just love a rousing (or would that be *arousing*?) challenge?

From the time I was a very small child I've been given to passionate crushes on the opposite sex. When I was six years old, I fell hard for Kurt Russell and his beguiling dimples in Disney's *The Computer Wore Tennis Shoes*. For five pivotal years of puberty Donny Osmond's blinding smile reigned supreme on the walls of my bedroom and in my heart. Darling Donny was my first muse, prompting me to pen Chapter One of a rollicking pirate novel in which Sir Donald Osmond abducted my intrepid heroine in a scene eerily similar to the kidnapping of the governor's daughter in *Pirates of the Caribbean*. To increase my chances of becoming The Donald's wife and bearing his many toothy children, I checked the *Book of Mormon* out of the local library and doubled my visits to the local orthodontist. I'm embarrassed to report that my ability to yearn wistfully for a total stranger resurfaced only last year when I developed a medical condition commonly known in Internet circles as RCO (Russell Crowe Obsession) and downloaded over 350 photos of the enigmatic actor in less than a month.

You might be asking yourself what Kurt's dimples, Donny's teeth and Russell's, well, everything have in common with the formidable Mr. Darcy. Mr. Crowe certainly does have a reputation for blunt speaking, and I have no doubt he'd be perfectly at home in a Regency drawing room delivering *bon mots* and direct cuts with equal ruthlessness. (After all, this is a man bold enough to publicly criticize Robert DeNiro for selling out!) However, it's not his prickly Australian nature that makes him a worthy successor to Darcy's mantle, but his chameleon-like ability to transform himself into every woman's fantasy with each role he plays. Whether slaughtering Barbarian hordes in *Gladiator*, rescuing Meg Ryan's hapless husband in *Proof of Life* or bellowing out orders in *Master and Commander*, he successfully evokes empathy while still playing hard-to-get with our yearning hearts.

We've always loved our stoic, enigmatic heroes. That's why so many women have chosen Spock over Captain Kirk through the years. Orlando Bloom's recent portrayal of Legolas in the Lord of the Rings film trilogy provoked a similar reaction from a new generation of teenage girls. He probably had three lines in the entire trilogy (and most of those were spoken in Elvish), yet the female sighs every time he appeared on screen were audible throughout the theater. His eyes spoke volumes although his mouth rarely moved.

In a similar fashion, it's not what we *know* about Darcy that intrigues us from his very first appearance on the page, but what we *don't* know. Jane Austen could have made us privy to every one of Darcy's thoughts and motivations long before they are revealed to Elizabeth. But she wisely realized that a hero stripped of his inscrutable nature is also a hero stripped of appeal.

From a very young age, we women need to have an object to personify our fantasies. Whether it's that first rapturous taste of puppy love or a high school crush, the more unattainable and inaccessible that object, the more we are able to endow him with all of the qualities we think we admire. And by the time we're done, he's usually *very* well-endowed indeed.

If we're consistently held at arm's length from the object of our desire, we can continue to view him through the tender glow of our rose-colored glasses. Our illusions will never be shattered by learning that he belches like Homer Simpson after downing a beer or that he always misses the hamper and leaves his dirty underwear lying on the bedroom floor. He can remain cloaked in a veil of mystery, and thus his perfection will never be impeached. He will always be an empty suit of clothes perfectly tailored to meet our needs—our soulmate without a soul.

In Mr. Darcy's case, that suit of clothes is a pair of buff-colored trousers and an impeccably tailored Regency tailcoat. From his first appearance in Meryton, we long to believe that his icy demeanor hides a warm and passionate heart, but Ms. Austen insists upon dashing our hopes at every turn and plot twist. Elizabeth herself pronounces him "very disagreeable" when discussing his character with the charming and amoral Mr. Wickham in Chapter 16, and Darcy condemns himself in her eyes as she recalls, "I do remember his boasting one day, at Netherfield, of the implacability of his resentments, of his having an unforgiving temper."

If the eyes are truly the mirrors of the soul, even Darcy's gaze is suspect. After her marriage to that obsequious toad, Mr. Collins, Elizabeth's dear friend Charlotte notes that Mr. Darcy "certainly looked at her friend [Elizabeth] a great deal, but the expression of that look was disputable. It was an earnest, but steadfast gaze, but she often doubted whether there were much admiration in it, and sometimes it seemed nothing but absence of mind." Mr. Darcy's empty suit of clothes is now complemented by an empty gaze. But it's precisely the vacancy of that gaze that allows us to color it with all of the ardor we imagine he is feeling for Elizabeth beneath his perfectly composed exterior.

Ms. Austen and Mr. Darcy continue to tease us until Chapter 35 when Darcy's impassioned letter to Elizabeth reveals his true motivations and a hint of his true character. Only then can we heave a collective sigh of relief as we learn that all of our hopes for him were not in vain.

The true beauty of Ms. Austen's characterization is that Darcy is slowly revealed to be everything we dreamed he could be. His haughty expression is simply the mask he wears to shield his vulnerable heart. His intentions toward Elizabeth and her family may be somewhat misguided, but it is not malevolence that informs them, but loyalty to his dear friend Mr. Bingley. Even Elizabeth can't dismiss the fine accounting of his character given by the housekeeper at Pemberley when he is revealed to be "thoughtful, kind, good-natured, a loving brother, and generous to those less fortunate than he." As she gapes at the housekeeper in disbelief, you can almost hear country singer Tim McGraw start to growl, "I may be a bad boy, but baby, I'm a real good man."

This fantasy is even more beguiling because in real life if we meet a guy at a party who seems like a jerk, he usually turns out to be...well...a jerk. Instead of apologizing for misjudging him as Elizabeth is eventually forced to do, we end up giving him a fake phone number or taking out a restraining order. By the time Elizabeth and Darcy have confessed their love for one another and earned their happy ending, we are confident he is fully equipped to satisfy her every romantic fantasy just as he has satisfied ours.

Our teen idols will grow up. Our high school crushes will marry the cheerleaders we hated and show up at our twentieth reunions with beer guts and balding heads. Our favorite actors will dump their young, pretty wives for younger, prettier wives and waste years spinning in the revolving door of rehab. But with Mr. Darcy so perfectly preserved on the page, we'll never have to worry that his dimples will turn into wrinkles, that he'll become a game show host instead of a pirate, or that his picture will be plastered all over the tabloids after he bites his own bodyguard in a drunken brawl. (Australians do that, you know.)

Thinner thighs and darker chocolate may not always be within our grasp, but thanks to Jane Austen, a brooding Englishman with an inscrutable gaze and good teeth will always remain just at our fingertips.

Teresa Medeiros wrote her first novel at the age of twenty-one and has since gone on to win the hearts of both readers and critics. All fifteen of her books have been national bestsellers, climbing as high as #12 on the *New York Times* bestseller list, #20 on *USA Today* and #9 on *Publishers Weekly*. She is a six-time RITA finalist and a two-time recipient of the Waldenbooks Award for bestselling fiction. Her next novel, *After Midnight*, will be released by Avon Books in September 2005. You can visit her Web site at www.teresamedeiros.com.

My Firth Love

LANI DIANE RICH

For anyone who's seen the BBC miniseries of *Pride and Prejudice*—and is there anyone reading this book who hasn't?—Darcy is forever Colin Firth, the Man in the Damp Puffy Shirt. Lani Diane Rich is a fan with a weak grasp on reality, but a strong grasp on what makes Darcy firth in her heart.

March 5, 2005

Hey, Diary. How ya been?

I realize I haven't written to you since the eighth grade, when I had that very intense crush on Andrew from my music class, remember? And I went on and on *and on* about he said this and I said that and he smiled at me and I wanted to throw up and does he like me or does he *like* like me? God. It's amazing you didn't corporealize yourself and kill me then.

Thank you for that, by the way.

I'd like to say not a lot has happened since then, tell you it's been a boring and colorless life, but I think we both know that's not true. I'm

staring down the barrelhead of thirty-four as we speak. I graduated high
school, went to college, got married, had kids. I've worked as a nanny, a
television producer and a pyrotechnician. (Not in that order.) I lived in
Alaska for a while. I'm a novelist now, and I teach part-time at the local
university. I don't know what happened to Andrew. I heard his brother
was dating a supermodel for a while, though.

Anyway, I'm coming to you now because something has happened
to me that hasn't happened since around the last time you saw me, so I
thought I'd see if you could help.

I have a crush. A bad one. On a man who doesn't exist. And if he did
exist, he would have died, oh, some 150 years ago.

It's all very complicated. More later.

March 10, 2005

Sorry these entries are short. My daughters are three and five, so I have
to grab these moments when I can. Right now, I'm writing at the kitchen
table as my youngest tries to ask me a question while chewing simultaneously on two pieces of toast. She's inherited her mother's grace, poor
thing.

Anyway, back to the crush. Sorry to shift gears so fast, but we both
know why we're here. I mean, if I wanted to discuss the existential angst
of motherhood I'd be writing in a journal. Diaries are for the down and
dirty, the stuff you don't want people to ever find out about you. Journals are the things you leave open around the house, hoping a literary
agent will wander in, read it and declare you the next genius of your
age.

So let's quit pretending, shall we? This crush. I was a little dishonest
with you. The crush isn't *exactly* on Darcy. (We both knew who I was
talking about. I mean, come on. It was either Darcy or Spike from *Buffy*
and . . . okay, well, I'm riding that train, too, but that's another discussion
entirely.)

My point is, like pretty much every woman between the ages of fourteen and dead, I read *Pride and Prejudice* sometime in the high school
era and fell instantly in love with Darcy. His strength. His integrity. His
quickness to jump to the aid of the woman he loves, defending her in
secret, expecting nothing in return for his heroism and gallantry.

Sigh.

But after I read *Pride and Prejudice*, I read *Emma*, and fell in love with Knightley. Then there was the David Addison thing, the Joel Fleischman thing...well, you get the point. What can I say? I've always had a weakness for fictional men. Nice, harmless little crushes. By the time I hit my mid-twenties, though, with the exception of the occasional dream starring John Cusack, they ceased. I'd finally gotten jaded enough by life to understand that real men didn't behave that way and never would. And I was okay with that because fictional men didn't....

Well, let's just say real men have their advantages, too.

And then, it happened. You know what I'm talking about. You've been dormant and lifeless, gathering dust for twenty-one years, and even you know what I'm talking about.

The BBC adaptation of *Pride and Prejudice*.

Oops. Gotta run. Baby's stuffing toast up her nose.

March 17, 2005

The Husband is taking care of the girls while I write. He thinks I'm working on my book. And I should be working on my book. Instead, I'm sitting in my office, watching *Pride and Prejudice* on the DVD player on my computer with my headphones on.

Isn't that one of the signs you have a problem? Lying to your loved ones? Altering your life to work around your addiction? Staying up until two in the morning bookmarking fan sites on your Internet browser? But I'm getting ahead of myself. I should start where it all started...with my mother-in-law.

Don't get me wrong; I adore my mother-in-law. She's smart and funny, and when I come to visit she takes my children and gives me wine. I only blame her because it's all her fault; she was the first to tell me that I needed to watch the BBC version of *Pride and Prejudice*.

"Darcy," she said, pushing a wine glass into my hand. Just the one word, speaking volumes. And I thought I understood. After all, I'd read the book. I'd fallen in love with Darcy, too. So I nodded knowingly.

"Yeah," I said. "I hear ya."

"No," she said, putting her hand on my arm, her blue eyes deadly serious as she drove her point home. "*Darcy*."

Then my two sisters-in-law joined in. "Darcy," they said, and swooned. But they were teenagers. They swooned over the pizza delivery guy.

The final straws were my two best friends, Monica and Wanda. They were older, wiser and even more jaded than me. They *never* swooned.

"Darcy," they said, in unison. Monica picked up a manila folder and fanned herself.

"Darcy," Wanda repeated, her deep southern tones tinged with a wanting so bone-deep that I began to suspect I might be missing something.

So. Fine. I rented *Pride and Prejudice*, grumbling, "I have two young kids, a husband, a job. Like I have time to sit around for six hours and watch people line dance 1800s-style while telling a story I know by heart already. And what could possibly be so great about this guy, anyway?" And then Darcy proposed to Elizabeth and he was awkward and nervous and so obviously in love and those eyes, *ohmygod* those *eyes*....

I swooned. I was over thirty at the time, and I was swooning, for Christ's sake.

I bought the DVD set the next day.

March 19, 2005

It's four in the morning. I can't sleep. However, as a working wife and mother, this is the only time in the day when I can actually get a moment to myself, so I came out to the living room and turned on Fox News for 3.5 seconds so I could feel like a reasonable adult person with reasonable adult concerns.

Then I popped in my *Pride and Prejudice* DVD.

Oh, shut up. I know it's pathetic. Do I at least get points for knowing? Anyway, I think it's time to finish this story, and get to the reason why, after over twenty years of no contact, I'm suddenly bothering you at all hours of the day and night.

Where was I? Oh. Yes. I watched *Pride and Prejudice*. I swooned. But the final nail in the coffin containing my own pride was when Darcy found Elizabeth after she got the letter from Jane telling of the horrible things Lydia had done to disgrace their family, thus making it impossible for any respectable man to marry any of the Bennet sisters, and you can tell that his heart is breaking for her and he doesn't know what to do and...

Jesus. I'm swooning now, just writing to you about it. Gah.

So, anyway. I swooned. *Fine*. That part doesn't bother me. Too much. What bothers me is what I'm doing now.

Oh. God. The five-year-old is demanding waffles. It's five in the morning. What kind of person gets up at five in the morning when they're not getting on a plane? Teenagers sleep until noon, don't they? Just eight more years...

March 22, 2005

His name is Colin Firth. I'm in my office at the university, and I have to start my class soon, so I don't want to waste any more of your time or mine. The first step to recovery is admission, right?

Colin Firth. I have a crush on a celebrity, and his name is Colin Firth. There. I've said it. And you're thinking, what's the big deal, right? Lots of perfectly smart, sensible women have little crushes.

Well, let me finish my story.

After watching Colin as Darcy, I became a little obsessed. I looked him up on IMDB.com. I visited fan Web sites. I read articles. I wrote an entire novel using him as the inspiration for the love interest. In the first draft, the character's name was even Colin; that's how transparent I was.

It's all so embarrassing. I'm a relatively intelligent, well-grounded woman in my thirties. I'm married to a gorgeous man. I have two beautiful daughters. I'm happy with myself and satisfied with my life. I know that my affection is full fantasy, that I don't know Colin Firth in the least, that I'm projecting onto this man everything I want to believe him to be, everything Darcy is, rather than having any idea about who he is.

I. Don't. Know. Him.

And yet? I think I love him.

God. This kind of thing doesn't happen to me.

But it has. And now comes the true confession, the reason I've cracked your spine once again after all these years to pour out everything about me and this fantasy I've projected onto a man I don't even know.

I've been asked to contribute to an anthology about *Pride and Prejudice*. I'm very flattered that they would even ask me, and I love the novel, and there are a million smart, intelligent things I could talk about. I'm thinking about doing my essay on the influence of Austen on postmodern romantic literary heroes as portrayed in film.

The really embarrassing part? The reason I'm confessing?

I don't give a crap about the influence of Austen on postmodern romantic literary heroes as portrayed in film. I'm using the anthology as an excuse to buy every Colin Firth movie I can get my hands on and take it off on my taxes.

I think I might need help.

April 5, 2005

Well, I've watched them all. Every Colin Firth movie I could get my hands on, including the one where he played a lawyer defending a pig. The Husband, not typically the jealous type, has taken to calling Colin "that poncy British poofter," which I think is unfair; any idiot can see that Colin is the pinnacle of manhood.

But that's not where I was going with this. The Husband and I will argue that tonight. No, what I wanted to report was that through my extensive research, I have discovered something.

While Colin is an incredible character actor and does a great blustering villain, it is only the Darcy or Darcy-like roles that are really swoon-worthy. Which leaves me to wonder, what is it about Colin Firth playing Darcy that creates this effect? Although the others who have played Darcy have done pretty well—Laurence Olivier must be given his props—no one has created the adolescent-reminiscent fervor that Colin has. Why is this? What is it about this particular man in this particular role that is so potent?

I'll finish that thought later. I have to organize all these receipts for my tax files, and try and write a respectable essay. Wish me luck!

April 21, 2005

The deadline for this essay is fast approaching, and the only thing I've written so far is, "Hemma hemma, what a hottie." Just a guess, but I'd say as far as *respectable* opening sentences go, that one ranks pretty low.

In the past week, I've watched Colin play Darcy no less than twelve times and haven't even opened the packaging on the other versions I got for the essay. If it helps mitigate that embarrassing admission at all, I fast-forwarded through all non-Firth scenes. Of course, The Husband has started using more creative language when speaking of Colin, but was slightly assuaged when I suggested we use the money from the essay to buy a new electric drill set. However, once the article is handed in, I think he's going to expect me to stop watching the DVDs.

And I'm not sure I can.

Anyway, it occurred to me that by isolating the specific things that cause all the swoonage, I might possibly be able to think a little more rationally about this whole situation. And hey, who knows, maybe some of it will be useful in the essay. So here's what it boils down to, the essence that makes Colin Firth as Darcy a more potent swoon elixir than Darcy alone, or Firth alone.

The accent. This may not be such a big deal to British women, who I imagine are pretty immune to the whole British accent thing, but for a certain faction of American women, the accent is swoon-worthy on its own. I will confess that the Darcy accent I concocted in my head while reading *Pride and Prejudice* for the first time was a huge contributor to my fictional man crush. But Firth's sandpaper voice softened by the elegant speech increases the swoon-factor considerably.

The eyes. Austen didn't waste a whole lot of time talking about Darcy's eyes, so the greater part of the swoon-worthiness of the eyes belongs entirely to Colin. There's a smoldering quality in every look he gives Elizabeth Bennet that could melt the white cotton panties off a ninety-year-old schoolmarm. (Note to self: Find a more dignified way to express that sentiment in the actual article. Don't want these people thinking you're a total idiot. Partial idiot will do just fine.)

The dancing. I don't blame men who don't dance; it's almost impossible to dance well and still be manly. (Deney Terrio, anyone?) The dances of the Austen era, with all the twirling and the sidestepping and the ducking-slash-walking under arm bridges, were particularly emasculating. But Colin, with his slight awkwardness and total focus on Elizabeth, makes Darcy seem not only sufficiently masculine while dancing, but damned sexy.

The lake scene. It is a truth universally acknowledged that any woman watching the BBC version of *Pride and Prejudice* will swoon upon seeing the lake scene. The lake scene was not in the original text, and no one really knows what genius decided to put it in the BBC version—I'm guessing the director—but damn, it's inspired. Wet Colin, instructed to play the scene as though he had an erection. 'Nuff said.

The passion. How is a movie with only one chaste kiss at the very end so passionate? I can't quite put my finger on it. Perhaps because Colin appears to be mentally undressing Lizzy during every scene they have together? Perhaps because whenever he handles anything he sort of...fondles...the object? Perhaps he was instructed to play the entire movie as though he had an erection? I don't know. It's a marvelous mystery.

The tight pants. See above re: the lake scene.

He goes for the smart girl. Okay, let's face it, the actress who plays Elizabeth Bennet is a knockout and any man would want her on first sight. But Darcy doesn't; he doesn't even realize how cool she is until he sees her intelligence, wit and integrity. That's what makes her beautiful to him. This is the way Austen wrote it, this is the way I read it and damned if Colin doesn't hit that nail on the head.

The interpretation. I think the final element that makes this particular Darcy portrayal turn otherwise intelligent and grounded women into panting adolescents is the fact that Colin brings to life the subtext we all read into *Pride and Prejudice*; his vulnerability. Laced underneath Colin's performance is a subtle insecurity that makes his behavior, although definitely not admirable, at least understandable. That sets the stage for total forgiveness once we see what he does for Elizabeth, with no hope of winning her affection, just purely because he loves her and can't stand to see her in pain. With this element, Colin has sealed the deal. He has given us what we always knew was there, the fantasy man who isn't what he seems, who is deeper than we think, who surprises us. Who loves us even though we rejected him. Who gives us a second chance. In a world where most women would be thrilled just to have a man who will take out the garbage without expecting us to throw a parade in response, Colin Firth as Darcy is the ultimate fantasy man. He smolders, he pines, he takes action with no thought of reward. He simply...loves. (Note to self: Not bad. Maybe spruce that up and use it in the essay. You might almost sound like you know what you're talking about.)

April 28, 2005

I'm off to couples therapy with The Husband. I'm in love with a fictional man, and he's threatened by one. What a pair. But, bonus, the police don't come to our home to break up drunken fistfights, so the therapist says we're head and shoulders above many of her other clients. I like her, although I'm not sure it's appropriate for her to say that. Makes me worry that she's using me to make her other clients feel better about themselves.

"So, you went after your husband with a knife. Big whoop. I've got a client who's having an emotional affair with a fictional dead guy and the actor who plays him." (Making twirly-finger gesture beside her head.)

But, what the hey, The Husband's company is paying for the counseling, and it probably can't hurt.

Anyway, I told the therapist about you, Diary, and she said I need to burn you as part of my symbolic release of this period of my life, blah blah blah. Don't freak out. I'm not going to burn you. I'm just going to rip these pages out and stuff them in an envelope and seal it and write "1999 Tax Receipts" on it to guarantee that The Husband will never touch them.

Anyway...thanks for letting me pour out my heart to you. Again. I'll let you know if I ever find out what happened to Andrew from eighth grade music class.

Date: August 1, 2005
From: Lani Diane Rich
To: Jennifer Crusie
Re: Little mistake

Hey, Jenny! I just wanted to tell you what a great job you did editing the *Pride and Prejudice* anthology. I mean, I haven't seen the final version yet, of course, but you...you're so good at everything. Really. Just super-spectacular. And I'm not just saying that.

Um...you haven't gone to press yet, have you?

The reason I ask is that I think there's been a little itsy bitsy mistake. I've recently been the victim of a freak audit, and while going through my papers I discovered that I may have accidentally sent you some pages from my personal journal as opposed to the essay I wrote and prepared for you. I hope that you will accept my apology, return to me the pages I sent, and publish the enclosed essay, "The Influence of Austen on Postmodern Romantic Literary Heroes, as Portrayed in Film," in the book.

And if we could never speak of this again, that would be super. Thanks!

—Lani

———

Lani Diane Rich is an author, college instructor, mother of two and...something else, but she can't remember. She lives in upstate New York where she is currently at work on her next novel which is about...something. She can't remember. But it'll be at your local bookstore soon. Look for it. She's pretty sure it's a good one. You can find her at www.lanidianerich.com.

Jane's Untold Stories

"All the Jane Austen characters are ready for an extended life which the scheme of her books seldom requires them to lead, and that is why they lead their actual lives so satisfactorily."

E. M. FORSTER

Not Precisely Pride

MERCEDES LACKEY

Austen created such a fully realized world that it's not surprising modern novelists long to wander through it again. In this story, Mercedes Lackey suggests that there was more to England than met Elizabeth Darcy's eye, and then goes on to show it to us.

IT IS A MISPERCEPTION universally accepted as a truism that a single woman in possession of her own fortune must be in want of a husband.

"I really do not know what I am to do about this invitation," Althea Lynncroft said to her companion, staring at the inoffensive pasteboard crossly. "I do not wish to accept it, and yet I cannot in politeness turn it down."

Her companion, Regina Sedgwick, blinked at her from behind the thick lenses of her spectacles. "Why do you not wish to accept it? Mrs. Darcy is a most amiable lady, and you have often rejoiced in her company when you have been together in London. Pemberley is by all accounts a charming estate in all seasons, but is said to excel in the spring. What possible objections can you have?"

"Only this: that Cordelia Hawthorne has also written me to warn me that Elizabeth Darcy has already secured the attendance of a gentleman of her acquaintance to this party with the intention of matchmaking."

Althea's stormy expression betrayed her feelings. "Lizzy is the most charming of friends, but really! This is ample proof for me that Elemental Magicians really should not seek for company outside their own circle. Outsiders cannot be told of our powers, and cannot understand why the attentions of a suitor with no magic whatsoever in them must be abhorrent to us! Now I must either lose the regard of Mrs. Darcy, or suffer an uncomfortable weekend fending off the attentions of some fellow who may be a fine gentleman, but can have nothing more in common with me than your spaniel and my parrot!"

Her companion sighed. "It is a difficulty. I have seen one or two marriages outside of the Talented, and they are fraught with tension. The hazards of being discovered place dreadful stress upon even the most affectionate of spouses."

"And one cannot disclose the Talent without risking being thought mad—or worse, making one's spouse think *he* is mad!" Althea frowned again at the card. "This really is vexing."

Regina gazed thoughtfully at her. "Mrs. Darcy is not known at all for meddling in the affairs of others; she is not the sort to engage in willy-nilly matchmaking. What could possibly have occasioned this?"

"Now there is the other vexatious point: I do not know! Cordelia tells me that the young man in question is a fine gentleman, perhaps not so well-positioned financially as I, but by no means impecunious. In fact, she speaks quite warmly of recommendations she has received from mutual friends outside of the Talented of our acquaintance. He is as book-loving as I and more musical; he, like myself, tends to shun the hectic company of Society in favor of a quiet country life; he is said to be warm in his cordiality and modest in his habits; in short, there is not a soul who says a word against him. I should probably like him a very great deal, and take pleasure in his company under any other circumstances! But it seems that I will not be able to do anything in this situation without offending someone!"

After hearing this recitation, Miss Sedgwick felt moved to voice a fear of her own. She was, after all, a specimen of that species known as the "paid companion," engaged for propriety's sake by single ladies to avoid the censure of the world by daring to live alone. If Althea married, her new husband might not care for the continued presence of Miss Sedgwick in his household. "My dear friend, if it is concern for *my* situation, should you wed, that prevents you—"

But Althea laughed. "By no means! First of all, any man who could not abide *your* continued company in our household I should hold odious in the extreme! You are my dear, dear friend, and I will not be parted from you, no, not by the most attractive of men! But secondly, I am not the only one of our circle for whom your company is a continual pleasure and support. You know very well that should you even hint that you might be willing to change households, Lady Denton, Charlotte Brighton and Mrs. Danvers will all be vying for your services!"

Miss Sedgwick acknowledged, with a blush, that this was true, and put her very fine brain to the problem at hand as Althea set the invitation aside for the moment in favor of other correspondence.

"I think," she said at last, breaking the silence, as Althea sealed the last but most contentious envelope, "You should accept this invitation."

Althea regarded her with surprise. "And—? I cannot suppose that this is all you have to say on the subject."

Miss Sedgwick smiled, showing that streak of mischief that so endeared her to her livelier friends—mischief not being a quality often found in a paid companion. "I believe you should take this as an opportunity to exercise your gifts of play-acting. You must find some way to make yourself mildly dislikable to this young man so that he is put off making love to you! Nothing extreme—" she added hastily. "You would not wish to make yourself into a—a guy, of course. But simply amicably disagreeing with him on most subjects, even those on which you secretly agree, would surely make him certain that you are not the sort of person to whom he wishes to be attached for life."

Althea considered this for a moment, then nodded. "This does seem to be a good solution to a difficult problem. I will not offend Elizabeth, I will not offend the young man and I will not find myself burdened with his company for very long if I 'agree to disagree' on all possible subjects." She smiled warmly at her friend and companion, and answered the invitation in the most cordial manner possible.

It was truly a pity, Althea thought with regret, that Mr. Trenton was so impossibly un-magical, for in all other ways she and he were admirably suited to one another. As an Earth Master, she found herself acutely uncomfortable in the environs of cities; she had not, in fact, met Elizabeth Darcy in London, but in Bath, which at least had the advantage of being less poisonous to her sensibilities than London. Her "London Season" when she Came Out and was presented at Court had been mercifully cut short by the death of her aunt, and she had not resumed it at the end of the requisite mourning period. While she had feigned the unhappiness her peers would have felt that the death of an unlikable relative whom she scarcely knew should "ruin" her debut in Society, she had been so far from feeling disappointment that she even accepted the dubious legacy of her aunt's parrot, an irritable bird that bit everyone who ventured within range of its beak.

She had amended its behavior by the simple expedience of explaining to it in plain terms—magically, of course—that biting meant being confined to its cage and no treats. It had, in turn, explained its needs to her, and now only bit strangers—and then only as a sort of warning that they were either too silly to abide, or not to be trusted.

Since that time, she had opened her London townhouse only for a few weeks at the very height of the Season, and chose to be the one giving the parties rather than attending them, venturing out only for the occasional play or opera. The rest of the time she much preferred the comfort of her family home in the country; while not an imposing place, it was generally considered one of the best examples of a modest Tudor structure of the "Hardwick Hall, more glass than wall" variety. Lord Percy—the parrot—had his own room, as much like his jungle home as it was possible for her to devise. She often spent a great deal of time in there herself, particularly in winter, when the spirits of an Earth Master were apt to be depressed.

And it seemed that the amiable Mr. Trenton was similarly minded. He confessed that he was something of a hermit, that he seldom left his own Ash Lodge, and described it so movingly that she longed to see it. But of course, she laughingly disparaged such stay-at-home attitudes, much to the quiet astonishment of Elizabeth Darcy, and declared that anyone who would not spend the entire Season gadding about London must incur her pity.

They liked the same sorts of novels and poetry; she was forced to feign a yawning disinterest in reading. She could not bear to profess to political opinions that were contrary to her own, so she confined herself to pretending that she had none, and discussed gowns and hats with the other ladies so minded with an animation that made Elizabeth's eyes go round. She eschewed the music-room for needlework, about which she was at best indifferent. She who was normally quiet and mild-tempered took to teasing the others just up to the point of torment. It pained her in a way to see Mr. Trenton's initial interest swiftly turn to indifference, but what was she to do?

She knew that when Elizabeth was able to find her alone, there would be questions about her sudden reversal of personality, so she did her best to be inaccessible. Finally, in what looked like a moment of despair, Elizabeth suggested a riding-party out to view the woods, knowing that Althea showed herself to best advantage on horseback, and that there had never been a horse in the stables of Pemberley that would not behave like an angel under her.

"Oh! No, no indeed, thank you!" was Althea's reply. "I never ride; it is far too dangerous a sport for one like me, who cannot keep her mind on which way the reins are to go!"

Elizabeth very nearly lost countenance at that point, and she was prevented from saying something only by the softly added confirmation of Miss Sedgwick, that indeed, it was so, and they would much rather walk in the gardens.

Since Mr. Trenton had already agreed eagerly to be one of the party, and clearly had no reservations on the subject, Elizabeth gave over with a sigh—and with a look at Althea that threatened that there *would* be an accounting for her behavior before the day was out.

When they were gone, and Althea and her companion were changing their shoes in Althea's room for sturdier ones, Althea gave vent to no few sighs of her own.

"Oh! It is *too* bad," Miss Sedgwick said, with remorse, "that my scheme has deprived you of a charming ride!"

"There will be others," Althea said, but not without regret. "At least, there will as long as I have not sunk myself below reproach in Elizabeth's eyes." The stables at Pemberley were as famous as their woods, and Althea loved to ride. She herself could only afford to keep the two carriage horses and one dear old hunter who ambled rather than ran, but whom she could not bear to be parted from, for he had been her first real mount, and she was determined he end his days in her good care.

"Well, let us at least make good on our pledge of walking," she said with determination. "And if I may not ride myself, I can at least watch the riders."

And so they did, walking out of the pleasant valley in which Pemberley lay and up to the woods ringing it about.

And that was as far as their travels took them. For no sooner had they set foot on the lane beneath the shadows of the majestic oaks of which the woods were formed, than cries for help, full of fear and pain, and the thunder of hoofbeats on the turf betrayed that something had gone terribly wrong with what was supposed to have been a pleasant ride.

There came a shriek of terror from somewhere ahead, and the sound of a fall. A moment later, a tall hunter, black as midnight and wild-eyed, burst out of the undergrowth and plunged toward Althea.

She had but a moment, but she was not an Elemental Master for nothing. Gathering her magic about her, she threw up her hand and her force at the same time.

She shouted out a Word of Power at the same time, creating a shield around herself and Miss Sedgwick, and a barrier to hold the horse should it not be stopped by the Word alone. Nor was Miss Sedgwick behindhand in acting; though not a Master, she was an Elemental Magician of the complementary power of Water, and she added her own force to Althea's.

The horse pulled up so quickly that he skidded on his haunches and nearly sat down like a dog. He stood at the very edge of the barrier, rolling his eyes and trembling in every limb, drenched with sweat.

"Oh! My heavens, it is Eclipse!" cried Miss Sedgwick, recognizing the horse the instant before Althea did, and seizing the reins. "My dear, he is a good fellow, and he would never so misbehave as to bolt if something dreadful had not happened!"

"Can you calm him?" Althea asked, for now that the immediate danger was over, her thoughts flew to the sound that had surely been that of someone falling, and by the soprano tones, a woman, confirmed by the fact that Eclipse was wearing a side-saddle. "I must go—"

"Of course I can, and of course you must!" Miss Sedgwick replied immediately. "If anyone is hurt, *you* are the one who can help, not I!"

"Then as soon as he is calm, mount him and ride him back to Pemberley for help," Althea ordered, secure in the knowledge that her companion was a sturdy and untimid creature, for all her retiring nature, and would have no difficulty in following these orders, nor in finding a rock or a stump to help her into the saddle. And with that, she plunged into the undergrowth.

She was not long in finding the victim—a Miss Caroline Nash, a friend of Georgina Darcy, Mr. Darcy's younger sister, and a member of the party with whom she was not well acquainted. Althea was obliquely glad of that; had it been someone she knew the disposition of the poor girl would have thrown her into a state of anxiety not at all conducive to prompt action. She had clearly taken a bad fall; she lay unconscious, in a pitiable state, and from the paleness of her complexion, it was to be feared that she had taken a serious injury to her head.

Althea knelt by the girl's side, stripped off her gloves, and went straight to work.

Most Earth Masters were also at least indifferent healers; Althea was quite more than merely "indifferent." In moments, she knew intimately every detail of the girl's injuries, knew that she had, indeed, broken her skull, and that in fact it would be a fatal injury unless something could be done, immediately. And it would have to be something only magic could accomplish, for the excellencies of modern medicine could not avail against such a terrible hurt.

And she had very little time in which to accomplish her work, both because the damage would shortly become irreparable, and because the others, either of her party or the aid summoned from Pemberley, would soon arrive.

Althea swiftly lost herself in The Work, and a moment later, sensed another mage kneeling beside her. She fully expected to be augmented by Miss Sedgwick's cooling Water magic, and indeed, had prepared to "clasp hands" with her friend, welcoming the support. But the "hand" that clasped hers was unfamiliar, and the magic much more powerful than she anticipated. Indeed, it was the Water Magic of another Master!

But she repressed her shock and surprise in the urgency of the moment, and concentrated on the healing. As she and the newcomer worked side by side, she knew that what was to be done could not have been done so swiftly nor so surely by her power alone. Indeed, it might not have been accomplished at all.

But by the time the summoned help arrived, along with the rest of the alarmed riding party, the repairs had been made, and a pale and shaken, bruised and head-sore, but otherwise unharmed Miss Caroline was helped to sit up, soon to be scooped up in the strong arms of an enormous footman, summoned for that very purpose, and carried down to the house to be made much of.

The rest of the party also departed, their minds much on the injured girl, and entirely forgetful of Althea and Mr. Trenton, who still knelt, side by side, on the moss.

"Why did you not—" she exclaimed, at the same time that he demanded, "Why did you conceal—"

They looked into each other's eyes and smiled and burst into helpless laughter.

"What a bother!" she said, recovering first, and holding out her bare hand to him. "I believe we must begin all over again. I beg your pardon for vexing you, Mr. Trenton."

"I hope you will call me William, Miss Lynncroft," he replied with a charming smile. "Mrs. Darcy arranged that we should meet precisely because we have so very much in common—I confess, however, that I did not expect to find we had Mastery as well!"

"And I," she replied, feeling well content for the first time since that fateful invitation arrived, "beg that you will call me Althea. And I believe that we have much to talk about."

Indeed, so much that by the time they walked down to Pemberley, leading William's horse, everything had been set for their wedding but the date.

FROM THAT MOMENT, much to Elizabeth Darcy's puzzlement, but also to her delight, her friend Althea reverted to her old self. And William Trenton, an acquaintance of Mr. Darcy's of whom she had grown quite fond, responded to the change in every particular that she could have desired.

"I am not the sort of inveterate matchmaker that we both abhor," she later wrote with much satisfaction, "But I could not think of one of those two without feeling that they *must* meet. And it does seem that I was right, after all!"

Viscountess Mercedes Lackey-Edgerton-Smythe has had a rose, a dahlia and a tulip named for her. A neck-or-nothing rider, she was the first ever female to be named Master of the Derbyshire Hunt. She raises peafowl and swans and is a notable expert on eleventh-century incunabula. And if you believe any of this, perhaps your copy of *Burke's Peerage* is not what it should be. She is the author of several fantasy series, including the Elemental Masters series in which this story is set.

Georgiana

Jane Espenson

Poor Georgiana, doomed to be a plot device of a little sister whose most exciting moments are behind her at sixteen. Here Jane Espenson swoops in to the rescue with a story that gives Georgie a second chance at love and readers a second chance at loathing Lady Catherine.

GEORGIANA HAD BEEN TO ROSINGS BEFORE, having been relegated to the upstairs schoolroom during family visits when she was a child. But she had not returned for many years now, and as she was led through the antechamber of the house, her alarm was every moment increasing at the prospect of facing her aunt, Lady Catherine de Bourgh. Lady Catherine featured in childhood memories as an imposing figure, forever conducting inquisitions of mathematical and historical knowledge without ever waiting for the answers. Encounters with her were a trial for a naturally shy child, and even now Georgiana dreaded offending her. She had yet to learn that the commanding of respect was not the same as the deserving of it.

Georgiana's brother and sister-in-law, who accompanied her, didn't display obvious agitation, although there was, to be sure, a tightness around Darcy's shoulders, and there had been a telling briskness to his gait as they approached the house that had forced the women to quicken their steps after him. Elizabeth glanced at her husband with a smile, trying to win its echo. This was not awarded to her, but she was not surprised or disappointed. At times, Darcy had a tendency to slip back into the kind of stiffness he wore in the earliest days of their acquaintance, and Lady Catherine de Bourgh, of all his relations, was the one most likely to bring about this change. This stemmed more from his fear that Lady Catherine would display vulgarity than any concern that Lizzy would. Elizabeth had tried to teach him the art of being amused by the excesses of one's relations, rather than mortified, but he had yet to learn it.

Lady Catherine rose to greet them as they entered the room, urging them to "Come in! There's no point in hanging about the doorway!" Georgiana was pleased and relieved to see Colonel Fitzwilliam, an old friend and her former guardian, smile at the newcomers from the mantel where he stood. Miss de Bourgh sat near the fire, accompanied by a pleasant-faced young man of about five-and-twenty, in company regimentals, who rose now to greet them. He was dark and neatly made, not especially tall, and with an open intelligent expression. Colonel Fitzwilliam performed the introductions, and she learned that this was Mr. Havers, who possessed a lieutenant's commission and who had come to this part of the country in the company of Fitzwilliam, his commanding officer. He had recently come into an unexpected elevation in income and prospects that gave him a grateful but unsure air. Havers bowed and spoke a few words of greeting, before Miss de Bourgh murmured something at his elbow that required him to return his attention to her. Georgiana supposed there might be an attachment of a sort between the two young people.

Everyone sat, Georgiana forcing herself to follow her sister-in-law's example and sit squarely on her chair rather than perch on the edge of it. Surely it would be Lizzy who would attract Lady Catherine's attention, freeing her from that sharp gaze. A marriage between Georgiana's brother and Miss de Bourgh had been the fondest wish of Lady Catherine's heart, and in her mind the fault for the miscarriage of this hope lay solely with Lizzy, Darcy himself somehow escaping the transaction with as little blame as if his marital state was due to no volition of his own. But, to Georgiana's dismay, it was not Lizzy at whom Lady Catherine stared, but rather at herself.

"So this is how you turned out, is it?" the lady began, and Georgiana found herself coloring. How did one reply to an opening such as that? Luckily, Lady Catherine was not inclined to need a response.

"You're very tall. I daresay you're more than seven inches above five feet. Some will say it's too tall for real elegance, but you must not believe them. The women in our family have always run toward height. I am tall myself and Miss de Bourgh would have been tall, too, had her constitution permitted it."

To her alarm, Georgiana saw that a reply was now expected, and to a statement so extraordinary she could imagine no sensible reply possible. "I am not above five-foot-six, ma'am," was all she could essay.

"Nonsense!" Lady Catherine looked affronted. "Lieutenant Havers, how tall are you? Stand next to my niece and we'll see what's what. Take those great tall boots off while you're at it."

It took the combined efforts of Darcy and Elizabeth to persuade Lady Catherine that the comparison would yield little of import, and soon the conversation turned to an examination of the ways in which Elizabeth ran her household. Georgiana settled back with relief, content to listen to her new sister's spirited defense of the way in which she chose to order sugar and flour. She knew she need have no fear of Lizzy's being equal to that task. In Georgiana's eyes, Lizzy was fearless.

Georgiana's own nature was quite the opposite. She ran naturally to shyness. She had been on her way to acquiring a measure of confidence at age fifteen, when a misadventure had so shamed her as to drive her back into her own shell with a force that those who knew her best feared now she might never overcome. She had entered, at that age, into an ill-advised intended elopement with George Wickham, the son of her father's steward. The elopement had been foiled when she was unable to conceal her plans from her brother, who had always been afforded by her the respect due to a father. Darcy had been able to patch up the situation and keep her reputation intact, but it had been a shameful episode that loomed in her mind so large as to remind her every day of what she had almost done. The fact that three of the people in this room, Darcy, Lizzy and Colonel Fitzwilliam, knew of her secret was enough to make her blush. The thought that without her brother's care, Lady Catherine might have known as well —that was almost too much to bear.

As soon as it was possible, in an effort to keep her aunt's attention from turning to her again, she took herself to the side of the room where

Fitzwilliam sat in quiet conversation with Miss de Bourgh and the young Lieutenant Havers, which is to say that Fitzwilliam and Havers spoke, with Miss de Bourgh occasionally softly mouthing a request for an extra pillow or for her footstool to be moved either nearer to, or farther from the fire, whichever move would cause the most inconvenience. Georgiana lowered herself onto a settee near the group and tried to look as though she had a part in their conversation while earnestly hoping she would be left quietly on the outside of it.

But her ex-guardian would not let her sit silently by. Colonel Fitzwilliam drew her into the discussion by mentioning one of her favorite poets. It turned out that Lieutenant Havers also had an opinion on the topic, and before she knew it, they were comparing verses. Each of them was so naturally deferential that whenever they discovered any difference of opinion, each of them was so eager to concede the point to the other, that several times they actually traded their positions, only to find themselves back in unintended conflict again.

Colonel Fitzwilliam called the phenomenon to their attention, making both of them blush. "I daresay it is only because she expresses her opinion so well," ventured Lieutenant Havers, "that once she says it, I see too clearly where my own error lies." Georgiana nodded her agreement. "And Lieutenant Havers makes such solid sense, there would be no point in my holding to my position after I've heard his."

"Excellent," smiled Fitzwilliam. "You both place perfect faith in the opinion of one who is willing to abandon that very opinion!"

Havers laughed and looked at Georgiana from under his thick lashes. "I think he has us. If he is requiring us actually to believe the things we say, then our conversation is indeed doomed."

"I suppose," Georgiana offered, "that if one ruled out faulty assertions, *all* conversation would be doomed."

Havers laughed at that, surprising Georgiana—whether with his reaction or with her own wit, she could not say. At this point, Miss De Burgh asked Colonel Fitzwilliam, with surprising force, to move her chair completely away from the fireplace. All of this resulted in such a stir and scraping that Lady Catherine was forced to inquire from across the room what they had gotten up to. "What is all that over there, then? Are you moving the furniture? I thought you were talking about poetry. I can't abide a poem when a proverb would do as well. It's just words upon words; I tell my nephew that all the time when he's sitting with one of those ridiculous great books of his. Don't I tell you that, Darcy?"

Darcy agreed that she had often said something very like that and the conversation became general again until dinner, Georgiana being very glad of it, as she found herself tired from the effort of her sally, and from all the feelings that assailed her when she remembered Havers' gratifying reaction to it. Georgiana had made someone laugh, just as Lizzy often did, and she found the experience deeply satisfying.

THE NEXT DAY, Darcy, Elizabeth and Georgiana went to call on Elizabeth's friend Charlotte and her husband, Elizabeth's cousin, Mr. Collins. With the encouragement of Lady Catherine, who approved of exercise for all but herself, they made the pleasant walk of about half a mile across the park. The outing was made all the more pleasant by the contrast with the oppressive atmosphere of Rosings. Darcy thought the sky had never seemed so high above him as he walked out with his adored wife and beloved sister. Even the prospect of an entire day spent in the company of Mr. Collins was not enough to dim his happiness at a respite from his aunt and her autocratic and ungenerous behavior. As they walked, Lizzy talked to Georgiana, preparing her for Mr. Collins as if he was a form of entertainment to be highly prized and anticipated. Darcy marveled again at his wife's temperament, and he knew himself to be a fortunate man. He had seen how his formerly timid sister was flourishing under the positive influence of his wife, and he smiled an indulgent smile on the two of them, managing, for the moment, to forget both the household that receded behind them and the one that approached.

The little group arrived to find the Collinses waiting for them. While Elizabeth happily embraced her friend, Mr. Collins waxed prolific in his greetings. He addressed himself particularly to Georgiana.

"Ah! This must be Lady Catherine's youngest niece, the renowned Miss Georgiana Darcy!" he exclaimed, beaming and bowing. "I should have known you anywhere! So like your aunt in height and complexion and general evenness of temperament! I hope I am not overstepping my bounds to make these observations, and perhaps you may wonder at my even presuming to generalize so about Lady Catherine, but I think you find that I, and my family, my dear Charlotte, are on terms of gratifying intimacy with Lady Catherine and the inhabitants of Rosings, so that my expressed thought is not so stupefying as it must at first have seemed."

Georgiana replied, "I was not wondering, sir, at your having knowledge of my aunt's general temperament, but rather at your having knowledge of mine!" This earned a smile, even half a laugh from Lizzy, who had overheard the exchange. Georgiana herself colored deeply. This new habit of speaking as she thought had its risks. Indeed, Mr. Collins now launched into a series of apologies so profound she feared she had really made him fear to have given serious offence. But as she attended his words she found that the apologies were of a wide-ranging sort, including his heartfelt sorrow over the unevenness of the ground in the park and the number and vigor of local burrowing rodents. Georgiana was just wondering if she was expected to defend the rodents when Mr. Collins steered his words through a steep turn and began showing off his wife's housekeeping to Mr. Darcy, who did his best to appear interested.

Darcy would have need of that skill again soon, as, after a luncheon, Mr. Collins took him off to admire some improvements he had made to the house's modest grounds. A stone walkway was talked of, and plans for a bower. This left the three women alone in the house, and with a much-lightened mood. Although, it must be said, Elizabeth never could witness her best friend's domestic situation without remembering her own role in bringing it about. It was not that she regretted turning down Mr. Collins' proposal of marriage to her, but rather she remained conscious that her turning it down had put Charlotte in the path of it. Elizabeth still found it hard to believe that Charlotte was satisfied with this lot in life, no matter how often she was assured of it.

Georgiana got a clearer picture of the felicities of married life as she observed the two women. Lizzy was clearly the more contented of the two, having found a husband who was her match in intellect and taste, but Charlotte was not unhappy. As her marriage entered its second year, she was finding her husband's company increasingly tolerable, as he abandoned some of his more elaborate affectations, at least in private. Both Elizabeth and Charlotte revealed through their exchanges that they found marriage to be a matter of accommodation, as every decision required weighing the opinions and preferences of another person. Listening to them, Georgiana was struck by how shallow her association with Wickham had truly been. Their imagined life—that is, the life as Wickham had sketched it for her—had none of the texture of two people accommodating each other. She saw now that impediments to perfect joy came even in the best of marriages, and made the man and the woman the happier for overcoming them.

Charlotte, of course, had more to overcome than most. She led them to view an oddity; her pantry, filled, floor to ceiling, with bottles.

"What is this?" Lizzy asked, perplexed.

"Local wine. At least that's what it purports to be," Charlotte replied, her mouth twitching at the corners. "Lady Catherine insists we drink it to support the family that makes it, without her having to drink it herself. She had these sent over for us."

"Is it so terrible?" Georiana asked, peering at the murky liquid, and wondering at what her aunt was thinking, giving a gift such as this.

"It's vile. But she looks in here every time she visits, to make sure they're disappearing."

"What do you do?" Lizzy asked.

"I've been emptying them in the garden. The roses don't seem to mind it, at least."

To demonstrate, Charlotte filled her arms with the bottles and the other two women followed her into the garden. They were shaking the last dregs of sour-smelling wine from the bottles when Lady Catherine's carriage pulled up the walkway. Lizzy looked in amusement, as Charlotte and Georgiana made haste to hide the empty bottles at the base of a particularly dense rosebush.

"What can have happened to bring her out?" Lizzy exclaimed with some surprise. "We left her only two hours ago."

Georgiana found herself to be not at all surprised. She was beginning to accept that, at least in this part of England, Lady Catherine simply was everywhere.

LADY CATHERINE descended from the carriage, and the three women moved to greet her. Charlotte was made to know that Miss de Bourgh was remaining in the carriage, and that Charlotte was welcome to chat with her there. Charlotte took that as the directive it was, and moved off to carry it out. Lady Catherine was left with Lizzy and Georgiana, the latter of whom felt herself not at all equal to something so very like a one-to-one meeting. Even with three people, she was sure the conversation would provide her with far too large a percentage of the Lady.

Elizabeth endeavored to invite Lady Catherine inside, but the offer was declined, and the three instead walked in the garden. Elizabeth found herself forcibly reminded of a similar previous meeting with Lady Catherine. That time, Lady Catherine had demanded that Elizabeth not marry Darcy. Elizabeth sensed that something of the kind might be forthcoming now, but she couldn't imagine what it was. Was she about to be bid to bear him an heir? The thought amused her and she had to stifle a laugh. Lady Catherine might have a very large notion of things she could command into existence, but even she might not imagine it to extend so very far.

"I've been asking some questions about you, Georgiana," Lady Catherine began briskly, once they were out of earshot of the carriage, "and I have discovered your secret."

Georgiana felt the blood drain from her face, and her feet almost faltered on the gravel walk. Whatever questions had been asked, there could be no question about what answer had been given. There was only one secret. Elizabeth wondered what powers Lady Catherine had exerted over Colonel Fitzwilliam, for he was the most likely source of the intelligence. But that was a secondary concern. Right now, her role was to prevent Lady Catherine from employing the knowledge. Lady Catherine continued:

"Obviously the elopement was prevented. And I understand you came forward yourself to confess it. But that doesn't change the fact that you chose to enter into it in the first place. I see by your face, Mrs. Darcy, that this is no surprise to you. That you were also involved in keeping these facts from me."

"Lady Catherine—" Lizzy began, but Lady Catherine wasn't done.

"I cannot tell you how disappointed I am. Both that a niece of mine would behave in this way and that, although I am your aunt, I was never told. Even now, I find I cannot determine whom the bridegroom was to have been."

Georgiana closed her eyes for a moment with relief. She accepted that news with the gratitude it deserved. As it now lay exposed, the adventure might devastate her in Lady Catherine's eyes. The same adventure, with Wickham, would render her below redemption.

Elizabeth had recovered her composure enough to venture into the until-now one-sided conversation. "I will not ask how you found out. But I will ask you why you chose now to make it your business to find out."

Lady Catherine looked at Elizabeth, taken aback, as always, by this girl who always found the mettle to stand up to her. Georgiana, walking on the other side of Lizzy, by contrast, had her face pointed down toward her feet. Lady Catherine found herself, as always, a bit impressed with Elizabeth, and became all the more imperious as a result.

"I ask because Lieutenant Havers is intended for my daughter."

Elizabeth was struck, more forcefully than before, with a need to laugh. It was happening again. Sickly, unpleasant Miss de Bourgh had had one intended husband denied her when Lizzy wed Darcy. And now Georgiana—tall, shy Georgiana—was apparently perceived to be repeating the offense. It was too perfect for words. Elizabeth considered asking Lady Catherine how often she was obligated to pay this very errand. Elizabeth had been party to it twice. Did it also occur during periods when she was not in the neighborhood? Only Elizabeth's genuine alarm at the release of Georgiana's secret kept the question from emerging. She was aware of the need to measure the depth of the danger.

"I assume you are not planning to share this with Lieutenant Havers," Elizabeth asserted.

"I do not see why you should assume any such thing!" Lady Catherine snorted back.

Georgiana found her tongue: "Because I should die of shame."

Lady Catherine fixed Georgiana with a cold stare. "You should have thought of that before you embarked on your romantic misadventure. Imagine, a child of fifteen having the will to throw herself into an alliance against the wishes of her family." The gaze shifted to Lizzy, and with significance: "But I suppose some of us can imagine that quite well."

It was a reference to Lydia, Elizabeth's younger sister, who had done exactly what Georgiana had come so close to doing and, unknown to Lady Catherine, with the same man. Elizabeth struggled against her anger to keep her voice calm.

"What Georgiana means, Lady Catherine, and it is a very good point, is that Lieutenant Havers would be the first one outside the family to have this knowledge. At that point secrets have a way of becoming the property of the community." Lizzy found herself growing more incensed as the truth of what she was saying grew in her. Lady Catherine was literally going to ruin Georgiana to keep Havers for Miss de Bourgh. "I doubt very much you want your niece to suffer this, not to mention the Darcy name—"

Lizzy was prevented from expounding upon the Darcy name by the arrival of one of the men who bore it: her husband, returned with Mr. Collins from their tour and surprised to find the odd trio of walkers. At this point, everyone was required to listen to Mr. Collins for a space of five minutes while he rhapsodized about Lady Catherine's condescension in favoring them with her presence and as he apologized for himself, his garden, and the amount of recent rain that had left mud where there ought to have been more attractive dirt.

While the effusions wafted around him, Darcy was able to read some of what had occurred on the faces of his sister and his wife. The former stood with eyes downcast and cheeks red, the latter, equally red, but from a different cause, fixed him with expressive eyes that conveyed the need to act. It was not difficult to settle on the course of action most likely to improve the peace.

"Aunt Catherine," Darcy said smoothly, "allow me to escort you back to your carriage. It's very good of you to come out to see us, although unnecessary."

Perhaps Elizabeth's invocation of the Darcy name had had its effect. Lady Catherine, whatever the cause, felt no need to continue her mission under the eye of Mr. Collins and allowed herself to be led placidly away, her work done. Elizabeth looked at Georgiana and feared the girl had been driven rather forcibly back into herself in a way that might be beyond remedy.

A SUDDEN RAIN, common for this time of year, kept the Darcy party at the Collinses' that night, providing a delay in which the various participants were able to rest and think. In their chamber, Lizzy and Darcy spoke about Georgiana. They neither of them felt there was serious danger of the girl disturbing any preexisting arrangement between Anne de Bourgh and Lieutenant Havers. That misapprehension, Lizzy felt sure, came from an overactive fear on Lady Catherine's part that events would repeat themselves. They talked until late, but arrived at no solution better than simply impressing again on Darcy's aunt the importance of keeping the knowledge of the intended elopement within the family.

Georgiana, alone in her chamber, had no one with whom to share her thoughts. All she could do was ponder a world in which her childish trust in Wickham, and her willingness to do as he said at the cost of her own future and reputation, would be known by all who knew her.

It was hard to bear, imagining the reactions of others whose respect she would like to deserve. And, inevitably, her actions would reflect badly on her guardians, on Colonel Fitzwilliam and on her beloved brother. That would be extremely trying and undeserved. She was surprised to find her thoughts returning, though, to another face. Even at this hour, she knew, Lieutenant Havers might already be apprised of her story. She hardly knew him. They had shared an acquaintance counted in the hours. And yet she had sensed a kinship in him, a delicacy of feeling and a quiet gentleness that she had liked. Such a man wouldn't understand what she had done. He would imagine himself wrong about her. He would characterize her as a wild girl with a rash disposition. He wouldn't see that she had been then a trusting soul, quite overwhelmed by a young man's declaration that she had become necessary for his happiness. She felt asleep worrying over that conviction, and hoping only that Lady Catherine's threats would come to nothing.

ACROSS THE PARK, another young head failed to find rest on its pillow, and not because of the pounding of rain on his window. Lieutenant Havers, still dressed, walked the floor of his chamber, his footfalls silenced by the thick rug—which had been imported at great inconvenience and cost over five hundred pounds, he had been assured by Lady Catherine. He had not been told Georgiana's secret, but he had been told there *was* one. This was conveyed, by the Lady herself, with such a dark tone, such a sense of delighted dread, that he found himself quite overwhelmed with curiosity and concern.

He had quite liked Georgiana, and he would be both surprised and troubled to find there was a hint of scandal about her. Second, he was startled to discover how *much* he had liked her. The sense of—what was it? The sense of *loss* which he now felt was out of proportion with what was appropriate for an afternoon's acquaintance.

He was the eldest son of a family with a noble history and little else. With no natural pretensions to fortune and no other path to it ever having been found, the entire family was shocked when, with the death of a long-forgotten relation, it happened upon them without warning like a sudden storm. Havers found himself transformed overnight from an impoverished officer to a wealthy officer, which was much the same but seemed to come with a need for new uniforms, many social engagements and, if possible, a wife. He was overwhelmed. Colonel Fitzwilliam had taken pity on the young man and had brought him to Rosings several times, hoping he might at least enjoy a few peaceful fortnights wandering the grounds.

Miss de Bourgh had seemed to Havers, at first, to be an ideal companion for him, and exactly when he found himself in need of one. She struck him as a quiet girl, very proper, accustomed to money and therefore not driven to try to impress. It wasn't until the afternoon with Georgiana that Miss de Bourgh had begun to tire him with her silences rather than refresh him. And in the day that had passed since then, her fretful requests and languid sighs had impressed on him what a future filled with such exhalations might be like. He had already been troubled, before the hints from Lady Catherine about Georgiana's past, that he had been too quick to demonstrate a partiality for Miss de Bourgh, and now, for the second time in two days, he again found himself doubting a woman of whom he had been sure. His friends told him he was in need of a wife. But they were of little help in selecting one. And he was starting to doubt his ability to do so on his own. He walked the length of the room again, vowing to forgo sleep until he had made a decision about how he might react to any information Lady Catherine might convey to him in the morning.

THE NEXT DAY dawned dark, with clouds that threatened a return of the rain and did little to soothe the nerves of the members of both households. The afternoon would bring the party's return to Rosings, and Georgiana spent the day dreading the evening in that way that ruins the day and does nothing to improve the evening. Darcy and Elizabeth shared her concerns, and her depression of spirits. Charlotte tried to entertain her guests, but there was little she could do, and it was with a small measure of relief that she saw them on their way, she herself left with the familiar, and increasingly endurable, company of her husband.

Georgiana followed the servants through the antechamber at Rosings again, flanked by Darcy and Elizabeth, wondering what she was about to face. She entered the room to find things much as they had been two days before. Colonel Fitzwilliam stood at the mantel, apology in his eyes, Lady Catherine surveyed the room from her chair, and Miss de Bourgh looked as if she was either too warm or too cold but hadn't yet decided which. For a moment, Georgiana thought Havers was not to be counted among them, but then she found him at her side, his having been sitting apart from the others. His face was impassive. Georgiana was unable to read whether or not he had been informed of her secret.

A glance toward the others found Lady Catherine questioning Elizabeth closely about the Collinses' household, and Darcy in deep conversation with Fitzwilliam. Georgiana found herself led, by Havers, to the pianoforte, where they were able to talk softly under the pretense of discussing the sheet music. His first words to her chilled her to the core.

"I know of the planned elopement."

Georgiana looked at the floor. This was it, then. He went on: "Your aunt, Lady Catherine, is an honest woman. She felt it her duty to tell me. I used to think her a foolish woman. But now I see she is something beyond that. She is *supremely* foolish."

She wanted to raise her eyes and look at him, but the effort was beyond her. He went on, "An impropriety of some years ago—an impropriety *not* committed—does not strike me as a very grave thing. What is grave is her risking your family's reputation for the sake of denying you the chance to make your choice where you will. If I have any complaint against you it is with your having an aunt who must indeed be the silliest person in the county."

Georgiana finally raised her eyes to find him smiling at her. She found her courage and smiled back. She heard herself say, "Oh, but you're wrong. You haven't met Mr. Collins."

No reply was possible, as Lady Catherine chose this moment to imperiously call them back to join the group. At that time, Lizzy and Darcy saw much on the young peoples' faces to reassure them, and the de Bourghs saw much that did not.

We leave them with little more than an afternoon's friendship. But it was from this that their mutual regard grew and thrived. They met again at Pemberley, the Darcy ancestral home, within the month, and then at his family's home. She grew in confidence, and he became more comfortable with the requirements of his new status. Lady Catherine was right to be concerned. Once again, there was a bride. Once again, she was not Miss de Bourgh.

Jane Espenson grew up in Ames, Iowa, where she was introduced to the writings of Jane Austen at an early age by her English-lit-major mother. She eventually found herself with a long career as a television writer/producer, but she never gave up the essential love of Austen.

She wrote for a number of half-hour comedies, including *Ellen*, then moved on to drama writing, including stints on *The O.C.*, *Gilmore Girls* and a five-year run on *Buffy the Vampire Slayer*. While working at *Buffy*, she was able to write a vampire-themed comic book story in the style of Austen, rekindling her love for that kind of storytelling. She continues in television, working under a development deal with 20th Century Fox television, creating shows of her own, and rereading Austen in her spare time. She's delighted to be included in this collection.

Charlotte's Side of the Story

MELISSA SENATE

I've always thought Charlotte was a smart cookie to have snagged Mr. Collins and the promise of a future at Netherfield. Melissa Senate thinks so, too, and vindicates Charlotte then and now with this modern tale of a woman who knows what she wants...even if nobody else will date him twice.

WILLY COLLINS WASN'T UGLY. He was no Viggo Mortensen, but then, who was? Willy had a great nose, a Roman nose. He had strong eyebrows, too strong for his buggy, watery eyes, but they added something necessary to his face, which was on the flat side. He also had remarkably clean fingernails. I didn't usually spend my lunch hours picking apart someone's looks, but as Willy sat across from me in the Sixth Avenue diner, poking at his eggs and droning on about how Elizabeth wouldn't go out with him, I took the opportunity to study his face. It was a face I saw every day, well, Monday through Friday. We worked together at Pushkin Publishing. Elizabeth and I were editors (me: cookbooks; Elizabeth: travel guides) and also best friends, and Willy was the managing editor, which meant he was in charge of production and schedules and bossing us around, even though he wasn't our boss. I'd never really looked closely at Willy before; when you were late with a manuscript or hadn't turned in your cover concepts and Willy came knocking with his clipboard and monotone voice and a ten-minute lecture about sticking to schedules, you didn't look him in the eye. You looked everywhere else so that he'd get the hint and move on to the next unlucky editor. The problem with Willy, aside from everything else, was that he never got the hint. Nudnicks rarely did.

"The man has no social skills!" Elizabeth had yelped at our last company Christmas party, when Willy asked her to dance at least ten times, arguing with her each time she turned him down.

ELIZABETH: Thanks, but no, Willy.
WILLY: [*Shakes his hips*] Oh, come on. I love this song!
ELIZABETH: [*Tight smile*] No, really, but thanks.
WILLY: [*Shimmies shoulders so that his chest is practically against hers*] Come on, *one* dance!
ELIZABETH: [*Steps back. Can't tell him to fuck off because he's the managing editor*] I really *don't* feel like dancing.
WILLY: [*Grabs her hand*] Sure you do!
ELIZABETH: [*Shrieks at top of lungs*] What part of *NO* don't you understand?
WILLY: [*Blank stare. Smiles*] That's funny! Did you just make that up?
ELIZABETH: Arrrrrrgh! [*Stalks off*]

This went on two more times until Elizabeth had had it and actually left. Not that Pushkin parties were a blast, but there was an open bar and the new V.P. of New Business Development, Fitz-something-or-other, *was* Viggo-esque.

Twenty minutes before lunch, I had come upon Willy and Elizabeth by the copy machine. I heard Elizabeth say, "Read my lips, Willy: *NO*." Then she walked away, Willy sighing after her.

"Willy, there's more tuna in the sea," I'd said.

He rolled his eyes. "Then why won't any of the women I'm interested in go out with me? Charlotte, I'm *forty* years old. I've been ready to get married for years. I want kids, two—maybe even more. If Elizabeth would just give me a chance...."

When Willy moped, his whole face moped with him. The strong eyebrows drooped. Even the Roman nose retreated. But instead of looking like Elmer Fudd, he suddenly reminded me of the hound dog I'd had as a child.

Ready to get married years ago…two kids…maybe more.…

"Willy, do you want to know what I think?" I asked, placing a hand on his shoulder. "I think you could use a comfort meal. Lunch is *my* treat."

And so off we'd gone to the diner on Sixth Avenue, where I began counting his use of the word *Elizabeth*. I was up to twenty-two times.

"I've asked Elizabeth out at least ten, maybe twelve times in the past month," Willy said, cracking open his boiled eggs. "She always says no. I just don't get it."

"Willy, maybe she's just not attracted to you. I'm sure women have been interested in you and you haven't been attracted to them."

He poked at the tops of his eggs. "No, that's never happened."

Oh.

He flagged down the waitress, who was struggling with a tray full of dirty plates and glasses. "These eggs are *not* soft-boiled," he told her. "A perfectly-cooked soft-boiled egg should be removed from the heat and set aside for exactly *two* minutes. These are at least *five*-minute eggs." The waitress stared at him. I wouldn't have been surprised if she grabbed the eggs and scooped out their mushy yokes onto his head. She asked if he wanted something else, and he snorted and said, "I can't eat anything anyway. I expect the eggs will be removed from the bill." She rolled her eyes and left, and Willy turned his attention back to me. "Has Elizabeth talked to you about me? You're her best friend. Do you think I have a chance?"

Were you recently dropped on your head? I wanted to scream at him.

"I don't think so, Willy."

He sighed. "I just don't get it. I'm so ready to get married and have a family. I'm tired of being alone." The buggy eyes began to mist.

I began arranging our imaginary baby's potential features. My doe eyes and his Roman nose. My heart-shaped face and his I-Mean-Business eyebrows. My willowy frame (he was short and stout) and his healthy nails (I bit mine). Of course, there was always the chance that the baby would get my too-long nose and his buggy eyes. His flat face and my blah brown hair.

"There, there," I said and put my hand over his, adding an unmistakable caress. He glanced up at me slowly, shyly, those buggy eyes opening wide.

I'D KNOWN ELIZABETH for thirteen years, since she started at Pushkin as a twenty-two-year-old editorial assistant. Then twenty-seven and an assistant editor, I was the older, wiser one, and she often came to me for dating advice since I tended to look at life through my crystal clear glasses.

He talked about himself all through dinner? That's what men do.

He ogled the big-chested blonde at the next table? That's what men do.

You weren't attracted to him? You won't be in twenty years when he's bald and pot-bellied, so what's the diff?

Elizabeth liked to shake her head and laugh when I went off that way. "Charlotte, there's a fine line between practical and cynical. I think you're crossing too far over."

I *pshawed* her. "Go rent the movie *Two for the Road* with Audrey Hepburn and Albert Finney. They go from making fun of long-married couples who don't talk in restaurants to *being* a long-married couple who don't talk in restaurants."

"It doesn't have to be that way," she said.

"Then why *is* it that way?" I asked her. "What's your parents' marriage like? I know what my parents' marriage is like."

She gnawed her lip, then smiled and shook her head. "Cynic," she sing-songed at me.

I was thirty-nine years old and had been dating since I was, what? Sixteen? That was twenty-three years. There's cynicism and then there's *been there, done that*. I hadn't always been so . . . *pragmatic* was the word I preferred. When I was young, in my teens and twenties, I had fun. An open mind. A big heart at the ready.

The guy was all wrong for me? What was a couple of months with a thirty-year-old grad student in philosophy who whispered life's big questions in my ear while making love to me on a futon?

Using me for sex? But he looked just like Colin Firth!

Won't commit? So? I was only twenty-five, twenty-six, twenty-seven, twenty-eight—

Which brought me to Nicholas, who told me I was The One until I discovered he had two other Ones. At thirty-two, when my very first maternal urge brought me to tears in Baby Gap, where I'd been buying my newborn niece a gift, I'd begun to wonder if I were doing something wrong.

I've been leaving it to chance, I'd realized during Thanksgiving dinner the year I turned thirty-five and was afraid to look too long or too hard at my aunt Rebecca, who was fifty-two, never married and burst into tears at the sight of children. *Chance!* For something so important as the rest of my life? And so I put a personal ad in *New York* magazine. Letters and pictures poured in. I had twenty-six first dates. I had only one second date, with a guy who told me he wasn't particularly bowled over by me on the first date but wanted to make sure with a second date; over Indian food he informed me he was sure. There were blind dates, too. Set up by friends, family, coworkers. *Have an open mind! Just enjoy yourself! You're not marrying him, it's just lunch or dinner or a drink or coffee!*

And it was. For a long time. Until now. Until *thirty-nine*. Until pure biology made it something else: a time issue. Until now, finding "the right guy" had always seemed like a real possibility. And when you were single, the possibilities were truly endless. Except when it came to whether or not you'd have a baby.

That people seemed to understand. When I said I wanted a baby, no one ever shook their head and accused me of wanting a man instead of a life. If you were single and thirty-nine (or, say, upwards of thirty-five) and dared admit that you wanted to have a baby, what people said, without meaning it, was, "Don't worry—you'll meet someone. He's out there."

Where? And trust me, I looked. And looked and looked. He wasn't there. And according to the tick-tock of my biological clock and my gynecologist Dr. Flynn, it was now or never.

"It's not now or never!" Elizabeth had assured me a few weeks ago, when I broke down in tears over the impending loss of opportunity, of choice, of hope to have a family, a husband and child. "It's now or *international adoption*!" she'd said. "Now or a *sperm bank*! Now or a gay friend who wants a kid too!"

THE GOSSIP BEGAN a week or so after my lunch with Willy. I was about to walk into the Pushkin Publishing kitchenette for some coffee when I heard my name.

"There's a rumor going around that Charlotte's dating Willy," I heard the editor in chief's assistant whisper.

I stood just to the side of the doorway, clutching my mug.

"Please," came Elizabeth's voice. "Charlotte's not desperate. Give the woman some credit!"

ELIZABETH AND I were on the train to Chappaqua, heading to Samantha Siegel's baby shower. Samantha was a coworker, a self-help editor who married one of her authors, a famous relationship guru. Elizabeth and I each carried matching Baby Gap shopping bags. I'd spent over an hour in the newborn section, marveling over tiny soft onesies in pale pink and baby blue.

"So, about this rumor going around about me and Willy Collins," I said to Elizabeth as we stepped off the train.

She smiled and shook her head. "I know. As if, right?"

"Actually, Elizabeth, Willy and I *are* dating."

She laughed and strained her neck to look for street signs.

"I'm serious," I said, my cheeks hot—and not from embarrassment, but from *anger*. "Just because you didn't want to go out with him doesn't mean no other woman would, Elizabeth. Or maybe you expected him to pine for you forever?"

She stared at me, her own cheeks turning pink. She was assessing. Possibly waiting for me to say, *Gotcha!*

"We've gone out five or six times," I said. But I was well aware it was *five* times. Our sixth date was tonight.

"I didn't know you had a thing for Willy," she said, still assessing. Still waiting.

"He's single. He's forty. He wants to get married and a have a baby right away. He's just looking for the right woman."

"*You're* the right woman for Willy?" she asked.

"Who's the right person for *anyone*? The divorce rate is fifty percent, Liz. That means half of all couples think they're marrying the right person and it doesn't mean *jack*."

She shook her head. "But the point is that they start out marrying someone they *love*—"

"I can love a *life*," I said. "I can love not sitting home on Valentine's Day or New Year's. I can love that I never have to hear my relatives tell me how bad they feel that I'm all alone, that 'my day will come, especially if I lose a few pounds and straighten my hair.' I can love that my mother will stop sending clippings for singles dances. I can love that I don't have to feel like no one *chose* me. I can love that I'll be *engaged*, *married.* That the option of having a baby isn't suddenly wrested away from me because I couldn't find the guy."

I was too close to tears and I shut the hell up fast. Besides, we'd found Samantha's house. We stood in front of a huge pale yellow Colonial with flowers blooming everywhere.

She squeezed my hand. "Charl, I understand, okay? I'm thirty-four! Right behind you, sister. Look, I know you're just dating Willy to rule him out. I do that kind of thing all the time when my mom or sisters set me up on blind dates with guys I know I'd never be interested in." She smiled. "Look at us—arguing over Willy Collins! You're just dating the guy, for God's sake. It's not like you're going to *marry* him."

Oh no? Just watch me, I thought as Samantha, having to turn sideways to make room for us and her belly, welcomed us inside.

IT WAS FUNNY (strange, not ha-ha) how the sight of the ring moved me more than the proposal. It was a round solitaire, six prongs. And it sparkled. It sparkled and shined and I started to cry.

"I know," Willy said, the buggy eyes misting. "I made you the happiest woman on the earth."

In a way, yes, I thought. I had a ring. A suitable man got down on one knee, asked me to marry him, and held out a sparkling diamond ring in a lovely velvet-lined box. A man who would be an attentive, if superannoying husband. He would be an attentive and doting father, of that I was sure. All I had to do was say *yes* and I would be *engaged.*

Pro: Husband. Baby.

Con: Nebbishy nudnick.

The *pros* had it.

"You have, indeed, made me the happiest woman on earth," I told Willy. "My answer is yes. Yes, yes, yes!"

He smiled and hugged me and slid the ring on my finger. We admired it for a moment, and then he said, "It's *platinum,* not white gold. Just in case anyone asks."

THE NEXT MORNING, a warm and sunny Saturday, I headed to Elizabeth's apartment. She always slept in, so I knew she'd be there. I'd seen little of her during the past two months. When I'd stop by her office for lunch, she'd claim she had too much work to do. When I'd ask about weekend plans, she'd say she was visiting her mother (yeah, right) in New Jersey.

When I asked if she wanted to go for drinks after work or see a movie or do anything involving me, she offered tight smiles and excuse after excuse. So I stopped asking.

At her building, I rang the buzzer to apartment 4B. A sleepy "Yes?" crackled through the intercom.

"Elizabeth, it's me, Charlotte."

Silence. And then *buzzzz*.

I climbed up the stairs, the ring sparkling on my hand on the banister. Elizabeth stood in her doorway, wearing an oversized Pushkin Publishing t-shirt from our last sales conference.

"I brought coffee and bagels and lox," I said, holding up the bag. "And two Krispy Kremes."

Her sharp eyes zoomed to my ring.

"He proposed last night," I said. "We're engaged!"

She stared at me. She stared at me and didn't say anything. Not a word. Not a fake *I'm happy for you*. Not a *good for you! I know how badly you want this!* Nothing.

We sat down in silence and opened our coffees and bit into our bagels, which tasted like wood chips.

"Do you know what Willy told me on our first date?" I said, my first bite of the world's best doughnuts turning to sludge in my stomach. "That he wants a baby. What man says that?"

Why am I defending myself to you? Why can't you just be my friend?

"But do you *like* him?" she asked, staring me down. Taunting me.

Judgmental bitch! "He has a great nose."

"Charlotte..."

I pursed my lips. I hated when I did that. "Elizabeth, Willy Collins might not be the best-looking guy or the most interesting and yeah, he has to work on those social skills, but he's making possible something that I want more than anything in the world. Why can't you understand that?"

She let out a deep breath. "Because marrying someone you don't love is *wrong*. I know you're not a romantic, Charlotte. I know you take pride in being practical. But what you're doing isn't practical." She twisted up her face as though she had to spit. "It's—" She dropped her bagel on the coffee table, shook her head and leaned back, her face flushed.

"It's *what*?" I asked, my voice cold, my breath held. *Go ahead and say it, Elizabeth-the-perfect.*

She didn't say anything.

"All that's required of you, Elizabeth, is to be happy for me."

"If you'll be happy, I'll be happy," she said.

I rolled my eyes. "But you don't think I can be happy with Willy."

"How could you be?" she snapped. "You don't even like him!"

"Well, I'm marrying him, so I must like him."

She burst into tears.

"I don't need a maid of honor anyway," I said, reaching for my jacket.

She grabbed my hand. "Charlotte, of course I'll be your maid of honor. I'm just *shocked*. Two months ago you didn't even like Willy. You couldn't stand him. You'd cringe at the sound of his voice! Then you go out with him, what—ten times, and you're engaged? You're going to spend the rest of your life with him?"

"The heart knows what it wants, Liz."

She gnawed her lower lip. "It's just that *I* want something else. Something special. Something magical. Something wonderful. And I want something else for you."

"But you're *not* me, are you?"

There was nothing left to say.

"EIGHT POUNDS, TWO OUNCES!" I announced when Elizabeth appeared in the doorway of my hospital room. Baby Ben, who looked exactly like me, except he had Willy's nose, was napping in my arms as I lay back in my bed, surrounded by flowers, *It's A Boy!* balloons and box after box from Baby Gap.

"He's so beautiful," she whispered, sitting down on the edge of the bed and caressing the baby's impossibly tiny knit cap. "Oh, Charlotte."

For a few moments, we ogled the baby and smiled. My heart was bursting and my hormones were raging and I was beyond exhausted, but the sight of Elizabeth almost made me cry. I'd rarely seen her in the past nine months. Several weeks after he proposed, Willy and I had eloped to Las Vegas since we didn't want to spend a fortune on a wedding and Willy was worried that every passing day aged my eggs even more. When Elizabeth received the wedding announcement, she'd stopped by the apartment with a bowl from Tiffany's. She asked if I was happy, but she didn't mean it; she didn't need an answer. I knew it and she knew it and that was the end of our friendship. Working together wasn't an issue; I'd had such awful morning sickness—and something of a broken heart—that I'd made a deal with my boss to work from home until my maternity leave. I was surprised that Elizabeth had come to my baby shower; she'd dressed up and brought an expensive gift (the Maclaren stroller I'd registered for), but kept to herself and left right after gifts were opened.

She was still the first person, aside from immediate family, that I called when I woke up in the recovery room, a mother. And she was the first non-family member to visit.

"Do you still think I compromised myself?" I whispered as I stroked Ben's cheek. "If I have everything I've ever wanted, did I still compromise myself?"

"You know what I think, Charlotte? I think you compromised. But I don't think you compromised *yourself*. There's a big difference."

It was a peace offering. And it was enough. It was never Elizabeth's validation that I needed or wanted; it was her *friendship*.

"I've missed you so much," she said, tears pooling in her eyes.

"Me too," I said, squeezing her hand.

We laughed like idiots, tears rolling down our cheeks, and then even Ben joined in the cry party. I rocked him in my arm and kissed his pale forehead. Magic. He stopped crying and closed his eyes.

"You'll never guess who I've been dating," Elizabeth said, her eyes twinkling. "Fitz Darcy."

"Fitz Darcy? The hot V.P. of New Business Development? I thought you said he was an arrogant jerk."

She burst into a smile, and I knew she was nuts for the guy. "He's not as bad as I first thought."

I grinned. "A lot of people are like that. And even the ones who *are* aren't as bad as they seem."

We squeezed hands again, the only way to hug when you had a baby in your arms. And then she told me all about her and Fitz Darcy. When Willy burst into the room, blathering on about the baby's feeding and napping schedule, which he was keeping track of in a little spiral notebook, she clammed up about Fitz, put on her jacket and said she had to get going. But when Willy invited Elizabeth to stick around the tiny hospital room and then launched into an explanation and step-by-step demonstration of proper swaddling techniques, she smiled at me and took off her coat.

Melissa Senate is the author of three bestselling chick-lit novels: *See Jane Date* (which was made into a TV movie for ABC Family), *The Solomon Sisters Wise Up* (which took her on a whirlwind three-city book tour of Italy); and *Whose Wedding Is It Anyway?* (chosen by *Marie Claire* magazine as a Top Ten must-read pick). Melissa has two books coming out in 2006: *The Breakup Club* (January), and her debut chick-lit novel for teens, *Theodora Twist* (May). Melissa lives on the southern coast of Maine with her husband and young son. Visit her Web site at www.melissasenate.com.

The Secret Life of Mary

Jill Winters

If there was ever a wet noodle of a sister, it's Mary: pedantic, uninspired and universally acknowledged to be the Bennet most likely to make somebody change his seat when she sits down beside him. Well, Jill Winters begs to differ. If you only knew, she says, what Mary was up to in the white space on those pages....

Absence Is the Thing

LET'S START WITH THE UNDERSTANDING that Mrs. Bennet has *five* daughters—not four—despite the amorphous existence of her third, Mary, throughout most of the book. While Jane Austen's *Pride and Prejudice* is not, nor is it intended to be, Mary Bennet's story, it nevertheless bears questioning as to why it is so much more the story of everyone *else*.

Throughout the novel I was struck by how infrequent a role Mary plays; distinctly underdeveloped, she drifts in and out of the narrative, inserting bits of rhetoric into the dynamic conversations of other characters, rather than engaging in real dialogue herself. Her appearances are sporadic; her choices are of little consequence. In light of this, Mary's function in the family is difficult to find. Austen frames her as the Socially Awkward Studious Daughter, but without developing her beyond the barely there, one-note caricature, the rendering never fully gels.

Rather, Mary becomes an enigma. What she lacks in characterization she makes up for in mystique. In fact, the more I read about the active, ever-changing lives of her sisters, the more I had to wonder: what makes them so special?

Or rather: what is Mary missing?

First let's look at the two eldest, Jane and Elizabeth. Beauty is a constant variable in both of their lives. Austen informs the reader repeatedly that Jane is beautiful—the "most handsome" of Mrs. Bennet's daughters—and suitor Bingley proclaims with certainty, "she is the most beautiful creature I ever beheld!"

Elizabeth is apparently a close second—"very pretty," according to Bingley—and her blatant attractiveness only serves to make Darcy's snubbing of her that much more appalling. Of course, it doesn't take long for Darcy to become enamored of Elizabeth's charm and beauty.

Just as we learn of Jane and Elizabeth's appeal, we discover Mary's lack of it. No one admires her looks or even seems to notice them. In fact, Austen blatantly declares her as "the only plain one in the family," which made me wonder: did *this* account for Mary's absence throughout most of the book? Did her bland austerity procure her near-invisibility?

The oversimplification of that theory becomes apparent, though, when we look at Mary's teenage sisters, Lydia and Catherine. While surely there is a sense of cuteness about them—with Lydia's exuberance and Catherine's too-cute nickname "Kitty"—they are rarely described in terms of appearance. Lydia is called "good-humored" and "tall," but never beautiful.

What Austen does describe at some length, however, is the girls' shallow nature—their silliness and their "vacant minds." According to Mr. Bennet, Lydia and Kitty are possibly "the silliest girls in the country." Meanwhile they are thoroughly validated by Mrs. Bennet, who is perhaps the most vapid, inane character in the book.

So, Lydia and Kitty lack not only their older sisters' striking looks, but also their substance. They lack Jane's benevolence and purity of heart. They lack Elizabeth's intelligence and articulation. Yet, somehow they are more interesting to Austen than Mary. Lydia and Kitty take precedence over Mary as on-the-page characters whose whims and movements impact the course of the novel. While Mary may not be particularly attractive or energetic, for a girl who reads constantly, forms opinions, and has a strong sense of morality, she comes off as oddly one-dimensional. Given her studious, reflective nature, she has to be at least somewhat substantive—yet we barely get to see her, and we never get to know her.

So let's look at what we *do* know—at the few traits that Austen allows us to glimpse. Mary is bookish. She's serious, solemn. To say she lectures would afford her too much space in the text—she makes statements, she has ruminations, she gives bits of wisdom, which are always simply brushed over, having no effect on her family members. In fact, when I break her down like this, I am struck by the similarities between her and Mr. Bennet's self-important cousin, Collins—who is not only a more central character to the story, but to the Bennet family itself!

Most of what we know about Mary and Collins does not actually come from the other characters; it comes from Austen's omniscient narrator, whom, for the sake of simplicity, let's identify as Austen herself. Austen assesses each as though her motivations can be assumed as empirical fact. She tells us flat-out, "Mary had neither genius nor taste; and though vanity had given her application, it had given her likewise a pedantic air and a conceited manner."

Regarding Collins, Austen assigns him "the self-conceit of a weak head"—declaring that he was educated by an illiterate father and compensates for it by putting on social airs.

Just as Mary is prone to "deep" study and reflection, Collins is prone to "meditating in solitude." Just as Mary is a bookworm, Collins spends way too much time in Mr. Bennet's library. And just as Mary takes herself quite seriously, so does Collins, and both are definitely alone in doing so.

So this made me think: why then is Collins—in light of such blatant similarity to Mary—given a more prominent place in a story largely about the Bennet sisters, than one of the sisters herself? The answer becomes clear only when we step back and look at the story as a whole, and we see the overarching context that frames the entire narrative.

Hooking a husband. All of the principal characters in *Pride and Prejudice* operate within the realm of this context except for Mary—and therein lies the crux of her dilemma. Simply put: unless she's there to hook a husband, she's barely there at all.

With no interest in suitors or courtship, Mary positions herself totally outside the one theme that truly drives the book: the quest for marriage. Jane is anxious to land Bingley, Mrs. Bennet is anxious for Jane *to* land Bingley, Elizabeth is determined to marry for love, Charlotte Lucas is determined to marry *period*, and Lydia and Kitty are both boy-crazy—and all of this works very well, thematically. The men play their roles, too. Bingley courts and eventually marries Jane, Darcy, who's all but engaged to Lady Catherine's daughter, ends up proposing to Elizabeth not once, but twice. Wickham, who'd first attempted to elope with Darcy's sister, ultimately elopes with Lydia. And finally, Collins, who is determined from the outset of the novel to marry, proposes first to Elizabeth and then, successfully, to Charlotte.

If the "business of [Mrs. Bennet's] life was to get her daughters married," Mary really has no prayer. With shrill proclamations and matrimonial schemes, Mrs. Bennet tends to overpower the family, determining, at the very least, the superficial roles the girls and Mr. Bennet play. To say, then, that Mary's role is minimal is almost misleading—rather, it is minimal*ized*, its irrelevance actively reinforced by everyone moving in one way or another toward the business of getting married, and Mary having little place.

A perfect example: at the beginning of the novel, when Mr. and Mrs. Bennet speculate as to which daughter Bingley might like, they discuss Jane, Elizabeth, and Lydia, but never even mention Mary. When Mrs. Bennet considers who Collins will marry, she debates between Elizabeth and Lydia, skipping right over Mary again—even though Mary is older than Lydia and therefore more marriageable. Collins does this himself; after abandoning the notion of marrying Jane, he shifts his attention to Elizabeth. After she rejects him, he proposes to Charlotte Lucas, rather than following the natural progression in selection from the Bennet household: Mary. Clearly, she is so outside the realm of the theme of marriage that she is not even a factor.

This goes far to explain why Mary's "displays" at a few of the parties—her singing and her piano playing—are rendered so tedious and almost burdensome by our omniscient narrator, Austen. Since Mary's performances have no intrinsic designs to catch male attention or attract a suitor, they're interpreted as nuisances to the plot and its players. Austen writes: "Elizabeth, easy and unaffected, had been listened to with much more pleasure, though not playing half so well." So even though Mary's performance is better, it seems to clutter up everyone else's fine time—simply because, in and of itself, it is without purpose.

And this brings up an important point: generally speaking, Elizabeth is not the least bit "easy and unaffected" as a character. Yet, if Austen states it as absolute fact, we as the reader, simply accept it. I think this is a critical mistake. *Behavior* is what defines a character, not the blanket dictations of the presumably omniscient narrator. Therefore we simply cannot trust without fail the assertions Austen makes throughout the text. And when it comes to Mary, specifically, we simply do not observe enough of her behavior to make a firm, certain judgment as to what motivates her, and who she really is.

The following conversation between Lydia and Mary—in which Mary is promptly ignored, as usual—reveals a bit more.

"Oh! Mary," said she, "I wish you had gone with us, for we had such fun!...We talked and laughed so loud that anybody might have heard us ten miles off!"

To this, Mary very gravely replied, "Far be it from me, my dear sister, to depreciate such pleasures. They would doubtless be congenial with the generality of female minds. But I confess they would have no charms for *me*. I should infinitely prefer a book."

But of this answer Lydia heard not a word.

This is a key exchange because it reveals that with Mary, it's not just a matter of being a stick-in-the-mud; it's a matter of not fitting in with the traditional female preoccupations, hooking a husband being the most important one.

Because of this, Mary's ability to move through the text is decidedly stilted. But Mr. Collins becomes a sort of substitute for her throughout the novel. He shares many of the quirks that Austen has ascribed to Mary, but because he fits well into the major driving theme of the story—the quest for marriage—he has a place on the page. He belongs. And interestingly, you can see the distinct trade-off between him and Mary. They never interact with each other, yet the two are very closely drawn.

At one of the balls at Netherfield, Mary mortifies Elizabeth with her off-key singing. Immediately following her performance, Collins jumps onto the page with a long, tedious "speech" about the importance of music and its role in a clergyman's life. Mr. Bennet is amused yet again by Collins, because as always, his cousin proves to be an absurd fool; this is, of course, right on the heels of Mary making a fool of herself, as well.

As soon as Collins comes into the story, in some ways, he assumes Mary's position as the self-conscious, pretentious buffoon. Because his traits so closely match hers, Collins can act as a surrogate for Mary while she is largely absent. A particularly symbolic example happens early on, and really sets up Collins' unique place in this story: "Lydia's intention of walking to Meryton was not forgotten; every sister except Mary agreed to go with her; and Mr. Collins was to attend them...." Here, Collins takes Mary's place in the family both literally and figuratively. And the more that Collins is on the page, the more his behavior *confirms* his character, as Austen has laid it out for us. The more we know of him, the more we feel certain of who he is.

And the less we see of Mary, the more we're forced to ask ourselves: where is she and what is she doing?

This is the genius of Mary's absence. Austen might tell us about Mary, but she never fully convinces the reader that Mary is truly as simple as all that. Set apart from *Pride and Prejudice*'s driving theme, Mary exists in a parallel space, outside the text. I argue that outside the rigid confines of the novel, Mary had her own life. A secret life.

Perhaps if Austen had lived longer she eventually would have written Mary's story. But in the absence of that, here's what I propose: Mary's sporadic appearances in *Pride and Prejudice* are like points on a map. The nature of her life in between those points is limitless, undefined. And the following is just one possibility.

Mary's Secret Life
(falling in love & other adventures)

*All text taken from *Pride and Prejudice* is in bold type.

It is a truth universally acknowledged, that a single man in possession of a good fortune must be in want of a wife. It was something Mary's mother proclaimed often—though not as succinctly, and with her own strident brand of ineloquence, but still—Mary couldn't help pondering the inverse of such a notion: a single woman in *no* possession of a fortune must be want of a husband.

If only it were that simple. The fact was that if she couldn't marry Rory O'Callan, Sir William Lucas' Irish footman, then marriage simply would not do.

Their affair had started innocently enough eight months ago, first with lingering looks, then with brief, evocative exchanges, whenever Mary had gone with her sisters to visit the Lucas estate. Eventually she and Rory made clandestine plans to meet in the wood, halfway between Longbourn and Meryton. Truly, Mary had never done anything so scandalous! But she'd been drawn inexorably to this brawny, dark-haired man, even though he was a servant and therefore quite unsuitable. She simply couldn't stay away from his warm, crooked smile, his quiet but flattering way, his sweet manner and gentle touch....

"What say you, Mary?" The sound of her father's voice jarred her out of her reverie, and she shifted in her chair, realizing that she had no idea what her parents had been talking about. Mr. Bennet continued, "For you are a young lady of deep reflection, and read great books, and make extracts."

Mary wished to say something sensible, but knew not how. "Uh..." she floundered guiltily, as warmth filled her cheeks. Surely her parents suspected something was amiss. But neither looked in her direction for more than a moment. Quietly, Mary exhaled a sigh of relief.

Two weeks later was a dreaded ball that Mary had no interest in attending. She tried to feign a headache, but her mother was unmoved. Quite predictably, the night unfolded with all the excitement of a wet noodle. When Charlotte Lucas came to visit the Bennets the next morning, the tedium of the past night's events lingered on. Endless prattle about how Jane danced twice with Bingley, and how Bingley's friend, Darcy, snubbed Elizabeth—whose assured opinion of herself was always on display. Though Mary loved her sister, she often wondered if anyone else tired of Lizzy's sharp tongue and haughty arrogance. In any event, no one seemed able to fathom how Darcy could have possibly snubbed Lizzy. It was all Mary could do not to roll her eyes and shriek, *Get over it already, you whiny baby!*

"What say you, Mary, about this?" Charlotte Lucas asked now. "You look deep in thought over the matter of Darcy's vanity."

Mary just shrugged and said, "In general, I suppose it's always a question of vanity or pride. **Pride...is a very common failing I believe. By all that I have ever read, I am convinced that it is very common indeed, that human nature is particularly prone to it, and that there are very few of us who do not cherish a feeling of self-complacency on the score of some quality or other, real or imaginary. Vanity and pride are different things, though the words are often used synonymously.**" She thought of Rory—how he was too proud to let her teach him how to read, but would listen kindly to her essays. Still, thinking of Rory, she continued, "**A person may be proud without being vain. Pride relates more to our opinion of ourselves, vanity to what we would have others think of us.**" Then she thought of her mother, who always seemed wholly vain and for little reason.

A few weeks later, with Jane and Elizabeth at Netherfield imposing on the Bingleys' hospitality, Mr. Bennet tucked in his library and Mrs. Bennet snoring loudly in her bed, Mary escaped through the back door. She met Rory at the small shed he'd built for them in the woods. Once they were nestled in, beside the kerosene lamp and atop the thick horse blankets, Mary told him all about the latest doings at Longbourn—about her mother's scheme to get Jane sick so she'd have to stay at Bingley's, and how Mrs. Bennet probably hoped that Bingley would offer a swift pity proposal, in between Jane's bouts of retching and nose-blowing.

Rory chuckled softly and stroked her cheek lightly with his fingertips. "You should be writing down these stories you tell," he said.

"Really?" Mary said, surprised by the idea. Normally her writing was restricted to serious themes of morality and social issues.

"These tales of your family," Rory continued, his gruff voice as always like a low rumble; sometimes it sent shivers rolling across her skin. "Your silly mother and how she preens your sisters. Your stories always give me great pause to laugh."

"Do they?" Mary said, smiling and snuggling closer.

"Aye," Rory said, "I enjoy them—even more than your essays. Of course, both entertain in good measure...."

Soon after, Mary had to return home, but she took Rory's words with her.

It was late, but she didn't dare come in through the back door just in case her father was still up and about. Instead, she climbed up the trellis on the side of the house, carefully pulled open the window, and landed on the frayed hallway rug with a *thud*. Just as she scurried to the bedroom she shared with Lizzy, she heard voices. One was Jane's... the other was Lizzy's. They'd finally returned from Netherfield!

Quickly, Mary slipped off her shoes, hopped into the desk chair, and threw open a book, just as her sisters entered—and they **found Mary, as usual, deep in the study of thorough bass and human nature**. They didn't suspect a thing.

Another week passed, and Mary took Rory's advice: she focused her writing efforts on the amusing doings of those around her. There was another party at Netherfield, the details of which she captured as deftly she could in her journal, details such as Mrs. Bennet squealing like a pig in the presence of any decent single man, and thereby ruining the family's chance for maintaining even a scrap of dignity at the affair. Or Mary taking her turn at singing and watching Lizzy blatantly cringe with embarrassment—undoubtedly thinking her sister's **voice was weak, and her manner affected**. (With cynical amusement, Mary noted that for all of Lizzy's talk about not caring if others found favor with her—Mr. Darcy in particular—she obviously cared quite a bit!)

And so it went. Weeks passed, and Mary recorded her impressions about the antics at home, including Collins' proposal to Lizzy. She read Rory her journal entries whenever they had chance to meet, and his interest and laughter always gave her great encouragement.

"Oh, and did I mention that Jane still hasn't heard from Bingley?" Mary said one night, as she set her journal down in her lap.

"Aye?" Rory said, furrowing his thick, dark brows. "Hmm..."

Mary added, "It's been weeks. We are all sure of his affection for her, but it's strange that he hasn't sent any letters to her yet. There must be good reason, of course."

"*Níl sé ró-mhór leí, sin an méid*," he murmured, and Mary looked quizzically at him. "It's an old Gaelic expression," he explained. "Roughly it means: he's just not that into her."

Nodding, Mary made a note of this in her journal.

With no greater events than these in the Longbourn family...did January and February pass away. And March, too. Unbeknownst to the rest of the Bennets, though, Mary's life took an exciting turn. It was at a social lunch in late April. She'd noticed a woman there who seemed troubled by something, but trying to conceal it. Mary wanted to make sure she was not in distress or any kind of peril, so she spoke to her apart from the other women at the lunch—one of whom was her mother, busy boring everyone to tears with her pointless blather.

This woman, Emilia, confided to Mary that her sister was ailing. Mary comforted her for a while, and as Emilia spoke more of her family, she mentioned that her brother was the editor of *The Weekly Gazette*. Mary's heart sped up. Sheepishly, she confessed her love for writing. Emilia, already moved by Mary's consideration, offered to show her works to her brother to see what, if any, publishing merit they might have. Overwhelmed, Mary told Rory the news that night, and he encouraged her to submit her humorous family pieces along with her serious musings, just in case.

And the wait began. May, June and July passed with no word from Emilia or her brother. By the beginning of August, Mary had all but given up on anything coming of her literary submissions. Meanwhile, Lydia's scandalous elopement with Wickham was quite a preoccupation—and not just for Mr. and Mrs. Bennet, but for Mary, too.

One evening, while everyone sat in the dining room discussing it, Mary remarked to Lizzy, **"Unhappy as the event must be for Lydia, we may draw from it this useful lesson: that loss of virtue in a female is irretrievable—that one false step involves her in endless ruin—that her reputation is no less brittle than it is beautfiul—and that she cannot be too much guarded in her behaviour towards the undeserving of the other sex."**

Instantly, Mary heard the hypocrisy in her own words. What rubbish! The truth was that ever since Lydia had disgraced the family, all Mary could think about was doing the same thing herself. What better time to elope with Rory than now, when a stir had already been created?

Elated at the notion, Mary set about making plans to run off herself, when something suddenly stopped her. It was a letter from Emilia's brother! He'd finally read her writing samples, and while most were unsuitable for his paper he'd apparently found her lighthearted pieces about a woman named "Mrs. Bettick" and her five daughters most delightful. He'd gone on to offer Mary the chance to write a serialized story about the "Betticks" and their daily misadventures.

Overwhelmed by excitement, Mary resolved to devote the next several months to this endeavor.

But with the success of her anonymous serial story, a few months turned into sixteen. By that time, **Mary was the only daughter who** remained at home; and she was necessarily drawn from the pursuit of accomplishments by Mrs. Bennet's being quite unable to sit alone. It was just as well, of course, because the more time she spent with her mother, the more material she had for her most popular character, "Mrs. Bettick."

It was only a matter of time before she had everything she wanted. She'd been stowing away her earnings from the *Gazette*, knowing that she and Rory would elope at the end of that winter. Their love seemed to grow stronger and more urgent with each meeting; he'd even let her teach him to read so that he would be able to read her stories on his own.

When Mary thought about the future, her enthusiasm was barely disguised by her poised, reserved countenance. An Irish footman and a female columnist—a writing career and a life of her own—Mary could hardly wait.

Jill Winters realized that she preferred fiction to term papers when she wrote her first novel, *Plum Girl*, instead of her Master's dissertation. Coincidentally, this was around the same time she discovered that sleeping was optional and coffee was not. A Phi Beta Kappa, summa cum laude graduate of Boston College with a degree in history, Jill has taught Women's Studies and is the author of four humorous novels: *Just Peachy*, *Raspberry Crush*, *Blushing Pink* and *Plum Girl*, which was a finalist for the Dorothy Parker Award of Excellence. Her fifth book, *Lime Ricky*, will be released in May.

Lord Byron and Miss A

CHERYL SAWYER

There are those scholars who are fond of pointing out that Jane Austen wrote at the dining room table, smiling indulgently as her nieces and nephews milled about, never having a thought that wasn't pure and good. Oh, please, people, have you read the woman's letters? Cheryl Sawyer obviously has; her excerpts from Byron's letters make it clear that whatever else Our Jane was, she wasn't milk toast. In fact, Byron might argue she was vinegar and bread.

Matcham, near Sittingbourne, Kent
Friday 12 July 1811

MY DEAR DAMNABLE OFFICIOUS HOBHOUSE—you have recommended worse things to me than staying with these friends of yours but none more threatening of tedium—what did you mean by it? Is flight from London so imperative that I must put up with a leg-of-beef-eater, his vegetative wife, and three daughters as fibrous as so many string beans? I arrived late, begged off supper, spoke two words to the Matchams (who are welcoming, I grant you) and repaired upstairs to write this—my head seethes with venom. Heaven spare you tomorrow if the *other* guests resemble the plain Jane I glimpsed, fixing me with the cursedest Dragon stare ever wielded by maidenhood. Byron.

Saturday 13th

Hobby, you are forgiven and forgot. Only an Angel could earn you this mercy, an Angel who may vouchsafe...but more hereafter. The day began abominably. I was up early for me (eleven) but late enough to hope for solitude at breakfast. Not so. I entered upon the same Dragon of last night, alone and a-contemplating of...not her fricassee, but a sheet of paper covered in writing. This she at once hid with sinister composure beneath her table napkin. Another damned female diarist!

My animadversions of last night were half-unjust, for she is not plain—indeed, the figure is light and the face pleasing—except that the eyes, being of a clear, accusatory hazel, still darted fire.

I said nothing, helped myself to a slice of bread (to which I would fain have added vinegar) and waited for her to leave, with a species of glower that might more deservedly claim the term *poetical* than any I have summoned. My eyebrows snapped into dark contiguity and I would have done the same with my *eyes* in order not to see an iota of the demoiselle, who sat on, with a silent censoriousness that pervaded the room.

Then an Angel walked in and we had a visitation, with an "O" of surprise, a settling at the table like a bird coming to its perch (complete with a mere crumb on the breakfast plate)—and a glance from heaven, blue as the Greek firmament. Whereupon, as casually as you please (and it did not displease *me*) she placed on the cloth a copy of *Childe Harold*! There I admit my quivering disarray might have turned to mirth had not the Dragon darted me a malicious spark from each of her glittering eyes. Whereupon I commanded my face to dignity, subdued other parts of my anatomy as best I could, and began a promising dialogue with the angelic one, which will no doubt feature in the other's journal, as "Lord B flirted outrageously with Mrs. C over the coddled eggs." I said little, however, leaving the delicious nub of the thing to Mrs. C. Yes, she is married, and if I am discreet with her name it is for the very good reason that I shortly mean to be *indiscreet* with her person. She is delectable and the husband absent—in fact her manners suggest he must be at least as far off as Terra Australis. I suppress the name of Miss A because I have already calumniated her enough and she had the grace to leave us alone at table. In a few days she will be back watering her kitchen garden in Hampshire—Mrs. C let fall that the father was a country parson—and hereafter she may thank me for many scandalous additions to her diary. Yours as ever, B.

Sunday, before the lark—or rather after it

Dear H,

Awake in every nerve, I shall not sleep for an hour, so permit me to amuse myself with some light diarising. Yesterday afternoon began tolerably and the other guests were not over-stupid, but Mrs. C having changed into something even more diaphanous than her morning gown, I found her Partialities more markedly on show than suited your worthy friends, so to preserve their countenances—and mine—went riding for hours about the country. It is in the main low, rolling pasture but with some handsome stands of trees which in this season are as rich in leaf as—but damn description, it is always disgusting. While cantering cheerfully down a green avenue I came upon Miss A, quite solitary and obviously wishing to remain so. There was a moment when we might have passed each other by, but courtesy prevailed—at least on my side—and we exchanged greetings. I said: "I would never have thought you rambled, Miss A" (we were full two miles from Matcham).

In like tone she replied: "I'm astonished you should even try to take my character, my lord. We have not said a word to each other until this moment."

"True," I said with a laugh, and some surprise, "so may I hope you are as cautious in taking *mine*?"

She smiled—and I would admit it a lovely smile, and the eyes alive with wit, if her riposte had been further from the mark. "Your work itself raises speculation, my lord. Indeed, don't you rather intend it to? You are so generous with your emotions in your poems, that no thinking reader can avoid being intrigued about your mind." *Or my habits*, she might have concluded, though delicacy closed this interrogatory.

A thinking reader. It intrigues me to think her so.

Supper was agreeable but after that they danced. What do country folk intend by ripping up the carpet and all one's expectations of company in one blessed fandango of an impulse? Miss A, dashing my good opinion of her intellect, consented to accompany, and Mrs. C, coaxed by her hosts, refused not the invitation to display. They danced like dervishes, I sulked like the devil and retreated onto the terrace, to a contemplation of Nature none too tolerant considering the unathletic equipment She was pleased to bestow on me at birth.

Then the lithe Miss A, having deserted the pianoforte and danced until she was blue—her stockings therefore being of another colour than I had suspected—rambled out unawares onto the terrace and startled me and herself. I was in no mood to speak, but at that moment she happened to glance up into the summer sky. "Look!" she said with the purest ravishment. "Aldebaran!" I turned to seek the star at once. We stood transfixed, and everything around us crystallized, as though I were subsumed into the universe, all my being concentrated in a single ecstatic instant. I felt positively Hindoo.

Then she seemed to come back to herself, and fixed me with a clear gaze and said, "Excuse me." No more—but there was a look that gave me the sole moment of ease I have felt at Matcham. There was no sympathy, or I should have turned from her in disdain. No—if I am not mistaken, it was a look of friendship. There was a moment of silent communion, then a subtle change in her posture, as though she might have stepped nearer—but she bade me a quick goodnight and quitted the terrace.

Mrs. C spent an hour or two in my chamber this night. It being your friends' home, before her arrival I confess to feeling wretchedly, ridiculously, fine-ladically *nervous*, but I have no complaints in the event. And having confessed all, I have my quietus. May your dreams be as natural as mine—though I leave you free as to the object! Byron.

Sunday evening

And now sermons and soda water. I am censured.

Mrs. C—who should be Mrs. H for Hypocrite—attended church this morning and Miss A, pleading a headache, did not. I came upon her without warning in the library as she was leafing through Thomson—dost call *that* any cure for the megrim?—and either the state of her cranium or the state of my morals—how does she guess?—caused her to give me a look fit to sear the heart, liver and entrails in one blast. Then she was gone.

What think you, Hobhouse, is it too late for me to betake myself to politics and decorum?

We dined in Gargantuan manner and then muddled about until I was so fed to the teeth I went riding again—brooding—what else does one do on the sabbath?—and returned to a somnolent household where the only conversable creature turned out to be your friend Matcham. Beefeater he may be, but he improves on acquaintance. Upon my idly mentioning Miss A he tells me she scribbles. And she's no diarist, by G—, but a three-volume novelist…though not, of course, published—yet. The devil! the devil! the devil!

After supper we played music, cards—and Mrs C and I sleight of hand—then in a respite from the last I gave my best impression of gliding to the library, where Miss A in her haste had left her loose-leaf diary that morning. In perhaps half an hour I sped through a swathe of pages: it is no journal but a sentimental novel!—dominated by a lofty timberhead of a character distinguished by a Plutonic scowl whom I perforce name Mr. D.

Then she entered behind me and shocked me so much I had an access of the *staggers* such as I've never suffered before. She relented a fraction, we sat opposite each other at the library table, uninterrupted—another wonder of this wondrous evening—and she would have me know in trenchant terms that the character I had discovered was a pure invention, of long date, and she was not going to ditch him just because I had found him out.

She fixed me intensely. "I have been working on this for years. It began as epistolary novel."

"Heaven help you," I said. "You'll never manage anything rational with letters."

"Samuel Richardson employed them."

"My point precisely."

She laughed—an instant, sunny transformation of the whole being—then said, "Well, it is called *First Impressions*."

"And? Is it your first novel, your tenth, your hundredth?"—She is

175

thirty-five if a day, and I've heard of women who can toss out one a fortnight.

"My first attempt. Another . . . that is, my first to be published . . . is . . . on the presses at the moment." She blushed more fiercely than she would have if I had caught her—or she me—*in flagrante delicto*! "It is named *Sense and Sensibility*. There is another called *Susan*, but the publisher seems to have lost it. One of my brothers is encouraging him to look for it." And she gazed at me with cheeks still aflame.

Ill-used by a pestilential publisher!—she could not have kindled my fellow feelings in a warmer manner. We talked.

She confessed to having read me, but there were no *blushes* at that! No, she takes me seriously—and being informed *I* do nothing of the sort will not deter her. She shows a very commendable admiration of Scott's poetry—on which count I am inclined to forgive her veneration of Thomson's. I told her the only Thomson I ever spent any time with was a merchant on board ship—no lie, Hobhouse, as you know—on the way to Sardinia, who joined me in pistol practice, firing at bottles lined up on deck. "Indeed an apt verse from your Idol sprang to my mind at once, Miss A: *Delightful task! To rear the tender thought—To teach the young idea how to shoot!*"

There was a dreadful pause at this—followed by what I can only call a Fit of the Giggles. Then we were decently launched, for to my mind there's no place in heaven or hell for a soul that cannot laugh at Literature.

Our slender understanding about poetry gave us no basis for agreement on prose. I argued that Scott would excel in narrative—what is *The Lady of the Lake* but a novel in disguise?—and she praised his dramatic gifts but doubted his ability not to *sprawl* if given the fatal option of prose. "I am persuaded," she said, "that wit, for instance, is only to be reached with economy."

"Do you care more for wit than drama, Miss A?"

"Must one exclude the other?" Her bright gaze said, *You* will not tell me so!

"Never, in a poem. But I'm by no means sure that anyone can make us laugh in a novel, and still retain the sense of life in full, deep flow. Rousseau—"

She shook her dark head vehemently. "I do not aspire . . . you have hit on the very thing I am *not* trying to write. There is no likeness between myself and Rousseau—except one. The little circle of his characters is neither grand nor strange. The domestic, the familiar, is his canvas. And mine."

Whereupon I found out more than I shall tell you, because it is probably much more than she ever wished to convey. She is as private an individual as I ever met. However *generous with her emotions* in her books, she will not put her name on them, and I only give you the titles because I'm convinced that they will be different on publication.

I offered to help move the blighted publisher, and she refused. I told her to dedicate the first publication to the Prince Regent or some such hollow figurine, and she laughed. If my affairs were not in such a lackadaisical posture I would have offered to fund the new book myself, for truth to tell, my stolen perusal gave me the sense of a *spirit* in this unusual creature that may yet prove the fortune of the subscription libraries—and hers.

When we returned to the music room, Mrs. C was jealous and disposed to give us a demonstration of high London manners, intending to show Miss A up as a country dowd. It was impossible to think better of my Angel for this, and at the zenith of her raptures about sophisticated society I made a caustic remark about fops and poesy and prate that silenced her at last, just before Miss A with quiet dignity left the room.

I am almost persuaded I shall not be disappointed if a Visitation is denied me tonight. B.

Monday . . . damn the date, who cares for it in the country?

Oh! Sophonisba! Sophonisba! Oh!

Dear Hobhouse, she is going today, not back to the rectory but to Kentish relatives at a place called Godmersham. We had another talk on the terrace, this time in frank daylight. I had pondered during much of the night—unvisited by heavenly bodies, I may say—which I could swear Miss A *guesses*, being of subtle, prescient mind and disposed as I am to think lowly of mankind—and I told her I had been weighing up that great character, Mr. D. "I'm concerned," I began, "with his looming, and silence, and scorn. I'm afraid if you make him a Stygian figure, Miss A, you risk destroying his seduction. In fact there is nothing so mercilessly *unromantic* as gloom."

She looked at me nervously, and I perceived she was not at all afraid of *me*, but of taking *bad advice* over her book! She ventured, "My lord, even in the silent, there may be the attraction of deep feeling—"

"What notion is this? Look about you. Despair does not draw sympathy, Miss A, it repels. Sorrow does not attract friends, it banishes them. Make a melancholic out of your D, and not a reader on earth will stomach five minutes of his company."

She examined me, undaunted by the bitterness in my voice, and so curious to search beneath it that I turned my eyes away. Then she said with a tremor in her tone, "My lord, let me reassure you. D has no melancholy. He is simply a man who considers himself so far above others in rank and intellect that speaking is a punishment to him."

I glared at her and discovered what made her voice uneven—the sly minx!—it was amusement! For an instant wrath flashed through me, but you know how I love satire, and what a satirist this unexpected person proves to be!

"I wonder, Miss A, when we first encountered each other, which was the worse, my pride or your prejudice?"

She paused so long I thought her frighted at last, but she grew resolute: "It may be that we each possess a little of both."

I laughed. "So you will go your ways without my counsel?"

"It would be most ungrateful of me not to consider it. But I suspect the damage may already be done." (Damage!) "If you have influenced my work, my lord, it happened the moment I read it and went too deep to be reversed. Even by yourself."

I bowed ironically, she curtsied. Unfortunately we were interrupted (you may fathom by whom) and now . . . she has left.

I return to London forthwith and hope to see you this evening after you have received this letter and I have sloughed off all Rustication.

She will forget me, more rapidly perhaps than I shall forget her. And I cannot even claim the distinction of having got into her *diary*—for she swears she keeps none, and there is a categorical ring of truth in the woman's every word.

Yours until the hour of darkness—and ever—Byron.

[*A note from the editor of the first edition of these letters, 1856.* This small sheaf of documents, now lodged in the British Museum Library, was first revealed to the public when sold at auction by bookseller-publisher John Murray in 1829, five years after Lord Byron's death at the age of thirty-six. They are not in Byron's hand, and Murray believed them to be a transcript from originals by the poet that were lost or destroyed. Debate over their authenticity has continued ever since. That they are forgeries cannot be discounted, and there has even been some speculation that they were composed in a spirit of fun by the author of *Pride and Prejudice*. However, since the papers are not in Jane Austen's handwriting either, scholars remain in doubt as to their true origin.]

Cheryl Sawyer is an historical novelist, author of *La Créole* and *Rebel* (Bantam, Australia). Her U.S. début, published in Signet Eclipse (NAL) in January 2005, was *Siren*, the love story of real-life pirate Jean Lafitte and his passionate rival, privateer Léonore Roncival. *The Chase*, a novel of the Napoleonic Wars featuring a beautiful English noblewoman who falls in love with a renegade French soldier, followed in June 2005. Cheryl has two master's degrees with honors in English and French literature and her career has included teaching and publishing. Cheryl's home is Australia, but during work on her current novel she is based in Costa Rica. You can visit her Web site at www.cherylsawyer.com.

Jane in the Twenty-First Century

"Jane Austen is weirdly capable of keeping *everybody* busy. The moralists, the Eros-and-Agape people, the Marxists, the Freudians, the Jungians, the semioticians, the deconstructors—all find an adventure playground in six samey novels about middle-class provincials. And for every generation of critics, and readers, her fiction effortlessly renews itself."

MARTIN AMIS

Pride and Prejudice. With Cell Phones

MICHELLE CUNNAH

The dishing and dissembling in *Pride and Prejudice* make it nothing short of a miracle that anyone in the story ever manages to communicate at all. Michelle Cunnah theorizes that the problem wasn't just social, it was technical: No cell phones.

JANE AUSTEN HAS LONG BEEN a favorite of mine, and I've always had a particular fondness for Elizabeth Bennet because she was such an independent, intelligent, sassy woman of her time. I wanted to *be* her! (And marry Mr. Darcy!)

With that in mind, I think that Goddess Jane would forgive me for taking such liberties as to rewrite Elizabeth's proposal scenes in parody style—it is done with much affection, and much borrowing of Goddess Jane's own words. And with the addition of cell phones, of course....

The Episode during which Mr. Collins Nearly but Not Quite Proposes to Elizabeth Bennet (Due to Cunning Use of Cell Phones)

"Lizzy, I *insist* upon your staying and hearing Mr. Collins," Mrs. Bennet told her reluctant daughter, Elizabeth.

Really! Early nineteenth-century gels could be so ungrateful and independent. But without a dowry said gel was obliged to grasp any nup-
tial opportunity that came her way, especially as it guaranteed that the
entire family would *not* be put out destitute in the hedgerows when Mr.
Collins inherited Longbourn.

But such fun to plan a wedding! Of course, it also meant a new bonnet for the mother of the bride. And new shoes! Who could resist such
a shopping opportunity? Mrs. Bennet flipped open her cell phone... her
new "Family and Friends" plan was such a comfort to her poor, long-
suffering nerves.

As her mother left the room (no doubt with the express intention of
calling the Entire World to discuss shoes and wedding arrangements),
Elizabeth realized that it would be wisest to either (a) let Mr. Collins say
his piece and get it over with, which might take the whole day, or (b)
think of a plan for averting the situation to the satisfaction of all.

"Believe me, my dear Miss Elizabeth," Mr. Collins began, "your mod-
esty, so far from doing you any disservice, rather adds to your other
perfections." And then he simpered.

Oh, dear. She just *knew* this was going to be a long-winded speech.
Plan (b) it was. If only there were some other future for dowry-less girls
of her social standing, aside from an arranged marriage with an idiot.
Possibly something involving romance and excitement and adventure.

Take that Mary Wollstonecraft, for example. Now there was an exciting woman! Up and eloped with poet Percy Shelley for love. Elizabeth
would bet her last penny, if she wasn't penniless and had one, that Mary
would write some poetry, too—or even a book. Percy Shelley would
introduce Mary to his editor, and bang! She'd be a bestselling author
before you could say...Elizabeth couldn't think of the word because
Mary had yet to invent it, but it featured a scary monster with a bolt
through its neck.

Oddly, when Elizabeth thought of excitement, Mr. Darcy sprang to
mind. Tall, dark, handsome, interesting...shame about the arrogance
and pride, though, even if he did have a great house in the country and
ten thousand a year. A girl could buy a lot of independence with that
chunk of cash. And there was always Wickham....No, elopement and
the subsequent disgrace it would bring upon the entire family wasn't
really Elizabeth's style....

"You would have been less amiable in my eyes had there *not* been this little unwillingness," Mr. Collins droned on, as Elizabeth had an idea for a television game show that involved phoning friends and lifelines and such (if only TVs and game shows had been invented, she was sure she could make her *own* fortune with that idea).

"But before I am run away with my feelings on this subject," Mr. Collins continued, "perhaps it will be advisable for me to state my reasons for marrying—"

Thinking longingly of phoning a friend and running away, Elizabeth glanced at the cell phone in her lap. Oh. Three new texts! Mr. Collins was so engrossed with his speech—he'd barely notice if she just had a quick look. Then she wished she hadn't.

"Aunt P. of opinion that pink a good color theme for wedding," said the first one from her mother. Talk about fast work. Somehow, Eliza just did not think of herself as a "pink" kind of gel.

"Collins? Pls. tell me not true!" read the second disbelieving message from Aunt Gardiner in London. At least someone was on Elizabeth's side.

"Congrats 2 U?" read the third from her friend Charlotte.

It was absolutely necessary to stop this now. But how?

If only Charlotte were here.... Charlotte was very good at distracting Mr. Collins.

"—convinced it will add greatly to my happiness—" Mr. Collins broke off, because his cell phone rang, which added greatly to Elizabeth's happiness. It was no doubt his patroness Lady Catherine de Bourgh. That woman called him at any time of the day and night to offer pearls of wisdom and brag about expensive, elegant chimney pieces that cost eight hundred pounds, and such.

"Do excuse me, my dear cousin," Mr. Collins simpered as he checked the Caller ID. "Duty calls."

And as Elizabeth heard Lady Catherine's voice booming down the cell phone (Lady Catherine had no need of a speakerphone), "Choose properly, choose a gentlewoman for *my* sake; and for your *own*, let her be an active, useful sort of person, not brought up high," a lightbulb went on in Elizabeth's head.

At least it would have been a lightbulb, if only someone had invented them.

A candle self-illuminated in Elizabeth's head as she recalled how readily Charlotte had entertained Mr. Collins at the Netherfield ball.

She had a sneaky suspicion that Charlotte coveted Mr. Collins for herself. All those smiles and hanging onto his every utterance. And Charlotte fitted Lady Catherine's description perfectly.

As Mr. Collins continued his irritating obsequiousness (didn't Mr. Collins realize that Lady Catherine couldn't actually *see* him bowing?), Elizabeth speed-dialed Charlotte. If previous phone calls from Lady Catherine were any measure, Mr. Collins would be engaged with her for at least another ten minutes.

"No, it's not true," said she quickly and quietly. "But Mr. Collins is *going* to make an offer to me, and I will not have him."

"Oh. Well, I am very sorry for him," answered Charlotte, sounding more flustered than sorry, and Elizabeth knew she had hit the proverbial nail on the head.

"He's on the phone to Lady C. at the moment, but would you be so kind as to come for a visit right now and listen to Mr. Collins? It would keep him in good humor, and I would be more obliged to you than I could express." There, that was discreet. She didn't want to sound too obvious. "And it would save him the embarrassment of my rejection if I didn't actually have to reject him. If you got here before he made the actual offer."

"I am already come," Charlotte told her. Did her friend sound just a little guilty? "Hill is just letting me in the front door, this moment. Um, it is such a fine day for a walk that I thought I might—call to make my congratulations in person. If congratulations were in order, of course."

Charlotte was hooked. Eliza was almost sure of it.

"Find such a woman as soon as you can—" Lady Catherine's voice boomed, as Elizabeth greeted the perfect candidate for that particular job, "—and I will visit her."

"I assure you of my satisfaction in being useful," Charlotte whispered, and Elizabeth decided that it was time to throw discretion out of the window.

"I am sure that you will be amply repaid for the little sacrifice of your time, and everyone one will be happy. You do want to marry him yourself, don't you?" she whispered urgently to her friend. "Because if you do, take your own advice and make it as clear as the nose on his face."

"I will most certainly, Lady Cath—" Mr. Collins said, as Lady Catherine hung up before he could finish. "Now, where were we? Oh yes. Now this has been my motive, my fair cous—" The expression on his face as he turned around and saw that Charlotte was in the room was comical. Well, more comical than usual.

"Mr. Collins, look who has come to pay us a visit," Elizabeth said, before he could begin to speak. Because once that man got talking it was hard to shut him up. "I'm sure you won't mind if I leave you in her capable hands and excuse myself for a moment, will you?"

Before he could answer, Elizabeth practically ran out of the room. And out of the house. She would take a good long amble in the glorious countryside. And when she called her mother, she could swear hand on heart that Mr. Collins had not made an offer.

She decided to walk in the direction of Netherfield. Not that she *wanted* to accidentally encounter that horrible Mr. Darcy on her ramble, of course....

The Revised Episode during which Mr. Darcy Nearly but Not Quite Proposes to Elizabeth, and during which Elizabeth Nearly but Not Quite Accepts (Due to Cunning Advanced Warning via Cell Phone)

"Mr. Darcy is such an intolerable man!" thought Elizabeth as the Collinses departed for Rosings, and as she settled herself in the Collins' drawing room for a night in by herself. Mr. Darcy had really gone and ruined things now! (And just as Elizabeth had decided that there was something appealingly charismatic about him, too, but she'd never tell a soul!)

Thank goodness the Collinses had gone to Rosings to drink tea with Lady Catherine. Thank goodness for an evening of peace and quiet without Mr. Darcy's distracting presence.

Every time Elizabeth went for a ramble around Rosings Park, there he was, all strong and silent, and insistent on walking with her. (Elizabeth would never admit this to a soul, either, but she deliberately went out for a lot of extra rambles these days. Secretly, she looked forward to meeting him. The strong silent treatment was...rather attractive.)

Every time they dined with Lady Catherine, there he was, all dark eyes and brooding haughtiness, looming down at her. Watching *her* all of the time, to the point where Charlotte had pointed it out. (Actually, Elizabeth secretly found the dark eyes and brooding haughtiness really exciting, too....)

And all the visits he made to the Collinses' house. Elizabeth had her own secret suspicions about his motives (i.e., to see her). All those double entendres when he did speak to her (a woman wouldn't want to be married and settled too near her family—i.e., Eliza).

Thank goodness for an evening of solitude!

And then Eliza's cell phone rang. Caller ID showed that it was Charlotte. Charlotte would only worry if she didn't pick up.

"Darcy alert, Darcy alert," Charlotte whispered down the phone. "The minute he heard you were unwell he was beside himself. He dashed out of the house in such a hurried fashion! I can only surmise that he's on his way to ensure himself of your good health. Lady Catherine is most put out."

"Insufferable man!" Eliza really didn't feel up to a meeting with him. Not tonight. (Although she secretly thought it was sweet that he was so concerned about her.)

"But what can he mean?" asked Eliza, but she had her own secret suspicions about his intentions....

"My dear Eliza, can you not see it?" Charlotte sounded just a bit exasperated with her. "I am sure that he is in love with you and that he intends to make an offer. Why else would he be so concerned?" Charlotte had a good point.

"Do you really think so? Not that I'm interested, because I'm not. Insufferable man!" Elizabeth was no dummy. She could see the writing on the wall, but it was always nice to have a bit of advanced reassurance from a friend. (And secretly, Eliza rather fancied herself in love with him. And being mistress of Pemberley and ten thousand a year were fairly big bonuses, too.)

But what a crushing blow, to discover that Mr. Darcy was responsible for ruining her dear sister's happiness with Mr. Bingley! And he had boasted about the part he played in separating them, according to Colonel Fitzpatrick! And of course everyone knew Darcy had ruined poor Wickham's life, too.

She never wanted to see Mr. Darcy ever, ever again! (Well, secretly she yearned to see him again, but how could she in view of the Jane and Wickham situations?)

"Eliza, do think carefully before you reject him," said Charlotte. "He does have ten thousand a year, after all. Oh, I must go. Lady Catherine needs me at once."

So it was not quite a shock (but secretly was a huge thrill of pleasure) when the drawing room door opened immediately after she'd pressed the off button on her phone, and in came Mr. Darcy. Gosh, but he looked all... gorgeously dark and brooding. Could Charlotte be right?

"Miss Bennet, I came with the express hope of inquiring after your health. I hope that I find you in better spirits," he said hurriedly.

"Yes, thank you," Eliza replied coldly (even though she was secretly smug that he'd come to see her—and so quickly—he must have run all the way from Rosings). Thank goodness Charlotte had warned her of his imminent arrival. And had shared her suspicions that he would propose to Eliza....

Darcy sat down. And then he stood up again and began pacing the room in an agitated fashion, and Elizabeth wished that he would just spit out whatever was bothering him. Hmm. Agitated, pacing, *nervous*, even?

She would bet her last penny, if she had one, that Darcy really was about to propose to her! Her heart beat faster as she imagined what it would be like to be married to such a man. But no, she couldn't do it. She had to think of Jane and Wickham.

After what felt like an eternity, but was in fact only a few minutes, he finally turned to her and thus began, "In vain have I struggled. It will not do. My feelings will not be repressed."

Excellent beginning, Elizabeth thought. Very well put, and she was particularly impressed by the acute level of emotion in his tone. It definitely sounded like the beginning of a proposal. Not that she was going to accept, or anything....

"You must allow me to tell you how ard—" he continued, then paused as the shrill tone of his cell phone completely ruined the moment. For a few seconds he remained speechless.

"Um, do you mind if I—?" he asked, holding up the phone.

She couldn't believe he'd take time out from his own proposal to answer a call! At least, she was almost sure it was going to be a proposal.

"What are you telling Miss Bennet?" Lady Catherine's voice boomed around the small room. "Let me hear what it is. I must have my share in the conversation, if you are speaking of her health. Does her head still hurt?"

That was the second time Lady Catherine had interrupted Elizabeth's proposal moment! Not that Elizabeth had minded during the Mr. Collins proposal. And not that Darcy had actually proposed, yet. Goodness, if she married Darcy she'd be related to Lady Catherine! What a terrible thought.

She *could* become a governess. That was an acceptable occupation for a penniless young woman. But she strongly suspected that someone would write a book about how horrible it was to be a governess in the not-too-distant future. Something gothic that would undoubtedly involve a certifiably insane secret wife in the attic, said wife having the unfortunate inclination to burn down the house and ruin your life. Definitely a *no*.

Maybe she should take Charlotte's advice and rethink her position on the Darcy proposal. If he ever got around to making one.

Ten minutes later, after much exasperation on Elizabeth's part, and after much instruction from Lady Catherine and not much from Darcy because Lady Catherine, like Mr. Collins, barely paused for breath, Darcy closed his cell phone and turned back to Elizabeth.

"Now where was I?" he asked, rhetorically.

"Something about struggling in vain, feelings not being repressed and me allowing you to tell me something," Eliza, who had the actual words committed to memory, prompted him.

"You must allow me to tell you how ardently I admire and love you," he said, and Eliza was so secretly delighted that she couldn't think of a word to say. Plus, she'd had second thoughts.

If she *was* married to Darcy, he could have no argument with his friend Bingley marrying Jane. And as Darcy's wife, Elizabeth would be able to help out poor Wickham. A win-win situation!

Taking her silence as assent (which secretly it was), Mr. Darcy proceeded to completely ruin the moment. It must be a family trait.

Instead of sweet declarations regarding her beauty, poise, accomplishments, etc., and actually getting around to asking her to marry him, he launched into a diatribe of why she was unsuitable, how awful was her family, and how low were her connections!

All of her secret hopes were crushed in one fell swoop. He'd use this as ammunition every time they had a fight. Elizabeth felt herself growing angrier every moment. He had to work his way through all these issues if they were ever to have a chance.

"I might as well inquire why with so evident a design of offending and insulting me," said she, as he finally stopped banging on about her mother's faults, "you chose to tell me that you liked me against your will, against your reason and even against your character? Insulting my family in such a manner does not tempt me to accept your offer." Secretly, she was sorely tempted despite his faults, but for his own good she had to be one of those young ladies who reject the addresses of the man whom they secretly mean to accept at a later date.

And then Elizabeth's own cell phone rang, and she flipped it open. Then wished she hadn't, because it was her mother.

"Good gracious! Lord bless me! Mr. Darcy! Oh! My sweetest Lizzy! I had it just now from Lady Lucas, who got it from Charlotte, that Mr. Darcy is in love with you!" Elizabeth blushed as her mother's words carried around the room. Mrs. Bennet, too, had no need of a speakerphone.

"What pin-money, what jewels, what carriages you will have! And such a promising thing for your sisters, your marrying so greatly must throw them in the way of other rich men! Oh, I must call Aunt Philips immediately!"

Darcy, having won that particular point, raised his eyebrows, and to cover her embarrassment Elizabeth immediately answered her cell phone again when it rang.

"Lizzy, what news!" Her youngest sister, Lydia. Unfortunately, Lydia took after their mother in every respect, including the loud voice.

"Tell Darcy we must have the engagement ball at Netherfield. And you must invite all of the officers! In fact, Denny and Wickham are with me right now. What fun we are having!"

Elizabeth got rid of Lydia. Darcy did have a valid point about her family, but if he loved her he would have to be prepared to compromise.

"Could you expect me to rejoice in the inferiority of your connections? To congratulate myself on the hope of relations, whose condition in life is so decidedly beneath my own?" said he, with such distaste that Elizabeth knew he had a long way to go before he'd be decent husband material.

"You could not have made me the offer of your hand in any possible way that would have tempted me to accept it," said she (secretly hoping that he *would* mistake her for one of those daring young ladies who risk their own happiness on the chance of being asked a second time)

As expected, he took off in a great sulk. And as Mr. Darcy left the building, Elizabeth was struck with a haunting yet attractive vision of him in a wet shirt.

Michelle Cunnah, born in Sheffield, England, had a normal child-hood—apart from six years in Central Africa where she developed a healthy dislike of spiders, snakes and crocodiles. She began writing in fourth grade—short stories and adaptations of well-known fairy tales into scripts, partly because she liked to spin her own happy endings, but also because it was a means to escape math lessons. Despite having written "hates math" on every job application form, she was very puzzled to get a variety of jobs in accounts departments. She moved to London, where she had more jobs that involved accounts (she never could figure out why). She also temped, worked in a gay bar and developed other people's vacation snaps. After moving to New Jersey, she was offered a three-book contract with Avon's Trade Paperback line. Michelle can currently be found in Rotterdam, the Netherlands or on the Web at http://www.michellecunnah.com.

Bennets and Bingleys and Bitches. Oh My!

ERIN DAILEY

You've taken the *Cosmo* quiz to find out if you and your mate relate. Now take Erin Dailey's quiz and find out who you'd be if fate dropped you into the Meryton Assembly. Hint: Watch out for those Bs.

OH, THE BENNETS AND THE BINGLEYS. Aren't they just the most delightful group of ...well...annoying and infuriating women you've ever come across in a work of fiction? The only saving grace is Elizabeth, and even she is somewhat hindered by the era within which she exists. How many times have you wished that at the precise moment the priggish Darcy generously bestows his good proposal upon Lizzy she would just up and smack him across the head with one of the fireplace pokers? But Lizzy...she, at least, is likeable. I mean, Jane's too nice, the Bingleys are too mean, Lydia's too silly, Mary's too serious and Kitty's...too...bronchial? I don't know. They're all too...girly for my tastes. Seriously. Are any of the ladies of Hertfordshire even remotely relatable? Can we see even a little bit of ourselves in any one of them? In the triumvirate of Lizzy, Jane and Caroline, can you find one iota of self-identification? Could you be one of them? Go on and ask yourself.

Which Lady Are You?

You just found out the guy you have your eye on has recently moved into a place across town. What do you do?

A. Don a frilly dress, copy the makeup off the model in the Lancôme ad, stroke for stroke, leave your coat behind because it makes you look fat, then head out into the rain to take two cabs, a bus and a train, only to arrive soaking wet and desperately ill, but who cares because your guy is just the sweetest and bestest guy on the whole planet!

B. Tell your friend's sister's friend to tell her brother that you certainly DON'T have your eye on the guy and that you resent the implication that you DO and if everyone would be so kind as to not mention his name ever AGAIN, you'd very much appreciate it because he is tacky and hairy and far, far beneath you.

C. Raise an eyebrow at the pouring rain, turn on BBC America, pour yourself a glass of wine and figure that if the rain stops before you've finished the bottle, you'll call a cab and head on over. If it doesn't, well, then at least you'll have a good buzz before Monty Python comes on.

There's a huge formal ball being given in honor of some hotshot foreign bigwig. Anyone who's anyone is going and so are you. Where will you be for most of the event?

A. Out on the dance floor, spinning your skirts, laughing your head off at the music, batting your eyelashes at your partner and generally being the belle of the ball. What use is beauty if you can't show it off once in a while?

B. Gathered with your gaggle of gal pals by the bar, commenting on every last nose job and bad hairline in the place. Who has time to dance when there are so many people to disapprove of? And has anyone SEEN Amanda Reardon's lips lately? Girlfriend looks like she accidentally pumped her mouth full of helium. What a loser!

C. Over in the corner, trading jibes with some of the politicians and diplomats who seem to think that just because you have boobs, you don't have a brain. "Hey, I may be wearing a damn corset under here, but it ain't cutting off the oxygen to my cerebral cortex, okay? And, while we're at it, could someone get me another drink? Hello?"

While at a cocktail party, you overhear someone say that your best friend is fat, ugly and probably will die an old maid. What's your reaction?

A. Well, obviously, that person is totally rude. But, you know, they kinda have a point. I mean, your best friend *is* on the chubby side. And she rarely goes out, so she very well *will* die alone. But that's not necessarily her fault because, you know, she has no legs. But she's a beautiful person on the inside. And so is that person at the cocktail party. When they're not being mean. Which, you know, you're sure they didn't intend to be.
B. You don't have a best friend, but if you did, she sure as hell wouldn't be fat or ugly and there's no WAY she'd die alone. Like that poor Melissa Kramer who choked to death on a shrimp gyoza or something and no one found her body until three weeks later and she'd already started to grow fungus? Man, she was fat. And ugly. And she had a HUMP. Gross.
C. All you can say is, they'd better not be in your immediate vicinity, or someone's going to wind up bitch-slapped. How RUDE is that? Like, they know you're at the party, right? Why would they be talking about your friend that way? Don't they KNOW you're capable of slinging a few barbs their way? In fact, you think you'll just walk over there right now and give them a piece of your damn mind: "FAT? I'll give them FAT. Bitches."

The guy who dumped you because his friend told him to is suddenly interested in you again. You:

A. Wonder how long you should wait before returning his phone call and then secretly start planning your seating chart and picking out china patterns because, honestly, there's only ever been one man for you and he is it and now that he's finally come to his senses, all is right with the world.

B. Scratch your head in confusion. What is this "dumped" of which you speak? That's a term you're not used to hearing. No one has ever dumped you. And no one ever will. Primarily because no one is good enough for you in the first place, you being the epitome of perfection and all.

C. Question his motives and try to think back to what it was you liked about him anyway. Was it his hair? No. His teeth? No. His hands? No. His wit? Oh, yeah. That. He was pretty funny. But, no. No way. He dumped you once before. He had his chance. Hell could freeze over and Satan could be triple lutz-ing his way to the damn A&P and you still wouldn't take that jackass back. Nuh-uh.

Your dad invites a total blowhard to dinner one night and Mr. Fatty McFatterton keeps making eyes at you and your sisters in between slurps of soup and wine. You:

A. Gently smile and share a stolen glance with your sisters. The poor man. He must be so lonely all by himself in that big house of his. Of course, he is rather...smelly. But some good grooming and a dash of cologne are all that's needed to cure him of that!

B. Wonder aloud about the effects of overeating on the constitution of men over the age of forty, and doesn't drinking wine after eight in the evening lead to heart attack and balding? You're sure you read that somewhere. Oh, well. In any case, double-breasted suits only look good on young mobsters circa 1945. Oh, but they look good on *him*, certainly!

C. Roll your eyes and think about the book you left out on the porch. You hope he sucks up the last of that wine fast so you can get back to it and find out what happened at the end of Chapter Five. Oh, damn. He's looking at you again. Look away. LOOK AWAY. Think happy thoughts! Think happy thoughts!

Your idea of the ideal way to spend a Sunday afternoon is:

A. Visiting people in and around the neighborhood, dropping off baked goods and care packages to the needy, enjoying the fine weather, spending time with your lover man, and, generally, thanking the gods for being alive. Oh, and chocolate. There'd probably have to be some chocolate in there somewhere.

B. Getting a manicure and a pedicure with your girlfriends and making fun of the woman behind the counter who has a moustache and wears a Justin Timberlake t-shirt and she's not even being ironic. I mean, does she have a *mirror* in her house or what? It's like she doesn't even know how hideous she looks! And that guy across the street? With the hat? Who's he kidding? The man is bald, honey, BALD.

C. Sleeping in. The *New York Times* crossword puzzle. A nice cappuccino. Or four. A walk in the park. A big lunch somewhere, preferably on a square, so you can watch people pass by and observe them. Reading in your favorite chair until the sun goes down. Then a quiet dinner and maybe a movie. Or…drinking Guinness at noon at the local pub until you forget what time it is. That's good, too.

The man whose proposal you refused is back in the picture again, only this time, he seems to be warmer, kinder and, in general, a much nicer guy. He was kind of dick back then, though, a point you haven't forgotten. What would you do if he asked you to marry him all over again?

A. Why did you refuse him the first time? Were you ill? Had you fallen? You don't remember him being awful or anything. You guess you had your reasons, though. If he asked you to marry him again, you'd most certainly say yes. And you wouldn't even make him beg for it!

B. Tell him to go screw himself. You refused him for a reason. The guy is trash, okay? He was trash then and he's trash now and someone as brilliant and beautiful as you can't go around just saying "yes" to some dillweed who can't seem to remember when he's been dumped already. Is he defective? Is he missing an ear? CAN HE NOT HEAR YOU?

C. Oh, hell. You'd marry the poor bastard. If only because he seems to have learned his lesson and become a better person. And he makes you laugh so hard you snort milk out your nose. There's something to be said for a man who can get rejected, turn his life around and come back for another potential dose of rejection, you know. Guy's got moxie, you'll give him that.

Results:

Mostly As: You're Jane, through and through. You're pretty and lively and generous and you keep running out of cash because you're always giving dollars to homeless people on the street. You see the world through rose-colored glasses and you're not afraid to admit it. Life is beautiful, people are beautiful, you are beautiful—what more is there to happiness?

Mostly Bs: Oh, great. You're Caroline. Really? Are you really Caroline? Because if you are, then, well, you're kind of a bitch. And a snob. And not someone anyone really wants to hang around with. There's a reason Caroline doesn't snare Darcy in the end—HE DOESN'T LIKE HER. And who would? Petty, insufferable and incapable of saying a kind word about anyone, the Carolines of this world should be taken out back and made to lick dirt. If you honestly are Caroline, honey, I'd suggest you get an attitude adjustment, like, yesterday.

Mostly Cs: Face it. You're Lizzy. And that's not such a bad thing. Lizzy's smart, temperate, quick-witted and generally fun to be around. That's you in a nutshell. You're always the first to come up with a plan or a solution, you see people for who they are and you never let anyone get away with anything. You're the kind of woman that novels are written about. Isn't that nice? Oh, stop rolling your eyes at me. It's true. Now go grab that six-pack and meet me in the living room. The Monty Python marathon is about to start.

Erin Dailey has never worn a bonnet or a petticoat, but she loves Jane Austen all the same. In her writing ventures, Erin has covered *Alias* for Television Without Pity (www.televisionwithoutpity.com) since its first season. Recently, she contributed an essay to BenBella's *Alias Assumed: Sex, Lies and SD-6*. She has written for such sites as This Is Not Over (www.thisisnotover.com), Shebytches (www.shebytches.com) and Metroblogging Chicago (chicago.metblogs.com). She lives and breathes in the delicious city of Charleston, South Carolina. You can catch up with her life ramblings at www.redhead-papers.com and her travel ramblings (and photos) at erindailey.typepad.com/journeygirl.

Pride and Prejudice: The Reality Show

Joyce Millman

Nobody suffers like Elizabeth Bennet. In fact, one might wonder how her plight could possibly be worse as she watches her life come unraveled under the pitiless eyes of stiff-necked society. Well, wonder no more. Joyce Millman knows: get out the sheep's eyeballs and let the cameras roll.

ANNOUNCER: You've seen *The Bachelor*. You've seen *Survivor*. You've seen *Joe Millionaire*, but you won't admit it. Now, from the creators of *Sense and Sensibility* and *Fear Factor*, comes a reality show that has as much romance, backstabbing and exhibitionism as those other shows—but with British accents, so you don't have to be embarrassed about watching it! *American Idol*'s Ryan Seacrest hosts... *Pride and Prejudice*!

Week One

[A pretty young woman in a Regency-era gown and bonnet strolls in a country garden.]

RYAN SEACREST: *[Voiceover]* Bachelorette Elizabeth Bennet, age not above one-and-twenty, has a quick mind, a lively manner and a pleasing appearance. But she's no society heiress, so her marriage prospects are looking dim. Lizzy's really going to have to work that lively manner if she wants to hook up with somebody rich and hot. Otherwise, her mom will marry her off to the first boring old dude who'll have her.

MRS. BENNET: [*To the camera*] I do not know what to do about Lizzy. She is so contrary! I am always telling her, "Lizzy, put down that book; no husband wants a wife who can read!" Am I not always telling her that, Mr. Bennet?

MR. BENNET: [*Dryly*] Lizzy is a horrid girl.

MRS. BENNET: [*To the camera*] Now, my eldest daughter, Jane, is much more obedient. And so agreeably weak and pale! I am teaching her how to swoon. "Jane," I told her, "No gentleman can resist a lady when she's unconscious!" She will be in top swooning form by the time we meet Mr. Bingley, our new neighbor from the estate at Netherfield. Yes, he is unmarried! And he has an income of five thousand a year, so he must be in want of a wife! [*Shouts up the staircase*] Jane! It's time for your beauty regimen! Come quickly, the leeches are restless!

Week Two

[*The five Bennet sisters happily hug each other.*]

SEACREST: [*Voiceover*] There is excitement at Longbourn! Bachelorettes Jane, Elizabeth, Mary, Kitty and Lydia have just learned that Mr. Bingley will be attending the upcoming dance at the Assembly Rooms. And he's bringing his posse!

MRS. BENNET: [*To Mr. Bennet*] I do hope that Lizzy can keep her contrary opinions to herself and not spoil Jane's chances with Mr. Bingley! Oh, husband, the anticipation of the dance has played harshly upon my nerves! I must take to my bed! I shall be indisposed for the rest of the day.

MR. BENNET: [*Dryly*] Trouble yourself not, my dear. I have urgent business to attend to in my study. [*Slips a copy of* Naughty Wench *magazine inside his waistcoat*]

ELIZABETH: [*To the camera, in a lively manner*] I am contrary, this is true! I refuse to stoop to swooning and flattery. I shall go to the dance and survey the bachelors, but looks and money do not sway me. I am far too discerning to let defects of character pass unnoticed. And of all defects, the most odious is pride! Depend upon it, I would never marry a proud man, even if he were master of the biggest estate in the county! Even if he were as handsome as Colin Firth! Even if he were Colin Firth himself, I would not yield! [*Reflects a moment*] Does anybody know if Colin Firth is married?

[*The Assembly Rooms. Young women and men are dancing in a line or engaged in conversation. Lydia Bennet, the bosomy fifteen-year-old bachelorette, is surrounded by soldiers of the _____ shire regiment. She is chugging punch.*]

SEACREST: [*Voiceover*] The big night is here and hook-ups are in the air! [*Shot of Bingley gazing starry-eyed at demure Jane*] Well, it looks like Jane has Bingley—or should that be *Bling*-ley?—on the line and she's reeling him in! Is that...? Yes, it appears the wealthy bachelor from Netherfield is offering her a rose!

BINGLEY: Jane, I would like to form an attachment with you. Will you accept this rose?

JANE: Yes. Oh, I feel faint.... [*Thud*]

SEACREST: [*Voiceover*] Meanwhile, all eyes are on Bingley's friend, Mr. Darcy, a handsome but haughty bachelor who bears a striking resemblance to Colin Firth. Darcy is an even better catch than Bingley! He has an income of ten thousand pounds a year and is master of Pemberley, an estate so huge a team of surveyors was sent to map it and was never heard from again. Let's listen in on the hidden microphone as the two bachelors compare notes.

BINGLEY: Dude, why are you not dancing? The place is crawling with foxes!

DARCY: Hmmmph. There is no one here foxy or respectable enough to dance with. They are all beneath me.

BINGLEY: What about Jane's sister Elizabeth? I wouldn't mind her beneath *me*! [*Giggles*]

DARCY: [*Turns to look, shrugs*] Eh. She's okay. Look, Bingley, I do not begrudge you some fun with Jane Bennet. But, good God, man, the family is trailer trash! The daughters are plain country girls of no consequence. Although, on second notice, Miss Elizabeth Bennet does appear to have a very fine pair of...eyes.

SEACREST: [*Voiceover*] Uh-oh. It looks like Lizzy overheard Darcy! She's in the confession room right now.

ELIZABETH: [*Heatedly talking into a video camera*] Oh, that proud Mr. Darcy! I detest him! I admit, he is handsome, but come on, he's no Colin Firth! If Mr. Darcy is considered a good catch, then I am happy to remain a bachelorette. I shall care for my parents in their old age and play bingo on Saturday nights and keep many pet cats, which I shall treat as if they are my children. It shall be a blissful life! [*Laughs shrilly. Twists a lace handkerchief around her hand so tightly, her fingers bleed*] Blissful!

Week Three

[*Jane rides side-saddle on horseback in a raging storm,
while Mrs. Bennet is heard in voiceover.*]

MRS. BENNET: "Jane," I said, "You must call on Mr. Bingley's sisters. If you do not, then Lady Lucas and her spinster daughter Charlotte will surely take the opportunity to turn Mr. Bingley's head." And then I sent her off in the rain. With any luck, she will catch a life-threatening chill and have to remain at Netherfield to recuperate. No gentleman can resist a lady when her cheeks are rosy with infectious fever! Isn't that right Mr. Bennet?

MR. BENNET: [*Furtively screwing cap back onto small flask and slipping it into his pocket*] What? Yes, yes, of course, my dear. Hic.

[*Jane tosses and turns in an ornate four-post bed, damp hair plastered to her semi-conscious face.*]

SEACREST: [*Voiceover*] Mrs. Bennet has gotten her wish. Jane has taken ill at Netherfield and Lizzy has been sent to nurse her. It's now Day Three of the mismatched housemates' confinement.

[*Elizabeth and Bingley's sister Caroline sit in the parlor. The air is thick with dislike.*]

CAROLINE BINGLEY: Miss Bennet, that is a darling frock you are wearing. But, does it not make you seem a tad thick around the posterior?

ELIZABETH: [*Not looking up from her book*] One who has the bosom of an ironing board and the face of a suckling pig should perhaps keep silent.

BINGLEY: Ladies, please do not start up again! It agitates Jane and she has already gone through my supply of laudanum! Pray, let us all be friends. Oh, look who comes! It is Darcy!

DARCY: [*Aloof, yet polite*] Good day, Miss Bennet.

LIZZY: [*Coolly*] I would not know if it is a good day or not Mr. Darcy, as I am only a plain country girl of no consequence.

SEACREST: [*Voiceover*] Rrrrrrrrr! Lizzy has the claws out! And Darcy can't deal! He's in the confession room.

DARCY: [*Into video camera*] I do not know how I gave offense! But why do I feel the pinprick of her sarcasm so acutely? It is beneath me to care! She is of no consequence. It is just that...in all my days... I've never...her fine...dark...eyes,,,*sputter ack*...dammit!

SEACREST: [*Voiceover*] As the week drags on, the tension between Elizabeth and Darcy mounts.

DARCY: The sky is quite blue, is it not Miss Bennet?

ELIZABETH: Perhaps if I, too, were blinded by pride, I would believe that the sky is blue, Mr. Darcy. But as I am only a plain country girl of no consequence, I can hardly see how my opinion of the sky could possibly be of interest to you. And, by the way, the sky is not blue, it is green.

SEACREST: [*Voiceover*] What about our other Bennet bachelorettes? With Elizabeth and Jane away, younger sisters Lydia and Kitty are looking for love in all the wrong places. [*Footage of Lydia and Kitty flirting with soldiers in town. They lift their skirts to show their ankles, which are censored on-screen by pixilated boxes. Britney Spears sings "I'm not...that...in-no-cent" on the soundtrack.*]

SEACREST: [*Voiceover*] Meanwhile, back home, the hapless Mary Bennet performs a pianoforte recital for her parents' dinner guest, one Mr. ___ Cowell of Fopshire. She is scathingly advised to "get thee to a nunnery." Seacrest...out!

203

Week Four

SEACREST: [*Voiceover*] It is a truth universally acknowledged that women always fall for the wrong guy. So we've thrown the wrong guy into this already explosive mix! [*A darkly handsome Colin Farrell look-alike gallops across the countryside on a white steed. Both his mane and the horse's are blown rakishly back by the wind.*] George Wickham is an Average Joe posing as a gentleman. He's a cad and a liar, and if this were *The Sopranos* his gambling debts would add up to several boxes of ziti. But Wickham knows how to use his impeccable manners and bad-boy good looks to woo the ladies. Will Lizzy be his next conquest?

[*Home of Elizabeth's aunt, Mrs. Philips. Wickham enters the room, and the women draw breath as one. The only sounds that can be heard are Lydia's throaty, "Hello, stranger," and a soft thud as Jane faints. Wickham sits down beside Elizabeth, who is frantically fanning herself.*]

WICKHAM: [*Gazing intently into her face*] Miss Bennet, I first saw you yesterday walking with your sisters in Meryton, and I have been unable to think of anything else since. You have the face of an angel. Did it hurt when you fell from heaven? May I tell you a tragic story about how Darcy has cruelly cheated me out of my inheritance?

ELIZABETH: Come to mama!

SEACREST: [*Voiceover*] Later, Lizzy and her spinster friend Charlotte Lucas have a heated discussion in a dark cupboard under the stairs. Our infrared camera and hidden microphone are there.

CHARLOTTE: Surely you cannot be considering an attachment to Wickham! You know nothing about him!

ELIZABETH: I know that his hindquarters are as muscular as a stallion's! Charlotte, I think I'm in love!

CHARLOTTE: Are Wickham's well-muscled thighs worth more than Darcy's ten thousand pounds a year?

ELIZABETH: Charlotte, dearest, you misunderstand me! It is not just his well-muscled thighs. It is also his broad shoulders, his soulful eyes and the way his lower lip quivered while relating how shamefully Darcy has treated him. Oh, Charlotte, give me a mysterious bad-boy of dubious means over a rich snob any day!

CHARLOTTE: [*Agitated*] Girlfriend, have you learned nothing from reading Miss Austen? We are living in a material world and we are material girls! The boy with the cold, hard cash is always Mr. Right—eventually.

Week Five

[*A self-satisfied-looking man in clergyman's garb walks up the lane to the Bennet home.*]

SEACREST: [*Voiceover*] Mr. Collins is a cousin of Mr. Bennet and the heir to Longbourn. And he's single!

MR. COLLINS: Thank you for inviting me to dine with you, Cousin Bennet. My most revered and condescending patroness, Lady Catherine de Bourgh, has decreed that I must take a wife. And since you have had the misfortune of being burdened with five daughters, I am here to lighten your load. Hmmm, let's see.... [*Points to Elizabeth*] That one is not as plain as the others. How much will you pay me to take her off your hands?

SEACREST: [*Voiceover*] Later that evening, after Mrs. Bennet takes to her bed from over-excitement, the rest of the Bennets hold a family council and secretly vote Mr. Collins off the Shire. But the determined Charlotte Lucas saves the castaway suitor's reputation by proposing that they form an alliance. Charlotte wins immunity from spinsterhood and Mr. Collins' torch for Lizzy is extinguished.

Week Six

[*Jane morosely looks out a rain-streaked window.*]

SEACREST: [*Voiceover*] Jane's boyfriend Bingley has left town with no explanation. Is their attachment broken? [*Elizabeth peers anxiously at Jane from the doorway.*] And Lizzy is so preoccupied with Jane's problems, not to mention her own mega-crush on Wickham, that she doesn't realize she has a secret admirer! [*Darcy stonily watches her as she plays the pianoforte for a roomful of guests.*] Yes, Darcy has fallen for more than just Elizabeth's fine dark eyes. And we're about to put Darcy's feelings to the test with a white-knuckle stunt like you've never seen before!

DARCY: [*To the camera*] My aunt, Lady Catherine de Bourgh, is giving a dinner party at Rosings for that obsequious parson and his bride. The Bennets have been invited. Oh, I have never known such fear! Mrs. Bennet's prattle, my aunt's unforgiving eye and Elizabeth's impertinence—all at the same table! [*Mops brow with handkerchief*] I shall be drinking early. And often.

[*Rosings. A dinner party is in progress.*]

LADY CATHERINE: I have had special delicacies prepared for my guests. [*Servants uncover silver trays.*]

MR. COLLINS: May I be so unworthy as to inquire of your most condescending ladyship what those extraordinary morsels might be?

LADY CATHERINE: [*Grandly*] Sheep's eyeballs, bull's testicles and earthworms. Tuck in.

JANE: Oh, I feel faint.... [*Thud*]

MRS. BENNET: I shall be happy to partake, Lady Catherine. I hear that earthworms are all the rage in London this season! [*Spears earthworm on fork, twirls it like spaghetti, chews with mouth open*]

MR. BENNET: [*Dryly*] This is very fine claret, Lady Catherine. Hic.

LADY CATHERINE: Mr. Bennet, you are drinking your finger bowl.

LYDIA: Who can guess how many bull's testicles I can fit into my mouth?

SEACREST: [*Voiceover*] Yow! The Bennets' table manners are so bad they could pass for Americans! Lady Catherine was in on the stunt and she looks pleased with herself, the sadistic old biddy. But wait...

ELIZABETH: [*With a defiant look in her fine dark eyes*] Lady Catherine, please pass the sheep's eyeballs.

SEACREST: [*Voiceover*] This is the moment of truth for Lizzy. Darcy is watching her and he looks worried. Can she salvage this disastrous evening? She's carefully examining her forks and spoons and...yes! Lizzy is the only one in her family who knows the correct utensil to use on a sheep's eyeball! It's the shrimp fork!

[*Elizabeth daintily chews the eyeball. Darcy's chest swells with affection. Lady Catherine slumps in her throne, defeated.*]

SEACREST: [*Voiceover*] Later that night, Darcy confronts Lizzy alone in the sitting room.

DARCY: Miss Bennet, your elegant manners as you ate that sheep's eyeball have made me realize how well-bred you are, despite your having grown up in a family of carney folk. I wish to form an attachment with you. Will you accept this rose?

ELIZABETH: Mmmph! [*Turns green, clasps hand over mouth, runs out of room*]

Week Seven

SEACREST: [*Voiceover*] After Elizabeth refused to accept his rose, Darcy videotaped a message for her. She's watching it now.

DARCY: [*On the tape, unshaven and disheveled*] Dear Miss Bennet, I have never been refused by a lady before, and I have spent the night and most of the morning in the wine cellar. I can no longer stand up, much less feel the pain of rejection, so what the hell, here goes. Wickham is a scoundrel and a gambler and a libertine. He tried to blackmail me and seduce my underage sister. Ha! Good choice! You should be very happy together! And by the way, it was I who talked Bingley out of marrying Jane. Why? Because her constant swooning annoyed me, that's why! [*Takes swig from bottle. Wipes mouth with sleeve*] An' another thing... you wanna talk about my pride? At least I have some, which is more than I can say for you! If I had a family like yours, I would have hidden myself in the Witness Protection Program by now! [*Staggers, takes another swig*] Good God, this Pinot is fantastic! You wanna know shomething elshe, Lizzy? You are predujiced. Tha's right, baby! Pridjidiced against rich people! Read my lips: Predi-juiced!

ELIZABETH: [*Distressed*] Till this moment, I never knew myself!

Week Eight

*[A downcast Elizabeth rides in a carriage with her Aunt
and Uncle Gardiner, who are not carney folk.]*

SEACREST: *[Voiceover]* Lizzy is ashamed of her prejudice against rich people, and she's having second thoughts about turning down Darcy's proposal. To torture herself with reminders of her incredible stupidity, she goes on a sightseeing tour of Pemberley, Darcy's spectacular estate. There, she meets Ty the Handyman, the son of the estate's old caretaker Pennington, and hears a heartwarming true story about Darcy's generosity.

TY THE HANDYMAN: Ye would not have recognized Pemberley before Mr. Darcy paid for the extreme makeover. People think this is the master's house, but Mr. Darcy really lives in that little cottage over there by the hermit's shack. The rest of Pemberley—twenty bedrooms, eighteen chamber pots at last count—were built for my father and mother and me and my fifteen brothers and sisters. Aye, 'tis true. Mr. Darcy couldn't abide having the servants all crammed together in poor quarters, so he built us this magnificent estate! Mr. Darcy an' me, we hammered and nailed side by side, using Craftsman tools provided by the good people at Sears. I still remember the look on my dear mother's face during the reveal. There is no finer man in all of England than Mr. Darcy! *[Elizabeth bursts into sobs, covers her ears and runs away. Ty the Handyman picks up a bullhorn and shouts after her.]* Miss! Wait! Have ye noticed how strongly he resembles Colin Firth?

Week Nine

SEACREST: *[Voiceover]* This week on *Pride and Prejudice*—the shocking development that changes everything!

[Mrs. Bennet runs through the house waving a letter.]

MRS. BENNET: Mr. Bennet! Happy news! Lydia has run away with Wickham! They are not married, but they have spent a week in each other's company, so she's as good as married, isn't she? Oh, and hear this, husband! Wickham requests that you pay all of his gambling debts in exchange for making an honest woman of our daughter. Oh, I am beside myself with satisfaction! Lydia's match shall be the talk of the town! Husband, where are you going with that pistol?

MR. BENNET: [*Dryly*] I am going to clean my weapon, my dear, while reflecting upon this delightful news. If fortune is kind, I shall accidentally blow my head off.

SEACREST: [*Voiceover*] News of Wickham and Lydia's elopement spreads as far as London. [*Footage of newsboy holding up paper with front page etching of Lydia sitting on Wickham's lap*] People can't get enough of the scandalous couple Fleet Street has dubbed "Wicks and Chlamydia."

ELIZABETH: [*Tearfully to camera*] This shocking development changes everything!

SEACREST: [*Voiceover*] What Elizabeth doesn't know is that Darcy has come to the rescue. [*Footage of Darcy riding at full gallop*] In order to save Elizabeth's reputation by association, Darcy has personally paid off Wickham's debts, forced him to marry Lydia and convinced his old college roommate, now head of programming for MTV, to give Wickham and Lydia their own reality series.

Week Ten

ANNOUNCER: This week on *The Newly-Shotgun-Weds*...

WICKHAM: Hurry up with dinner, woman, I'm starving!

LYDIA: Hang on, Wicky! I'm trying to stuff a turkey but the dopey bird won't eat!

Week Eleven

SEACREST: [*Voiceover*] Well, our first bachelor and bachelorette, Bingley and Jane, have made it down the aisle. [*Footage of wedding guests showering the happy couple with rose petals. Jane faints.*] And our more interesting bachelor and bachelorette, Darcy and Lizzy, are ready to say "I do" in a two-hour prime-time event, *Pride and Prejudice: The Wedding*, followed by a Diane Sawyer exclusive—Mr. and Mrs. Fitzwilliam Darcy's first interview as husband and wife.

DIANE SAWYER: Lizzy, who is a happier bride, you or Jane?

ELIZABETH: [*Looking playfully at Darcy next to her*] Diane, I am much happier than Jane! She only smiles, but I laugh! And do you know why I laugh, Diane? Because I married for love, but I got money too! Ten thousand a year and an estate to die for! And look upon him, Diane! Under this lighting, does not Mr. Darcy bear a strong resemblance to Colin Firth? Oh, I shall laugh and laugh and laugh, till the end of my days!

SEACREST: [*Voiceover*] Unfortunately, no one is laughing at Rosings, where Mr. Collins has been called on the carpet by his employer.

LADY CATHERINE: Why did you not stop my nephew from marrying that impertinent low-born woman?

MR. COLLINS: [*Bowing deeply*] My most revered and condescending patroness, I did all I could to counsel Mr. Darcy against such an unsuitable match, but he would not be moved! Can we not look to the future, your most forgiving ladyship? I humbly bring you a proposal that could generate boundless income for us. I have an idea for a reality show in which handsome women like yourself and my wife could become even more handsome through cosmetic surgery.

LADY CATHERINE: Mr. Collins... *you're fired!*

Joyce Millman's essays about television have appeared in the *New York Times*, *Variety*, Salon.com and the *Boston Phoenix*. She was a finalist for the Pulitzer Prize in criticism in 1989 and 1991 for television columns written for the *San Francisco Examiner*. She was a founding staff member of Salon.com and has contributed essays to Smart Pop Anthologies about *NYPD Blue* and *Alias*. A lifelong Jane Austen fan, she admits to a perverse and lingering crush on Colonel Brandon.

The Evolution of Envy

ALESIA HOLLIDAY

The book club is becoming a chick thing, a chance for women to discuss not just books, but lives. Alesia Holliday brings together the spiritual descendants of the Bennet sisters and their friend Charlotte and listens in while they dish on *Pride and Prejudice,* men and each other. They haven't changed much from their nineteenth-century forbearers. Except for the margaritas.

It is a truth universally acknowledged, that a single man in possession of a good fortune must be in want of a wife.
> —JANE AUSTEN, *Pride and Prejudice*

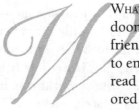WHAT IS NOT universally acknowledged is the doom, despair and dismay this can cause in the friends of the wife so wanted. Are we more prone to envy today than in Austen's time, or should we read her work as gentle fiction with our rose-colored Prada sunglasses firmly in place?

Envy, a Modern Book Club Discussion:

[H]is friend Mr. Darcy soon drew the attention of the room by his fine, tall person, handsome features, noble mien—and the report which was in general circulation within five minutes after his entrance of his having ten thousand a year.

LIZ: See, this is a problem. It's easy to be deliriously happy for your best friend when she bags the rich guy who looks like Winston Churchill in his declining years, or the gorgeous deadbeat who sprawls around her apartment mooching off of her. But when she falls in reciprocated love with a guy who's got both looks AND money, it's tougher.

JANE: That's not true at all. Look at the example Jane Austen sets: the sisters are delighted for each other's good fortune and miserable in empathy with each other's setbacks, and even Charlotte, who got the "runner-up," is happy for Elizabeth. If we can't be unconditionally happy for our friends, *especially* when they find a life partner who represents all of the best possible qualities, we are sending out negative energy into the universe and doomed to receive it back times three.

CHARLOTTE: You've been listening to that New Age crap on CD again, haven't you, Jane? After you made us all do that fire-walking seminar (and don't get me started on explaining away blistered heels to my pedicurist!), you promised no more *woo woo* for at least six months.

LYDIA: What's *mien* mean?

MARY: Countenance.

LYDIA: What's countenance mean?

LIZ: Oh, go look it up, for God's sake, Lydia. I'm just saying—and let me add here that I seem to be the only one in the room being completely honest—that it's human nature to be envious when somebody else gets something better. Better guy, better job, better house, better nose job, you name it. Jane Austen's world is fiction in more ways than one. Name me one set of sisters who would be that supportive of each other.

JANE: Easy. Charlotte and her sister. And, by the way, I'm tired of hearing about the blisters, Charlotte. You were supposed to transcend the flames. If you'd self-actualized—

CHARLOTTE: Yeah? Self-actualize, my ass. Flame is flame. Should I make another pitcher of margaritas? I have a feeling this is going to be our longest book club discussion in recent history. Plus, my sister quit speaking to me for at least three months after my wedding, so leave us out of the "supportive sisters" category.

LYDIA: Totally yes on the margaritas. And why did we have to pick *Pride and Prejudice*? Why couldn't we read that book about the call girl who went around the world? *Around the World in Eighty Lays*?

JANE: [*Patting her stomach*] No margaritas for me until after the baby is born and I'm done breastfeeding. Did you know there's an actual organization that's all about breastfeeding? I was reading about the inverted nipple problem...

ALL: STOP!

LIZ: You promised no breastfeeding stories. You're grossing me out.

MARY: Lydia, you're hopeless. We're trying to discuss the evolution of envy here, and how Austen's fiction resonates with today's woman.

LYDIA: Well, this today's woman needs a drink. Especially after that inverted comment.

When Jane and Elizabeth were alone, the former, who had been cautious in her praise of Mr. Bingley before, expressed to her sister how very much she admired him.

"He is just what a young man ought to be," said she, "sensible, good-humoured, lively; and I never saw such happy manners!—so much ease, with perfect good breeding!"

"He is also handsome," replied Elizabeth, "which a young man ought likewise to be, if he possibly can. His character is thereby complete."

JANE: You see? Elizabeth is entirely happy for her sister; not a hint of envy. Why do we have to see sinister motivations everywhere? Envy is a waste of energy. There will always be someone who has something better. It is a far better path in life to learn to appreciate what we have.

LIZ: Why do you always sound like a fortune cookie? And Elizabeth is just a teensy bit effusive, if you ask me. "His character is complete." What does that mean? What does being handsome have to do with his character?

213

LYDIA: What's effusive mean? That *Eighty Lays* book had a great chapter on losing your underpants in France....

MARY: Look it up, Lydia.

JANE: I do NOT sound like a fortune cookie. Life is lived in the seasons of calm we experience between moments of great drama. Why should we waste any of it being envious of our friends? They are the people we love the most. The problem today is that we've heard so much pop psychology—"own your inner child," "embrace your negative emotions"—that we all behave like spoiled children and feel compelled to tell the world whenever we experience the slightest frisson of unhappiness.

Then we blame our parents for it. It's a *me, me, me* culture combined with a victim mentality; the worst of all possible mindsets. Austen's world may have been fictional, but I choose to think of it as aspirational—don't we all aspire to have friends who would love and support us so well?

LIZ: I'm not an inner-child embracer, by a long shot. And I'm not saying that we should share our envy with the world, just that we do sometimes experience it. It's like taking your PMS out on your husband. It's not that we *want* to do it; it's just that he's there. Whose brilliant successes do we see as up-close and personally as those of our friends? It drives a kernel of anguish into our hearts, somewhere deep down underneath the happiness, that it's not happening to us, too. How do you think Charlotte felt when her best friend married the richest guy around?

CHARLOTTE: Hey, leave me out of this. Bill was a cheap bastard who hid money in the Caymans. We're using a forensic accountant in the divorce now. God knows THAT'S going to rack up the legal bills.

LIZ: Not *you*. Charlotte Lucas, whose best friend got Colin...er, Darcy. In the book. You know, the *book* we're supposed to be discussing?

CHARLOTTE: Oh, right. The book. *That* Charlotte is as practical as I am—she took the best chance she had for a good marriage and ran with it, then didn't waste time on envy or unhappiness. In fact, I think she was delighted for her friend. What was that passage? Hang on.

[*Flipping through pages*] Oh, right. Listen:

Before any answer could arrive from Mr. Collins, or any congratulations to Elizabeth from his wife, the Longbourn family heard that the Collinses were come themselves to Lucas Lodge. The reason of this sudden removal was soon evident. Lady Catherine had been rendered so exceedingly angry by the contents of her nephew's letter that Charlotte, really rejoicing in the match, was anxious to get away till the storm was blown over.

Charlotte really rejoiced in the match. You can't get any less envious than "rejoicing."

Anyway, Jane, not to bring up old news, but you *were* kind of distant and unavailable when Bill and I got married. What was that about? You sure weren't unconditionally happy for *me*.

JANE: [*Silence*]

LYDIA: I loved the guy who played Wickham. He was totally hot. And Colin Firth in that white shirt? Dude! I could sink my teeth into him.

MARY: Didn't you read the book at all?

LYDIA: I kinda ran out of time....

CHARLOTTE: Well, Jane?

JANE: It was a tough time for me. Bing had just dumped me, and, honestly, it was tough to be around all the wedding stuff. I mean, my God, Charlotte, seven different bridesmaids' events? You didn't think that was rubbing everybody else's nose in the fact that you were marrying a dot-com millionaire who looked like a *Playgirl* centerfold?

LIZ: Ah HA! So you admit to feeling envious of Charlotte's marriage?

JANE: If I felt anything like that then, I sure got over it fast when we found out Bill was banging everything with two legs.

LYDIA: He came on to me, once.

CHARLOTTE: He came on to everybody. And that sounds like denial to me, Jane.

LIZ: The POINT is that the women in Austen's book are in serious denial. Charlotte wouldn't be envious of her friend's love match, when she herself had married Mr. Brown-Noser? She'd even accepted the man her best friend had refused the day before. (By the way, can we say low self-esteem, much?) Lydia wouldn't be envious of Elizabeth and Darcy's money, married to that slacker Wickham? Mary wouldn't be envious of her sisters' looks, when even her own Mommy Dearest compares her unfavorably to them? You definitely can't tell me that *today* we're not envious when one of our friends finds a better job, or loves a better man, or lives a better life.

CHARLOTTE: Envy isn't one of the seven deadly sins for nothing.

LYDIA: I LOVED Brad Pitt in that movie. And did you see him in *Troy*? The abs on—

LIZ, Jane, Charlotte and Mary: Shut UP, Lydia!

JANE: That's a two-pronged argument, Liz. Taking the second first, regarding envy today, I think it's normal to feel a twinge or two when someone achieves something we wish we had. But when it's our friend, we get past that twinge to feel true happiness for her.

Regarding your first point, I think you're ascribing your own biases to the characters in *Pride and Prejudice*. The more interesting question is: what's going on in your life to make you so bitter? None of tonight sounds anything like you. What's up, Liz?

LIZ: Nothing's wrong with me. I'm just saying that in a post-feminist world, or at least a post-feminist United States, we should all be empowered by our own opportunities for growth and achievement, not still stressing out over what we *don't* have that our friends *do*. But, and again with the total candor thing, we still do. Why?

LYDIA: Because it's human nature to strive for emotional happiness, material success and the outward signs of success that will inspire respect from others.

LIZ, JANE, CHARLOTTE AND MARY: [*Shocked silence*]

LYDIA: [*Rolling her eyes*] What? Can't I ever contribute to your snooty discussions? Also, of course you know that Dante groups Envy with Anger and Pride as the sins of Perverted Love. The other two groups are Insufficient Love and Excessive Love of Earthly Goods. Envy is perverted because it loves what other people possess, rather than what is Good, Beautiful and True. Sort of like it *eats away* the heart of the envious person.

LIZ, JANE, CHARLOTTE AND MARY: [*More shocked silence*]

LIZ: *Lydia*???

LYDIA: [*Downing her margarita*] Fine. So I may have Googled. Sue me.

CHARLOTTE: Google or not, Dante had it going on. Envy is definitely about eating out the heart. I know I spent some time eating my own heart out about *your* wonderful marriage, Liz, when I found out that Bill was the horndog of the century. It wasn't that I was unhappy for you; just that I wondered why I couldn't find a good man, too.

JANE: I'm not going along with Dante, with all due respect. He says envy is perverted because it loves what other people possess, rather than what is good and beautiful. What if—

LYDIA: Good, beautiful and *true*.

MARY: Lydia, did you really write crib notes on your *wrist*?? What is this, eighth grade?

LYDIA: Like *you'd* remember that whole "perverted love" crap. Gimme a break.

JANE: Back to my point, what if we envy what other people possess simply because what they possess is good and beautiful?

LYDIA: And true.

JANE: And true.

CHARLOTTE: Like your new convertible!

JANE: I think it's okay to want what our friends have, but in an abstract way. Happy lives, good marriages, fulfilling work. But when our envy focuses on the specific—I want *your* husband; I want *your* job—that's when we veer into Dante's perversion.

CHARLOTTE: Dante's perversion, Dante's *Inferno*. I bet he was a fun dude to have around at parties.

LYDIA: Yeah, maybe at an S&M club.

LIZ: [*Begins to cry*] What's the resolution? How do we fix this so that women aren't still suffering from envy in the year 2205?

JANE: [*Crosses to Liz, hugs her*] Liz, you have to tell us what's going on.

ALL: [*Surround Liz*]

MARY: What is it, Liz?

LIZ: [*Crying*] We had the second in vitro fertilization procedure this month. Thirty grand in medical expenses that insurance doesn't cover; all of those damn hormone shots. And today I started my period.

JANE: Oh, Liz! Why didn't you tell us? We could have been there for you.

LIZ: I couldn't. I just couldn't. Sometimes it's hard for me to be in a room with you, honestly. You didn't even want to have a baby for another year or two, but you forgot birth control one time and *poof!* You're pregnant. It just seems unfair and I...I'm so eaten up by envy I feel like I'm dying, sometimes.

JANE: Oh, God, Liz. I'm so sorry. If I'd only known, I wouldn't have been so insensitive as to blather on and on about the baby.

LIZ: That's just it. You're *not* insensitive. I want so badly to be happy for you...I *am* happy for you. It's just easier to be happy for you when we're not in the same room. I guess that's why I read *Pride and Prejudice* through the filter of my own emotions. I'm so sorry—I want to be like Austen's characters and be sweet and supportive and not so caught up in my own dramas. It's been two hundred years since she wrote that book, and yet I feel like I've evolved backward. What can I do?

JANE: First, you need to know that we love you. Maybe it's as simple as this: We talk more; we communicate. We share our doubts and feelings of inadequacy, so that we know we're all going through the same kinds of things. Only hidden secrets have the opportunity to turn vile and noxious in the darkness of our minds; the light of reason and glow of friendship illuminate our shortcomings as further illustrations of our humanity.

LIZ, CHARLOTTE, LYDIA AND MARY: [*Silence*]

CHARLOTTE: You've been writing bad poetry again, haven't you?

JANE: Even bad poetry has the ability to convey truth.

CHARLOTTE: How about this: let's always tell each other when the envy monster grabs us by the gut so our friendships are never in danger? And we're all going to your next IVF treatment with you, Liz, to cheer on your happy little eggs and sperm!

LYDIA: I'll drink to that!

MARY: A toast to love and friendship, the enemy of envy!

LIZ: [*Smiling*] A toast to Jane Austen. May we live more in her world from now on!

ALL: [*Toasting*] Hear, hear!

LYDIA: Okay, next month is totally *Around the World in Eighty Lays*.

Alesia Holliday graduated from Ohio State University, then summa cum laude from Capital Law School, in Columbus, Ohio, then spent several years as a trial lawyer in complex class action and mass tort litigation. Now she is a "recovering" attorney turned bestselling author.

Alesia's first novel, *American Idle*, launched Dorchester Publishing's first trade paperback line and is a double finalist in the prestigious RITA awards for women's fiction. Alesia now writes chick-lit for Berkley Publishing, and she's starting a new subgenre with chick-lit legal thrillers coming soon from Berkley Prime Crime. Please visit her online at www.alesiaholliday.com.

Jane and Me

KAREN JOY FOWLER

Karen Joy Fowler gets the last word at the party—she does that a lot in real life, too—by thinking about what it is that makes Austen ever-changing and ever-new. How much of who we are do we read into Jane Austen's work? And how much of who Jane is reads into us?

I. "What is all this about Jane Austen? What is there in her? What is it all about?"

—JOSEPH CONRAD TO H. G. WELLS

I'VE BEEN THINKING ABOUT Austen again. We haven't had a new Austen movie since Bush took office (coincidence?) so there's less smoke blowing around the novels, a clearer view of the books as books. According to BookScan, 100,000 copies of *Pride and Prejudice* sold last year with no help from the movies at all.

In other news, a tearoom in Bath, planning to market Jane Austen teas and coffees (in "distinctively nineteenth-century flavors") found the name already trademarked for restaurant and catering services by a Mrs. Rachel Mary Morton of Dorchester, Dorset.

Plus, I've already seen my monthly quota of writer's lists of recommended reading in which no woman author's name appears (Carol

Shields' last book, *Unless*, has resensitized me to the issue) and we still have three weeks of the month to go.

But the real reason Austen has my attention again is that I recently published a work of fiction entitled *The Jane Austen Book Club*. Before it was published I passed out galleys of this book at the Northern California Independent Booksellers Association Convention. (So much more fun than selling them. I recommend it.) Several people there talked to me about Austen. Many women told me that they read her books over and over again. One woman said, "I read *Mansfield Park* four times before I liked it." Another, "I didn't really get her until I was forty years old." And from almost every man who picked up a galley, "I'm getting this for my wife."

Some months ago I showed an early draft of my book to a close friend. He is himself an enormous Austen fan and quotes her aptly when explaining soccer strategies, video games, California politics. The presence in my book, he told me, of one Austen-reading man was perfectly plausible. The appearance of a second was not.

Although my own circle contains multiple Austen-reading men, I suspect he's right, and have rewritten accordingly.

So among the questions I've been asking myself are these:

If I were a man and I liked Austen, would it be for different reasons? (If I were a man, would I ever have read her at all?) And just why is it that I like Austen so much anyway?

II. THE ORIGIN STORY

When I'm not steering it, the conversation these days turns more often to comic books than to Austen. Classic comics inspire a peculiarly reverent, but noisy nostalgia.

Now that someone has explained, I understand why Marvel is so much better than DC. I watched *Buffy the Vampire Slayer* right up until the final season when it got unwatchable, and am willing to talk to anyone, anywhere, about why it was good and when it stopped being so. I see the advantages of superpowers; I see the disadvantages. With great power, great responsibility, I so get that.

(The corollary—with little power, little responsibility, while inarguable on its face, is a political philosophy designed to let super-villains get and stay in office. Power is a slipperier concept than superpower. But I digress.)

Jane and Me

As a kid, I read comics only in those minutes while I waited to see the dentist or, later, the orthodontist. The Fantastic Four are linked forever in my brain to the drill and the way the wires of your braces cut up the inside of your upper lip so you tasted blood for four years running.

My dentist preferred not to use Novocain. He strung tiny pieces of cotton on the drill wires so that they slid up and down as he worked, and he told me to imagine they were little rabbits hopping about. He told me there was no more effective painkiller than my own brain concentrating on something else. (He may have escaped from some home for the criminally insane. This is only just now occurring to me.)

So I saw *The Hulk* this summer and I thought Ang Lee told it like it was—not nearly diverting enough.

That comic-sized space in my brain was filled with fairy tales instead. Fairy tales bear a superficial resemblance to comic books—mythic plots and magical powers, an inclination toward the poetry of glass mountains, ice fortresses, golden balls. A fondness for secret identities.

But mostly they're different. Fairy tales are nowhere near as hip. They're too old, too likely to have had parental approval. The characters in comic books save the city; in fairy tales, they can barely save themselves. No one returns in later episodes for the intimacy (and frustration) of long story arcs.

I suspect that the fairy-tale-reading experience is significantly less stable. Things you care about as an older reader undermine and overwrite your original readings. Because of this, fairy tales do not lend themselves to nostalgia. (Except for maybe the loathsome Disney versions.)

Skip ahead a few years to where I'm eleven or so. If I make myself imagine what I imagine to be a classic scene—two boys reading comic books together, belly down, comics opened on the floor; if I then turn those boys into girls; if I then turn one of those girls into me, the other becomes my best friend, Margaret; the floor becomes the twin beds in her bedroom; the comics become magazines. These magazines belong to Margaret's older sisters. We're not supposed to be reading them, but only because they're not ours, not because there's anything in them anyone thinks we shouldn't see.

These magazines are entitled *Seventeen* and *Teen* magazine, and maybe *16*, though the latter was a little celebrity-focused for us; we weren't so into that. I love the makeovers (who doesn't?) and the advice columns.

I'm engrossed in how to get and keep boys interested, long before I'm engrossed in boys. I read with fascination how the right hairstyle can add needed width to a thin face, how the right clothes can mask a short waist, even though my face is not thin and my waist not short. All these years later I can still quote random lines from such articles verbatim.

From an alphabet of beauty tips: "B is for brushes. Bless the whole kit and caboodle of them. When they sparkle, you sparkle, too."

From an advice column: "Laugh at his jokes." (They'll be fart jokes. And not funny ones. *Seventeen* doesn't care.)

More advice: "If you see him admiring some girl in the hall, say, 'She *is* pretty, isn't she?' Chances are he'll turn back to you with new interest. You've agreed with him and that's not bad!" (A writing teacher once told me that Jane Austen used to satirize mawkish sentiment or doubtful advice by putting the words "So true!" in the margin. He suggested we should all write "So true!" in the margins of our own work. He suspected much of our wisdom would not survive the juxtaposition.)

At eleven years old, I was deeply, puzzlingly riveted by these things. I spent hours reading this stuff. I never did graduate to the adult market of *Cosmo* or *Redbook*. I don't even read those magazines at the dentist. I don't even take the quizzes.

Okay, sometimes I read the medical stories.

This is not a nostalgic reading experience either. I can find sites on the Web that suggest some women are nostalgic about it, but my own feelings are chilly.

I was about thirteen when I read my first Austen novel. I don't remember how this happened; I don't remember which one it was. It wasn't assigned to me in a class or I would remember the class. I didn't see it first at the movies, because they weren't making movies of Austen books then. (I saw the Greer Garson/Laurence Olivier *Pride and Prejudice* for the first time eight years ago. I remember it vividly. It was on television. I wore blue.)

But I can guess why I loved it. In this Austen book, whichever one it was, some young woman battled adversity and disappointment, and probably a villainous seducer, too, and ended married to the right man. I thought Austen was surprisingly funny for someone two hundred years old, and romantic. I loved her young heroines. I found her easy to read and I was more impressed with myself about that than I was with her.

I seemed to have been pointedly prepared for her. How does a poor woman marry? She lets a man believe she can spin straw into gold. She gets a flattering haircut and laughs at fart jokes. She captivates him with her "fine eyes and pert opinions."

The reader of fairy tales, the reader of *Seventeen*, does not ask herself, "Why can't Elizabeth just tell Darcy she's changed her mind? One honest conversation would solve the whole problem," because this reader understands that a girl's job is to wait. "Boys don't like to be chased," she has read more times than she can count. "They like to think that they're the pursuers." (So true!)

This reader is comfortable at home in a place where courtships are conducted according to rigid rules, where happiness is achieved by following the rules, where deviation from the rules results in ruin and regret. Should you kiss a boy goodnight? Sure thing, just as long as you're willing to "run the risk of having yourself foot-noted as an 'easy number.'" Just as long as you never plan to marry some nice boy someday.

Fewer men than women seem familiar with fairy tales. I cannot find a single one who admits to reading much of anything in *Seventeen* magazine. This may have been my route to Austen, but if it were the only way, no man would get there.

III. THORNS AND BRAMBLES

"I have never read anything Austen wrote. I just never got at reading *Pride and Prejudice* or *Sense and Sensibility*. They seemed to be the Bobbsey twins for grown-ups."
—ANDY ROONEY

There are other barriers. Austen is a specialist in all those things that women's fiction has been criticized for over the years.

Let's review the list:

1. Her books are about women. With only a few exceptions, *Northanger Abbey* perhaps, her women are more interesting than her men.
2. She structures her books around the marriage plot.
3. Her focus is domestic. In one of the few serious reviews of her work published during her lifetime, Sir Walter Scott put a faintly

positive spin to this (he was more genuinely enthusiastic on this
same subject later) when he wrote:

The turn of this author's novels bears the same relation to that
sentimental and romantic cast, that cornfields and cottages and
meadows bear to the highly adorned grounds of a show mansion,
or the rugged sublimities of a mountain landscape...the youthful
wanderer may return from his promenade to the ordinary business
of life, without any chance of having his head turned.

4. Her presentation is genteel. Her books lack what Anthony Burgess
   has called a "strong male thrust." Burgess himself can only enjoy
   books with a "brutal intellectual content," but I would argue Austen has that.
5. Her own sexual history is highly suspect. She probably died a vir-
   gin. I find I have nothing further to say in regard to the apparent
   importance of this item.
6. And look who reads her.

Women.
And men.
Men of a certain sort.
In D. A. Miller's *Jane Austen, or the Secret of Style*, in the chapter en-
titled "Secret Love," Miller says:

...if Austen meant Woman, then perhaps in turn Woman might
mean Austen, and a girl's command of the language of the one—a
dialect, apparently, of her native tongue—would increase....
   But the same discovery...made the boy all wrong. Plied with a
Style whose unknown strength went straight to his head, he had fancied himself conquering the world with his swank Excalibur; now
he woke to sobering sounds of derision and found that, during his
intoxication, just as Lydia Bennet had done to another would-be soldier in *Pride and Prejudice*, Jane Austen had put him in a dress....

In one of the Austen chat rooms online a man has asked if there's something strange about him because he loves Austen. He has trouble attract-
ing women; he wonders if his lack of machismo, as represented by his

love of Austen, is part of the problem. Even the Austen-loving women on the list are not sure. Some of them say they find Austen-loving terribly attractive in a man. Others warn that this list is not a representative sample of women. *Their* husbands don't read her, they hasten to add.

Only the college professors seem to know significant numbers of men of the Austen-loving persuasion. One man recounts a semester of high-school English in which Austen was assigned. He says that all the boys' grades went down.

A quick and dirty survey of some of my male friends produces surprisingly uniform results. With only one exception, those men who say they like Austen (five of eight—my friends are a classy lot) also say they first read her because some woman made them. When I ask what it is they like about her, they mostly say that she's funny.

I ask the ones who don't like her (two), what it is about her they don't like. One says she's annoying. One says he just can't bring himself to care much about who marries whom. I get the same answer when I ask the one remaining man why he's never read her.

Question one, part two: if I were a man, would I have ever read Austen? By now I've persuaded myself that the answer is no. I might have read *Pride and Prejudice* in high school, where I would have been given a bad grade and blamed Austen for the whole mess. Or, if I was never assigned to her, I might have believed, based on word of mouth, that she wrote light, girlish romances. If I were a man, would I be man enough to pick up a girlish romance all on my own? I'm sadly sure not.

I think this is a shame. I think I would still have liked her, and I think, in my first readings of her, I would have liked her in ways that reflected better on me, ways I would be happier remembering. More interesting ways.

Question one, part one: if the male me had liked her, would it have been for different reasons? I feel certain the answer is yes. Even as I can't imagine what those ways might be.

IV. NEGUS AND SHOE ROSES

"We will, however, detain our female friends no longer than to assure them, that they may peruse these volumes...with real benefits, for they may learn...sober and salutary maxims for the conduct of life."

—*One of Austen's first reviews, unsigned*

Which brings me to question two: why do I like Austen so much? What *is* it about Austen?

The most important thing to know about the answer is that it can only ever be provisional. What I like most about Austen, so far, has changed with each rereading.

Let me begin by stressing that the way I first read Austen suited me at that time. I could not have been more pleased. It's only now that I wonder how the books might have looked if I'd come in on some other road—horse books, say, or through Patrick O'Brian's Austen-with-boats books.

Or comic books. Professor and critic Brian Attebery tells me, "There is little Austen in some of the comics—Metal Men maybe, and certainly the Lois Lane editions of the Superman series. A lot closer to Austen than fairy tales are."

Seventeen had me reading the books as if her world were familiar to me. I wonder how they would have looked if I'd been focused on what was strange. I could have done some world-building out of entailments, shoe roses, Gretna Green, negus, private estates whose housekeepers led tours for anyone who asked. The books didn't have to be romances. They could have been science fiction. Or fantasy. Or Marxist social realism.

Most irritating to remember is how I read her books as if there were a didactic content. This is a ghastly misreading; it's a testament to her genius that the books survived it.

Although I am not the first to do this (see review above) it seems to me, now, rather hard to make Austen read that way. The fault here is clearly not hers.

It cannot lie with fairy tales, whose morals and morality are seldom instructive and often appalling. One wonders really why any parent would approve of them.

The fault cannot lie with me. I could take full responsibility for it as is so fashionable nowadays. But what am I, some kind of superhero? I blame *Seventeen*.

V. FROGS AND TOADS

"In order to enjoy her book without disturbance, those who retain
the conventional notion of her work must always have had slightly
to misread what she wrote."

—D. H. Harding

I am not trying to tell you how to read Austen, nor how not to read
her. That project has been well in hand for more than a hundred years.
Surely no one else's fans have been scolded so often for so long over the
wrong-headed ways they love her. Even Austen herself has been appro-
priated for this project. She would be so ashamed of you, her fans are
told. You'd embarrass her.

I've only recently begun reading the world of Austen studies. So var-
ied, so vituperative! Now that I've started, I can hardly stop.

What a lot of male critics have wished to a marry her! Probably only
Marilyn Monroe has elicited more rescue fantasies. And what a lot
of male critics have made it clear they wouldn't fuck her even if they
could.

Rudyard Kipling (whose story "The Janeites" is a fascinating study
in gender, war and Austen, but told in such thick dialect I hardly know
what's happening at any point, so maybe it's not any of the above) wrote
a sappy poem about Miss Austen marrying her own character, Captain
Wentworth, in heaven.

But D. H. Lawrence called her, some hundred years after her death,
"a mean old maid." "Thoroughly unpleasant," he said.

Frederic Harrison described her to Thomas Hardy as "a rather heartless little cynic." (The "little" bugs me. Otherwise, he can have his own
opinion.)

And Mark Twain: "Every time I read *Pride and Prejudice* I want to dig
her up and hit her over the skull with her own shin-bone." (Samuel,
Samuel. Stop rereading the damn book.)

Even skimming the criticism, you can't help but see how Austen's
work has been put to every imaginable purpose, made to serve every
imaginable agenda. Corporate mergers, political movements, self-ag-
grandizements.

The more I learn to think as a writer, the more I notice and am impressed by the trickiness of her narration. Austen's voice is both dis-

arming and subversive; you're simultaneously lulled and put on your guard. It's both intimate and abstract; you feel you know her when she's revealed nothing, nothing about herself. She invites you, in the words of Virginia Woolf, to "supply what is not there," and your reading of her is partly determined by what you choose to supply. Apparently this can be whatever you want.

So here's what I'm liking best about her right now: no other author has ever managed to be simultaneously so authoritative and so absent. Her books are both solid and stretchy.

How does she *do* that?

VI. JANE AUSTEN, SUPERHERO

"Jane Austen and Dickens rather queerly present themselves today as the only two English novelists...who belong in the very top rank with the great fiction writers of Russia and France....That this spirit should have embodied itself...in the mind of a well-bred spinster, the daughter of a country clergyman, who never saw more of the world than was made possible by short visits to London and a residence of a few years in Bath and who found her subjects mainly in the problems of young provincial girls looking for husbands, seems one of the most freakish of the many anomalies of English literary history."

—EDMUND WILSON

I am not the only reader to discover that Austen's books have changed since the last time I read them. Katha Pollitt's poem "On Rereading Jane Austen" begins: "This time round, they didn't seem so comic."

Ray Davis, on his *Bellona Times* Web site, has posted the following explanation for why he didn't go to *Mansfield Park* the movie. "I was too young to deal with *Mansfield Park* the first time I read it, and I can't picture a living commercial movie director who isn't."

Plus, those women from the convention in California. "I didn't really get Austen until I was forty," the one of them said. The other, "I read *Mansfield Park* four times before I liked it."

But a third woman told me she thought *Pride and Prejudice* was almost a great book. "It would be so easy to fix," she said.

I asked her what she would change, but she couldn't answer; she said she'd read it too long ago. I don't know, therefore, what she found problematic or if she'd still find it so. I don't care. Let me go on record as someone who dislikes the fixing of Austen.

When I published my first novel, I used a great deal of Emily Dickinson's poetry. The work I used was written in 1872 and '73; I assumed it was all public domain.

I was wrong. I was told later that, when Dickinson was first published, her work was heavily edited. Someone had smoothed out the odd rhythms, straightened up the odd rhymes. The publications of her poems as she had actually written them were relatively recent, and this involved me in a complicated and bracing post-publication copyright process.

Something similar often happens to the work of Austen when it's filmed. The most interesting bits, the bits that most powerfully undercut the easy reading, are removed. So Willoughby's final speech has been cut in Ang Lee's *Sense and Sensibility*, the entire troubling personality of protagonist Fanny Price from Patricia Rozema's *Mansfield Park*. The first thing any Hollywood version fixes is those unsatisfying men. As with Dickinson, some effort has been put into making the work more formulaic, more ordinary. More of a standard romance.

I did this myself, without knowing I was doing it, in my own early readings. Now when I reread I'm also in dialogue with an earlier me. How did I miss *that*? I find myself wondering. How could I ever think *that* marriage was a good idea? I can't quite imagine the books without this double vision, though I'm confident they wouldn't suffer. Austen is far too wily to depend on your reading her any one way. She's proved as unstable and, for me, as invulnerable to nostalgia as the fairy tales. Which is one reason I continue to be interested in both.

Austen's voice is so addictive I lose my own the minute I read her. It takes copious medicinal amounts of poetry to break her hold on my prose, and it's never a clean escape. My favorite Austen novel is sometimes *Pride and Prejudice*, sometimes *Emma*, and sometimes *Persuasion*. It's telling that I can't narrow it down further than these safe and easily defensible choices.

But I am not done with her yet and I doubt she's done with me. I have a suspicion that the true Austenite loves *Mansfield Park* most of all. (Among the many critics who seem to like *Mansfield Park* best are Virginia Woolf, Vladimir Nabokov and Edward Said. *You* go argue with them.) I think that I might get there someday, the way sushi lovers start with California rolls, but one day find themselves longing for a bite of sea urchin.

Recently *Mansfield Park* has begun to seem the most interesting of the books. I still don't like Fanny Price nearly as much as Austen does. I still don't like the hateful Edmund at all. But it's gratifying to feel—after all these years, after all those readings and rereadings and misreadings—that exciting new progress remains to be made.

Karen Joy Fowler is the *New York Times* bestselling author of *The Jane Austen Book Club*, which has also been an Oprah Book Club book. She is also the author of *Sister Noon* (a PEN/Faulkner finalist), *Sarah Canary*, *The Sweetheart Season* and the story collection *Black Glass*. She lives in Davis, California.